T3-BSE-263

BANANA WARS
The Anatomy of a Trade Dispute

BANANA WARS
The Anatomy of a Trade Dispute

Edited by

T.E. Josling
Institute for International Studies
Stanford University
California
USA

and

T.G. Taylor
Food and Resource Economics Department
University of Florida
USA

CABI *Publishing*

382, 414
B212

CABI *Publishing* is a division of CAB *International*

CABI Publishing
CAB International
Wallingford
Oxon OX10 8DE
UK
Cak

Tel: +44 (0)1491 832111
Fax: +44 (0)1491 833508
E-mail: cabi@cabi.org
Website: www.cabi-publishing.org

CABI Publishing
44 Brattle Street
4th Floor
Cambridge, MA 02138
USA

Tel: +1 617 395 4056
Fax: +1 617 354 6875
E-mail: cabi-nao@cabi.org

© CAB *International* 2003. All rights reserved. No part of this publication may be reproduced in any form or by any means, electronically, mechanically, by photocopying, recording or otherwise, without the prior permission of the copyright owners.

A catalogue record for this book is available from the British Library, London, UK.

Library of Congress Cataloging-in-Publication Data

Banana wars: the anatomy of a trade dispute / edited by T.E. Josling and T.G. Taylor.
      p.   cm.
Includes bibliographical references and index.
   ISBN 0-85199-637-X
   1. World Trade Organization.   2. Banana trade--European Union countries.   3. Banana trade--Latin America.   4. Banana trade--Caribbean Area.   5. European Union countries--Foreign economic relations--Latin America.   6. Latin America--Foreign economic relations--European Union countries.   7. European Union countries--Foreign economic relations--Caribbean area.   8. Caribbean area--Foreign economic relations--European Union countries.   I. Josling, Timothy Edward.   II. Taylor, T. Geoffrey (Thomas Geoffrey), 1918-   II. Title.
   HD9259.B3 E773 2002
   382′.414772′098--dc21

2002005732

ISBN 0 85199 637 X

Typeset by AMA DataSet Ltd, UK.
Printed and bound in the UK by Cromwell Press, Trowbridge.

Contents

University Libraries   v
Carnegie Mellon University
Pittsburgh, PA 15213-3890

Contributors

Rachel Anderson, *Institute for International Studies, Encina Hall, Stanford University, Stanford, CA 94305-6055, USA*

Esteban Brenes, *INCAE, Apartado Postal 960-4050, Alajuela, Costa Rica*

Dale Hathaway, *National Center for Food and Agricultural Policy, 1616 P Street NW, First Floor, Washington, DC 20036, USA*

Timothy E. Josling, *Food Research Institute and Senior Fellow at the Institute for International Studies, Room E113, Encina Hall East, Mail Code 6055, Stanford, CA 94305-6055, USA*

Kryssia Madrigal, *INCAE, Apartado Postal 960-4050, Alajuela, Costa Rica*

Mechel S. Paggi, *Center for Agricultural Business, Adjunct Professor – Department of Agricultural Economics, California State University, Fresno, 2910 E Barstow Ave. M/S OF115, Fresno, CA 93740, USA*

Thomas H. Spreen, *Food and Resource Economics Department, McCarty Hall, University of Florida, PO Box 110240, Gainesville, FL 32611-0240, USA*

John Stovall, *National Center for Food and Agricultural Policy, 1616 P Street NW, First Floor, Washington, DC 20036, USA*

Stefan Tangermann, *Food, Agriculture & Fisheries Directorate, Organization for Economic Cooperation and Development, 2 rue André Pascal, 75775 Paris, Cedex 16, France*

Timothy G. Taylor, *Center for Agribusiness, Food and Resource Economics Department, McCarty Hall, University of Florida, PO Box 110240, Gainesville, FL 32611-0240, USA*

Preface

The idea for a book on the banana dispute originated in December 1998 in the corridors of a meeting of the International Agricultural Trade Research Consortium, the premier professional association for the discussion of agricultural trade policy issues. The editors found that they had a mutual interest in the saga of the banana dispute, Taylor as a student of the behaviour of food corporations and the prospects for Caribbean agribusiness and Josling as a follower of WTO issues and long-time observer of EU agricultural and trade policy. The idea was hatched to involve other colleagues who had expertise in various aspects of the issue, and to put together a volume that looked at the many dimensions of the banana market dispute within a comprehensive framework. We approached several colleagues to join us in this effort and found an enthusiastic response.

The preparation of the book was greatly helped by two workshops, the first held at the European Forum, Institute for International Studies, Stanford University in April 2000 and the second at the National Center for Food and Agricultural Policy in Washington, DC, in February 2001. These workshops gave the authors a chance to discuss drafts and to make a more coherent volume. Research support, mainly in the form of travel funds, is gratefully acknowledged from the European Forum, Stanford University and from the Center for Agribusiness, University of Florida. These institutions should not, however, be held responsible for the content of the book.

The editors would especially like to thank the authors for their efforts and for the cooperative spirit in which the manuscript came together. At Stanford, Rachel Anderson did sterling work on editing and formatting the manuscript, besides co-authoring one of the chapters. The cohesion of the book as well as its presentation owes much to her efforts.

Finally, we owe a debt to our families who bear the brunt of the frustrations and preoccupations associated with authoring and editing a volume such as this. To them we dedicate our efforts.

Tim Josling and Tim Taylor
April 2002

Introduction

Tim Josling and Tim Taylor

1

On 11 April 2001, the US and the EU announced an end to the trade dispute over the sale of bananas into the EU market. The dispute had arisen from the complex licensing system developed by the EU to regulate banana imports into the 'Single Market' in 1993. The mechanism used for allocating the licences had been found to violate the WTO rules, as it discriminated against suppliers from Latin America. The compromise agreement sets up an interim allocation of licences based on historical market shares, prior to the dismantling of the licence system altogether by 2006. Though not entirely happy with the outcome, producing countries in the Caribbean and Latin America generally have accepted the compromise.[1] Chiquita, the company that claimed to have suffered most under the EU banana regime, has been granted improved access, at the expense of other firms in the market. So, at least for the next 5 years, a truce is likely to prevail in the intercontinental banana war.

The long-running trade conflict in the banana market presents a fascinating excursion into the realm of trade regulation, commercial diplomacy and development policy. The complexity of the banana conflict is itself noteworthy: it has proved a test case for several aspects

---

[1] Ecuador subsequently had separate discussions with the EU to ensure that its own interests are taken care of in the allocation of licences. The remaining objections to the banana deal were finally resolved at the time of the WTO Ministerial in Doha in November 2001, when the waiver for the EU's replacement for the Lomé Agreement (the Cotonou Agreement) was agreed.

©CAB International 2003. Banana Wars: the Anatomy of a Trade Dispute
(eds T.E. Josling and T.G. Taylor)

of trade policy, including the authority of the World Trade Organization (WTO), and its General Agreement on Trade in Services (GATS) and Dispute Settlement Body (DSB); it has challenged the development policies of the EU, as laid out in the Lomé Conventions as well as the policies of the producing regions; and it has exposed some sensitive issues of domestic political influence, not least in the US. Each of these aspects of the story would merit examination and reflection. But it is the interaction of these different policy issues that renders the banana case unique in the area of recent trade policy disputes. Solving such a complex puzzle involving a heady mix of political interests on both sides of the Atlantic was not easy. The negotiated outcome will affect vitally the trade position of a number of actors from small island economies to large US and European companies. If well-meaning governments and their trade experts have sorted out this tangled web effectively, then trade diplomacy will have passed an important test. And if that solution leaves the trade system stronger, then the countless diplomatic and legal hours spent on the matter may yet have been worthwhile.

The facet of the story that elicits most emotion is that of the threat to the production of bananas in the Caribbean, in particular in the Windward Islands, as a result of the dependence of several of those economies on the continued sale of the crop at preferential prices in the major markets of Europe. The loss of such access undoubtedly would cause major economic and social problems in several of the islands. Thus one of the key policy issues posed by the banana conflict has to do with the problems of small island states threatened by the weakening of post-colonial trade arrangements.

Many Caribbean countries are uncertain what lies ahead down the road towards fuller integration into the global economy (and that of the Americas) and are apprehensive about the journey. Are these countries best served by the perpetuation of a trade system that in effect has tied them to the EU as a supplier of tropical fruits? Or would they be better off in the longer run if they could find other markets and products that were not quota controlled and at the political whim of European countries? But if such a move was desirable, how can it be accomplished without significant economic, social and political disruption? Most would agree that some help is required for such countries if they wish to change their trade patterns, but the best form of such aid is at present uncertain.

A second and related facet of the banana story concerns the private sector, which in the main does the marketing of bananas from the Caribbean Region and Latin America in both Europe and the USA. A small number of firms market the bulk of the crop, some focusing on Caribbean bananas and others bringing 'dollar' bananas from Central and South America. Considerable profits are to be made from this trade, and the firms have been competing actively for market share. But the firms themselves have changed over the years, through an intricate web of buying and selling parts of their enterprises. The current market structure is as much a reflection of company policy as commercial fundamentals. The firms have used their access to political representatives to push for diplomatic initiatives, and have helped to establish the parameters for the solution to the conflict. Thus what appears to be public policy is closely related to private-sector planning decisions. Changes in such policy have a significant bearing on the profitability of the marketing of bananas by particular companies. The tenacity with which the companies that felt disadvantaged by the EU policy changes have pressed their case certainly has distinguished this conflict from most other trade policy arguments.

A third aspect of the story is centred in Europe, where two very different banana import regimes had to be harmonized in 1993, when the 'single market' programme was implemented. EU policy previously had reflected the different interests of the members: no single import regime had been possible. In the UK, France and a few other countries, banana prices were held high by quantitative restrictions over and above the Common External Tariff to benefit the producers in the Caribbean and Africa. Germany had argued successfully for a derogation from the duty on 'dollar' bananas, on the grounds that it had no former colonies to favour. The two regimes were merged by imposing a quota on 'dollar' bananas at the EU level, a solution not popular in Germany. Added to the complexity of the internal EU issue, there is some banana production in the EU itself, mainly in the Azores, Crete and Madeira.

Thus the banana regime is strictly a part of the Common Agricultural Policy (CAP), with all the complexities and political tensions that are associated with that regime. The policies were formed largely at a time when the GATT rules were not thought to have much impact on a country's behaviour. The clash between the imperative to complete the internal market, the pressure to protect domestic banana producers and the obligation to preserve the benefits to overseas suppliers was potent enough in itself. The additional constraint of a rules-based WTO with a presumption against trade preferences proved too much.

A fourth aspect of the banana story is that of the domestic political influence of the banana marketing firms in the USA. The US is not a major banana producer, and normally would not take much interest in the commodity; but the firms that market the 'dollar' bananas exercised their right to point out to the authorities actions of a foreign government (in this case the EU) that appeared to contravene agreed trade rules to the disadvantage of the US. In this they were assisted by support from key members of Congress and from some astute political donations. As sometimes happens, domestic political interests clashed with diplomatic considerations. US policy towards the Caribbean was subjugated to the need to uphold commercial interests. An issue that might otherwise have been treated as one between the EU and some dissatisfied Central and South American countries became a beacon for the US in the fight for fairer trade rules. The case of the EU banana regime thus became a major transatlantic trade dispute almost by accident of domestic political timing.

The fifth facet of the banana story is that of the WTO and its Dispute Settlement Undertaking, painstakingly negotiated in the Uruguay Round, which has been tested rigorously by the banana case. The dispute procedure has been taken to the limit of appeal and referral, arbitration and retaliation. It has served as a way of identifying ambiguities in the system as well as testing domestic political commitment to the implementation of rulings. In addition, the banana case gave an opportunity to test some other aspects of the WTO systems, such as the General Agreement on Trade in Services (GATS), as the complaint was in part based on violation of this agreement as well as that on trade in goods. But in a broader sense, the banana issue has become a metaphor in a number of small countries for their treatment under the new trade rules. The WTO is not popular in those countries that see themselves as having to abandon established export industries for the sake of trade liberalization. The fact that these countries appear to be caught in the middle of a conflict between the EU and the US reinforces the notion that the small country is being ignored in the push for opening up markets.

This study is an attempt to relate each of these five stories and then to show their interrelationship. The policy observations that arise from the banana wars are brought together to see what lessons can be learned for future policy. Is this case *sui generis*? Or does it illustrate a number of different trade issues that need to be fixed? Are we seeing the natural tensions in a period of adjustment? Or is a range of incompatible expectations being placed on a trade system that cannot possibly deliver them all?

The organization of the study is as follows. The next chapter gives a brief description of main characteristics of the world market for bananas. This is followed in Chapter 3 by a discussion of the role of private firms in this market, tracing this role from the 19th-century development of the US market for Latin bananas by American firms to the introduction of this commodity by European firms in the British Caribbean as an alternative to sugar. Chapter 4 discusses the system of production and marketing in Central America, and the relationship between the firms and the governments in that region. That these countries have diverse objectives when it comes to the regulation of the banana trade is illustrated by their different actions in the WTO: some signed the Banana Framework Agreement with the EU, some joined the US in the WTO complaint, and one (Ecuador) took independent action, dissatisfied with either course. Chapter 5 traces the introduction of bananas into the Caribbean, the benefits of bananas as a small farmer cash crop, the growth of banana handling firms and the role of the unions. The significance of bananas in production and exports in the Islands is explored along with the benefits from the preferential access agreement and the experience with filling quotas.

Chapter 6 addresses the issue from the perspective of the EU policy debate. The early compromise on bananas in the EC is discussed, along with the issue of access for French overseas bananas and the derogation for German imports. The enlargement of the EU complicated the problem, first when the UK joined and later with Greek, Portuguese and Spanish entry. In Chapter 7, the EU single market scheme for bananas is discussed along with proposals for quota consolidation and the negotiation of the Banana Framework Agreement. In Chapter 8 the economic and political interests of the US in the banana industry are explored. This chapter discusses the filing of a Section 301 case that influenced the US decision to join the other plaintiffs in the WTO complaint, as well as the impact of Congressional pressures and election politics, and the links between bananas and other WTO cases.

The issue of the WTO banana case is examined in some detail in Chapter 9. This examination includes the historical position of GATT on preferential systems for developing countries, the question of the allocation of quotas in a non-discriminatory trade regime and the obligations that countries adopted when they agreed to the GATS. In addition, the question is addressed as to how the banana conflict became a test case for full panel–appeal–sanctions sequence under the DSU, and what was clarified by the case.

A concluding chapter draws some lessons for the trade system and for avoiding or resolving other such trade conflicts in the future. What can the banana issue tell us about trade policy conflicts? What does it say about preferences and developing countries? What implications are there for TRQ administration? Does the banana case hold lessons for small developing countries dependent on preferential access? Did the WTO serve the small countries well in this case? What can we learn about the internal EU market and the way in which the two regimes were harmonized? Did large companies have too much influence on trade diplomacy in this case? Did the US allow domestic electoral politics to cloud the foreign policy issue? Were there possible private sector solutions to what appeared to be a public policy problem? Can one improve the dispute settlement process on the basis of experience from the banana case? Whether or not there are clear answers to such questions, the act of raising them is itself a useful exercise for the understanding of trade policy.

Overview of the World Banana Market

2

Mechel Paggi and Tom Spreen

Introduction

Bananas are a highly palatable and nutritious fruit grown throughout the tropical and subtropical regions of the world (Fig. 2.1). Over the past century, they have established themselves as one of the most readily available fruits in the supermarkets of developed countries, as well as being consumed widely in regions where they are produced. The world banana market is influenced by a number of physical, structural and policy characteristics that play an important role in its

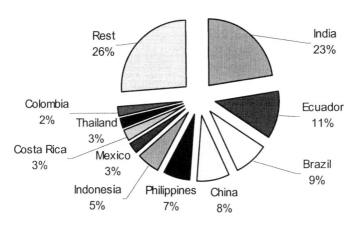

Fig. 2.1. World banana production, 2001 (Mt). Source: FAOSTAT (2001).

©CAB *International* 2003. *Banana Wars: the Anatomy of a Trade Dispute*
(eds T.E. Josling and T.G. Taylor)

structure, conduct and performance. The fruit of the banana plant is highly perishable and the plant itself is subject to disease and wind damage. International trade has therefore reflected the need for an effective marketing chain. This has in turn raised long-term issues of control and risk-bearing, and has contributed to the dominance of a small number of companies in the marketing chain.

The banana and its relative the plantain are native to South-east Asia.[1] Bananas were believed to have been introduced into Africa in prehistoric times and may have reached the Western Hemisphere (Ecuador) as early as 200 BC. More recently, bananas were introduced into the Americas by Spanish and Portuguese explorers in the early 16th century, and into the Canary Islands and the Island of Hispaniola during the 1500s (Crane and Balerdi, 1998). Bananas are a hetero-geneous product, with the varieties of bananas produced for local consumption often significantly different in quality from the varieties grown for export. The traditional export banana has been the Gros Michel, a variety of *Musa sapientum*, developed in Jamaica in the mid-19th century. Among those countries focused on export markets, however, the Cavendish banana is now the most favoured variety. Niche markets are also developing for organically grown bananas and those marketed with assurances about the conditions under which they were grown, such as the Fair Trade bananas.

National banana import policies have become entrenched and rooted in foreign policy. Far from being one global market, the banana trade reflects the different commercial traditions of the importing countries. It is one of the products benefiting most from patterns of preferential trade. Ironically, as a sector that represented an early example of globalization, the banana market now finds itself on the fault line between different trade regimes.

Production, Consumption and Trade of Bananas

Bananas are produced in more than 123 countries throughout the world. But the bulk of banana production is quite concentrated, with ten countries accounting for 63% of the total (see Table 2.1). In some countries, such as India, Brazil, China and Indonesia, bananas are a locally produced food staple. In other countries, such as Ecuador, Colombia, Costa Rica and the Windward Islands, bananas are primarily an export crop. The proportion of banana production that is exported

---

[1] The banana plant is a member of the *Emusa* family of palms, which include manila hemp (*Musa textilis*), plantains (*Musa paradisiacal*) and two groups of bananas (*Musa sapientum* and *Musa cavendishii*).

ranges from virtually zero in India to 99% in Colombia (see Table 2.1). Latin American countries such as Ecuador, Colombia and Costa Rica produce bananas mainly for export, which has given them a pivotal position in the global banana market.

More than half of the bananas produced are consumed in the world's main banana-producing countries. Only two of the top nine banana-consuming areas are not main banana producers: the EU and the USA. These two areas consume 13% of the bananas produced globally (Table 2.2). Their mutual dependence on a few key exporters of bananas, such as Ecuador, Costa Rica and Colombia, is a constant source of friction and trade disputes. The size and economic importance of these markets as the two key consumers of bananas from exporting countries in the Americas strongly influences the competitive nature of the negotiating positions of countries in Latin America

Table 2.1. Banana production, exports, and exports as a percentage of production, selected countries, 1998. Source: FAO (1999).

Country	Production (t)	Exports (t)	% Exported
India	11,000,000	0	0
Brazil	5,506,080	68,555	1
Ecuador	4,563,442	3,889,217	85
China	3,733,814	72,930	2
Philippines	3,560,800	1,149,552	32
Indonesia	3,176,749	77,433	2
Costa Rica	2,098,333	1,800,000	86
Thailand	1,720,000	1,297	0
Mexico	1,525,836	244,992	16
Colombia	1,516,640	1,508,487	99
World	55,988,655	13,504,107	24

Table 2.2. Banana consumption, per cent of world consumption, selected countries, 1999. Source: FAO (1999).

Country	Consumption	% of world
India	11,111,890	22
Brazil	4,617,420	9
China	4,309,120	9
US	3,652,888	7
EU	3,062,359	6
Indonesia	2,919,792	6
Philippines	1,848,658	4
Thailand	1,483,989	3
Mexico	1,335,955	3

and the Caribbean, whose economies are heavily dependent on revenues from banana exports.

Global trade in bananas has been steadily increasing in quantity and value during the last few years. The quantity of bananas traded has doubled over the past 20 years (see Fig. 2.2), while the total value of banana exports has more than tripled between 1980 and 2000, rising from US$1.3 to US$4.2 billion during these two decades. However, as shown in Fig. 2.3, this trade is fairly concentrated. About 94% of all exports originate from ten countries and the Windward Islands. Within this group of countries, Ecuador, Costa Rica, Colombia, the Philippines, Guatemala, Panama and Honduras account for over 88% of total world exports (see Fig. 2.3).[2]

The banana export marketing system is a major source of export earnings in many countries, especially in the Windward Islands. For example, in St Lucia the relative share of export earnings from bananas to total merchandise exports was 69% in 1998. In other areas, however, banana exports account for a relatively small share of export earnings. For example, in the Philippines, a major regional banana exporter, bananas account for less than 5% of export earnings.

In addition to contributing to export earnings, the banana industry is a major source of income and employment in many of the

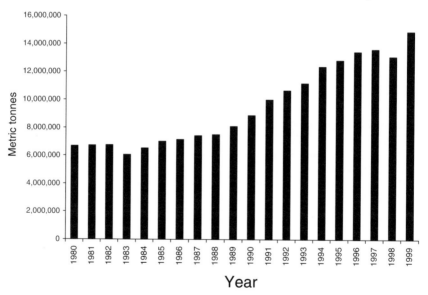

Fig. 2.2.   World banana trade, 1980–1999. Source: FAO (1999).

---

[2] It should be noted that exports from Honduras fell to 109,000 t in 1999 from normal average exports in excess of 500,000 t as a result of the devastating effects of Hurricane Mitch.

banana-producing countries. The dependence on the banana sector is most pronounced in the Windward Islands. In Dominica, St Lucia and St Vincent, it was estimated that around 33% of the labour force was involved in the banana industry in 1998. Most employees or smallholders are also heads of household: this adds to the number of people indirectly dependent on the banana industry for their economic well-being. In St Vincent, it was estimated that in 1998 up to 72% of the population was dependent on income derived from the banana sector (Liddell, 2000).

More than 100 countries import bananas: however, imports go predominantly to a few large markets. The largest two import markets for bananas are the US and the EU, accounting for around 58% of total world banana imports. The top seven markets for bananas account for over 80% of all imports. They are, in order of size, the USA, the EU, Japan, China, Russia, Canada and Poland. Banana imports are increasing steadily throughout most of the world.

Structure of the Banana Industry

The production and distribution of bananas involves several stages. Bananas are produced on a range of farms from smallholdings to large estates. The bananas are purchased from the producer by cooperatives and representatives from marketing firms. Export certificates and import licences are matched before the bananas are transported to the packing station. At the packing station, the bananas are culled, washed and boxed before being transported by land to the loading wharf. At the wharf, the export and shipping documents are executed and the bananas are loaded on to a ship. The bananas are then transported to market by sea. At the port of destination, the bananas are discharged from the ship. They must clear customs, import duties must be paid and the discharged fruit is deducted from import licences. The bananas

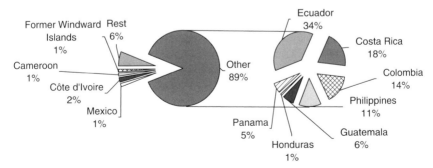

Fig. 2.3.   World banana exports, 1999 (1000 t). Source: FAO (1999).

are then transported by land to warehouses or ripening rooms where they are stored, ripened and repackaged for retail sale. Advertising and promotional activities also take place at this stage. After they are ripe, the bananas are transported to the retail point of sale. These numerous stages involve an extensive infrastructure between the producer and the final consumer that is characterized by high transport and transaction costs (US Government, 1996).

The global market for bananas is characterized by sharp regional market segmentation. For example, the Asian and Mid-east markets are the major destination for shipments from the Philippines. In 1997 (the last year for available data), 89% of Philippine banana exports went to six countries: Japan, Saudi Arabia, Republic of Korea, United Arab Emirates, Hong Kong and China. Banana exports from African, Carribean and Pacific countries go almost exclusively to the EU. The countries of Latin America ship bananas primarily to the EU, the USA and Canada, although Colombia, Costa Rica and Ecuador also supply bananas to the Mid-east and, more recently, to markets in Eastern Europe and China (FAO, 1999).

The main implication of the regional segmentation of the world market for bananas is that at the present time, for all practical purposes, the USA, Canada and the European Union operate in a market that is independent of the Asian market. If the Chinese market continues to expand, however, it is expected that there will be an increased presence of Central and South American bananas in Asia, effectively establishing a link between the Eastern and Western markets.

A variety of trade regimes are employed by banana-importing regions. The USA and Canada are notable in that both countries impose neither tariffs nor quotas. They also do not give preferential access to any particular banana-exporting countries. With the exception of the EU, the other banana-importing regions apply an *ad valorem* tariff on banana imports. Tariffs range from 3.8%, imposed by Hungary, to 15%, in Japan. The theme of this book involves the intricacies of the European trade regime, which are described in Chapters 3 and 4.

For the most part, global banana trade is conducted by a handful of multinational companies (see Chapter 5, for the history of these firms and their role in the banana controversy). Three firms – Chiquita Brands International (25%), Dole Food Co. (26%) and Del Monte Fresh Produce (8%), with a total of about 59% – currently dominate world banana trade. Other important players in regional markets, such as the EU, include Noboa (Ecuador), Geest and Fyffes. The latter two companies source bananas from the Windward Islands, Jamaica, Belize and Suriname for export to Europe (Loeillet, 1999). These companies rely on production both from their own plantations and from independent growers to provide supplies for export.

In some countries, such as Costa Rica, production is divided almost evenly between the two systems. On the other hand, Colombian production is dominated by independent producers who pool their production for export under the corporate structure of the Unión de Bananeros de Urabá (Uniban). In the Windward Islands, independent producers united to form a central marketing group known as the Windward Islands Banana and Development Export Company (WIBDECO). In Ecuador, production of bananas lies in private hands, with no foreign companies owning local production facilities (see Chapter 6).

While there are a few larger independent national companies (Uniban and Banacol in Colombia; Caribana and Difrusa in Costa Rica), some have had to link to the multinational firms in order to export to the European market (Banacol and Del Monte; JP Fruit Distributors and Dole; Caribana and Chiquita). Ecuador, Costa Rica, the Philippines and Colombia, are the chief suppliers to Dole and Del Monte, while Chiquita's main suppliers also include Panama, Guatemala and Honduras. In addition to the role of multinational corporations, the banana market is defined by differences in production costs, structures and marketing.

Differences in Production Costs of Bananas Among Countries

A diverse set of banana cultivation systems has developed over the years, ranging from small-holdings to sophisticated plantations. In addition, production costs vary considerably throughout the exporting countries. Data on the cost of production of bananas are not readily available. Comparisons between countries based on the data that are available are difficult, due to the lack of a consistent methodology for reporting production costs. Despite these limitations, analysis of alternative production costs estimates suggests that Caribbean Island producers are at a great disadvantage on a per-unit cost of production basis. For example, one study suggested that production costs in St Vincent are almost three times as high as those in Ecuador (see Table 2.3). Among major exporting countries like Ecuador and Costa Rica, the difference is much smaller.

Given the high degree of perishability associated with bananas, a prime challenge facing banana producers is the transportation of bananas from production regions to consumption regions. While differences in labour costs partly explain differences in production costs, another important factor is economies of scale.

Scale effects play an important role, especially in the harvest, assembly and transportation components of the production and

Table 2.3. Banana production costs, selected estimates (US$ per box). Source: van de Kasteele (1999).

	FAO 1994 (ex-financial)	CIRAD (FOB) 1995	BANDECO (FOB) 1997	Novotrade (FOB) 1997
Ecuador	2.95	2.95	3.29	5.01–5.81
Costa Rica	3.25	3.25	4.78	
Colombia	3.64	3.64		
Honduras				5.52–6.22
Côte d'Ivoire	3.40*	8.53		
Martinique	12.38			
St Vincent		8.39		
Dominica		9.37		

*Data for 1995.

marketing system for bananas. For example, in Costa Rica, large growers have installed a conveyor system that connects the banana-growing production area to sheds where the bananas are washed, graded and packed for export. Pickers remove bunches from the banana trees and then attach the bananas to the conveyor, which is fitted with hooks. The conveyor system facilitates the assembly process, and brings the bananas to a central facility. At the packing house, the bananas are separated into smaller bunches, sorted by size, graded and washed. A fungicide is applied to extend shelf life. Then the bananas are packed into cartons, placed on a pallet and transported to the port.

Due to the size of Costa Rica's banana industry, several ships per week leave its ports with bananas destined for North America or Europe. This is important because harvesting and packing occur on a nearly continuous basis; there is little need to coordinate the timing of harvest with the availability of ships (Hernandez and Witter, 1996). In sharp contrast is the banana industry of St Lucia, which is characterized by a large number of small producers scattered throughout the island. The Fyffes ship arrives once every 2 weeks. It makes two stops in St Lucia and then goes to Dominica for additional bananas. Harvesting is labour intensive, with the bananas hauled by hand to a nearby packing shed. Washing, application of fungicide, sorting and packing into boxes for export are performed by a few workers, who may pack as few as ten boxes per day. The boxes are loaded by hand on to small trucks for hauling to the port. Given the mountainous terrain of St Lucia and the large number of growers, the assembly process is long and tedious. It may take 4–6 h to haul the fruit from the farm to the port.

The basic elements that account for the variation in production costs include higher wage rates and social benefit cost in the Islands, economies of scale in Central and South America, and relative differences in outlay for disease-control expense. For example, in Costa Rica, as a result of problems associated with the disease black sigatoka, fungicide is applied 45 times in each growing cycle, while in Ecuador, less than one-half as many applications are required (Hernandez and Witter, 1996). In addition, the complex marketing system for bananas from procurement to retail delivery places a competitive premium on efficient transport and handling operations.

The differences in production costs, in combination with the structure of production and marketing, have resulted in widely varying conditions in banana-exporting companies. These differences have the potential to become, and in some cases have already become, sources of contention and divergent policies, interests and preferences as the global banana market becomes more competitive.

Conclusion

Bananas are the most important horticultural product traded in world markets. Global consumption of bananas is increasing. Production is very concentrated and a few countries provide most of the bananas traded in the international market, and three firms handle much of that trade. The USA and the EU are the dominant importers. As the developed economies of the USA, Canada, Japan and the EU are limited in their ability to produce bananas domestically, several less-developed countries have specialized in banana production for export. The paramount economic importance of bananas in exporting countries and differences in production costs, in particular within and between Latin America and the Caribbean, are two of the main reasons why banana trade regimes have become highly contentious.

References

Crane, J.H. and Balerdi, C.F. (1998) The banana in Florida. *Fruit Crops Fact Sheet*. University of Florida-IFAS, Cooperative Extension Service, Gainesville, Florida, pp. 1–8.

FAO (1999) *Banana Statistics*. CCP: BA/TF 99/3. FAO, Rome.

FAOSTAT (2001) FAO statistical database. Available at: fao.org/es/ESS/index.htm

Hernandez, C.E. and Witter, S.G. (1996) Evaluating and managing the environmental impact of banana productions in Costa Rica: a systems approach. *Ambio* 25(3), 171–178.

Liddell, I. (2000) *Unpeeling the Banana Trade*. Fairtrade Foundation, UK.

Loeillet, D. (1999) Reform of the CMOB: future still uncertain. *FruiTrop* No. 62.

US Government (1996) European Communities regime for the importation, sale and distribution of bananas. First submission to the WTO Dispute Settlement Panel. Government of the United States, Washington, DC.

van de Kasteele, A. (1998) The banana chain: the macroeconomics of the banana trade. On behalf of IUF, Amsterdam, February; International Banana Conference, Brussels 4–6 May, conference document.

European Interests in the Banana Market

3

Stefan Tangermann[1]

Introduction

While the whole extended drama of the Banana Wars is a multifaceted saga of policies in conflict, the EU aspect of the story in itself, the core and cause of the banana wars, has elements of a true classical Greek tragedy. It has elements of an inescapable conflict. Strong emotions are involved and, whatever the actors might have chosen to do, they would have encountered some of these emotions. The EU story is also multifaceted in the sense that so widely divergent interests are involved in it, at so many levels, that a whole panorama of essentially irreconcilable perspectives emerges.

In some way, the core of the EU story is one that can be found in many agricultural policies. There is a conflict between the interests of domestic producers, consumers and traders, and policy makers tend to solve that conflict at the expense of taxpayers and foreign economic interests. However, around that core we find a configuration of further conflicts that make this story very specific, and hence even more difficult to solve than the typical agricultural policy problem. As a matter of fact, Agriculture Commissioner Franz Fischler is on record as

[1] The author is grateful to Patrick Verissimo for his assistance in the analysis of developments in the EU banana sector. Parts of this chapter are adapted from his doctoral dissertation (Verissimo, 2001). Thanks are also due to Thomas Jürgensen for helpful comments on an earlier draft.

©CAB International 2003. *Banana Wars: the Anatomy of a Trade Dispute* (eds T.E. Josling and T.G. Taylor)

having commented in 1995 that 'no other market regime in the history of the CAP had been the subject of such controversy' (*Agra Europe*, 13 October 1995).

Developing-country interests enter the story very forcefully. However, in addition to the well-known conflict between developing and developed countries' views, in this particular case we also find a strong clash of interests between different groups of developing countries. This dimension of the conflict is exacerbated because political elements, originating from the old colonial ties between some developing countries and their 'friends' among EU member states, cut across diverging economic interests. Concerns regarding potentially strong social implications in the developing countries come into the picture and heighten the 'purely' economic conflicts.

At the same time, and closely related to the different histories of EU member states as far as their entanglement in colonial ties are concerned, there are unusually pronounced conflicts of interests among different groups of member states – much stronger than in many other agricultural affairs. The dimension of internal conflicts among EU member countries is further enhanced by the fact that this is one of the few cases where the commodity concerned is produced in only very few member states. The structure of conflicts among EU member states has kept changing with successive rounds of EU enlargement, including the 'accession' of the former German Democratic Republic. In that latter case, to an extent bananas played a role at the highest level of international foreign policy making to overcome the consequences of the long-lasting Cold War. In the EU, diverging national interests have been mirrored, to an unusual degree, in diverging perspectives of different individuals and institutional elements of the European Commission.

Lobbying has played an extreme role in the EU banana story because of the large stake that different companies have always had in the various compartments of the EU banana market. What makes this dimension of the conflict special, moreover, is the fact that the different types of trading companies have had much more widely diverging interests than we find in most other agricultural markets, depending on the nature of their historical involvement in specific parts of the market. The particular type of policy regime established by the EU, moreover, has contributed to partly confusing and partly heightening the diverging company conflicts, occasionally to the extent that some companies found it difficult to determine which future policies would meet their own commercial interests best. Should they be happy to skim off the rents resulting from the interventionist policy, or should they lobby for a more liberal regime?

Another dimension of this conflict story is the strong involvement of legal proceedings. Law has been brought to bear on EU banana policies, with widely differing degrees of success, at all conceivable levels, within individual EU member states, at the level of the European Court of Justice and internationally in the GATT/WTO system. The conflicting 'power' of the differing levels of law has been fully exposed in this story. Attempts have been made at using bilateral negotiations in order to erode the power of law, more or less effectively. It appears that there has been no other case, so far, in which EU agricultural policies have been tested to the same extent in legal proceedings at the various levels. Another very special aspect of the legal nature of the conflict is that different legal commitments of the EU appear, at least in the view of some, to clash in this case. What the GATT/WTO requires is considered to be opposed to what the EU's legal commitments *vis-à-vis* the African, Caribbean and Pacific (ACP) countries demand, and the legal and practical requirements of the EU's Single Market have forced policy changes that were, in the way designed by the EU, inconsistent with the law of the GATT/WTO.

Finally, the case is so complex, in terms of the facts, the economics, the politics, the legal implications and the policy instruments involved, that it tends to impose a heavy tax on the knowledge and intellectual capacity of even the analyst with the best intentions.

This multifaceted EU story is told here mostly following the historical sequence of events, starting with the negotiations on the Rome Treaty, turning then to the national policies in the original six member states of the EU[2] and the various rounds of EU enlargement. The emergence of the Common Organisation of the Market for Bananas (COMB) is finally discussed. Developments in the context of the Uruguay Round and the EU responses to the third banana panel, as well as later events, are examined in Chapter 4.

The First Encounters: Negotiations on the Rome Treaty

Bananas were a controversial product right at the beginning of the process of establishing the European Economic Community. In 1957, during the negotiations on what was to become the Treaty of Rome, establishing the European Economic Community, it became apparent that the future member states had different interests in the banana sector. While some member states wanted to go for a regulated and protective regime, others had a strong interest in liberal banana trade.

---

[2] The designation 'EU' will be used here in most cases, even in historical contexts where European Economic Community or European Communities would have been the appropriate designations.

Germany was the strongest proponent of free imports of bananas. Before the Second World War, bananas gradually had become a tropical product of interest to German consumers, considered a healthy food in particular for small children and people suffering from certain diseases, but also as an interesting addition to the choice of domestic fruit. During the war, banana imports into Germany ceased. After the war, however, with the German Economic Miracle unfolding in the 1950s and hence with growing purchasing power for imports from the rest of the world, bananas again began to be of much interest to German consumers. German politicians, therefore, wanted to keep the option to import freely a product that was considered an example of gradually growing wealth among German consumers.

Germany, which already had lost its former colonies in the First World War, no longer had special economic and political links with developing countries that exported bananas. It also had no overseas territories and, therefore, no producer interests whatsoever in that sector. Hence the natural option for Germany was to be concerned with no more than the interests of consumers and domestic trading companies (some of the latter being closely linked with banana trading companies in the USA). That there could possibly be a more general political alliance of interests among the traditionally protectionist domestic farm lobby in Germany and overseas producers of a tropical commodity obviously did not occur to German politicians at the time. At some point much later, a president of the German Farmers Union showed sympathy for the concerns of ACP banana producers, and in this context emphasized the importance of international standards for social and environmental policies (Leeb and Lipper, 1995: 23).

As other member states of the emerging European Economic Community had rather different interests in the banana sector, it proved impossible even at that early stage to find a compromise among the future member states on a common policy for bananas. One outcome of the difficulties was that bananas, unlike other fruits, were not included among the products to which a future Common Agricultural Policy was to apply (the then so-called Annex II products, according to the Annex to the Rome Treaty that listed those agricultural products to which common rules were to apply). But that was not sufficient. Rather than applying at least a Common External Tariff (CET) to all banana imports into the European Economic Community, even though no common domestic market policies for bananas were envisaged, Germany wanted access to completely free banana imports, while other member states, above all France, envisaged a much more constrained regime.

When it turned out that this was to become a highly controversial issue and negotiations on a common regime failed, Chancellor Adenauer from Germany went as far as blocking the overall negotiations on the Rome Treaty for 3 days in order to emphasize the intensity of Germany's interest in this matter (Leeb and Lipper, 1995: 33). In the event, Germany secured a special Protocol, annexed to the Treaty of Rome, in exchange for Adenauer accepting that France could constrain the sources of its banana imports to its overseas departments (Départments d'Outre-Mer, DOM) and former colonies. The special Protocol exempted Germany from having to apply the CET on bananas. Instead, it was agreed that Germany could import a given quota of bananas at zero tariff. This quota was to be adjusted, on an annual basis, in line with the actual level of imports (Verissimo, 2001). As a result, banana imports into Germany in effect remained completely free. Germany, therefore, traditionally has imported bananas from the cheapest and most competitive sources, i.e. from the Latin American countries.

Among the EU member states, Germany has always exhibited the highest per capita consumption of bananas in the EU. In 1991, Germany's consumption per capita was 16.55 kg per year, as compared to 10.35 kg on average in the EU-12, 8.44 kg in France and 8.47 kg in the UK (Behr and Ellinger, 1993: 35). Germany also has been the largest banana importer, importing at the end of the 1980s (average 1987/89) as much as 27.5% of total EU-12 import, and after German unification (and before the establishment of the COMB) even 34.6% of all EU imports (average 1991/92) (Behr and Ellinger, 1993: 34).

As far as competition on the German market is concerned, all companies could compete on the German market essentially without restrictions. In line with sourcing nearly exclusively from the dollar banana zone, the German market traditionally has been dominated by the big transnational companies from the USA and their local German partners and subsidiaries, though national German companies, sometimes in the form of joint buying conglomerates, and exporting companies from Latin America also have played some role.

National Policies in the Six Original Member States

At the other end of the spectrum of banana policies among the original six member states of the EU was France. France had 'domestic' banana production in its DOM of Martinique and Guadeloupe. Moreover, France maintained close economic and political links with its former colonies, among which some, i.e. the African countries of Côte d'Ivoire, Cameroon and Madagascar, traditionally supplied the French market with bananas. France, therefore, had a completely different interest in the banana sector from Germany. It wanted to protect both its domestic producers and producers from the Franc Zone in Africa.

France accepted in principle the EU's CET on bananas of 20%, later consolidated in the Dillon Round of GATT negotiations, but in effect established a national regime that reserved its market largely for banana producers from its DOM and the Franc Zone. Bananas from the DOM continued to have free access to the French market after the establishment of the European Economic Community. Bananas from the three countries of the African Franc Zone were also given free access to France, originally under a bilateral arrangement, and later covered by the two successive Yaounde Conventions (Yaounde I, signed in 1963, and Yaounde II, signed in 1969), providing preferences to 18 former French, Belgian and Dutch colonies. When, after the 1973 EU enlargement to include the UK, Ireland and Denmark, EU relations with the former colonies of the then nine member states were covered by the Lomé Convention with the ACP countries (Lomé I being signed in 1975), duty-free access to the French market for bananas from the three African ex-colonies of France became part of this wider arrangement. Banana imports into France from the rest of the world, i.e. essentially from the dollar zone, remained regulated through a tight regime of quantitative controls.

Consequently, prior to 1993 the French market was divided to accommodate bananas from mainly five different sources regulated by duty-free quotas: two-thirds for the two DOM, and one-third for the three African countries. The share of domestic production had further been split, whereby Martinique supplied twice as many bananas to France as Guadeloupe did. Similarly, the ACP quota had been further divided, with a ratio of 75/140 allocated to Côte d'Ivoire, and the remaining equally distributed between Cameroon and Madagascar.[3]

The administration of the French banana market had been performed under the authority of the Comité Interprofessionnel Bananier (CIB), a semi-private entity whose members were, among others, representatives of producers, importers, ripeners and retailers. Its main task was to estimate month after month the domestic demand for bananas, to maintain a certain balance between demand and supply in order to secure a stable income for all market participants along the distribution chain, and to allocate market shares following the distribution pattern described above. By doing so, the competition between the banana suppliers on the French market had been virtually non-existent prior to 1993. If a supplier could not fill the quota it had been allocated (e.g. due to hurricane damage), the remaining quantity would be transferred to other suppliers within the same category (i.e. DOM or ACP) and, if that proved not to be practicable, to suppliers from the other category.

In the pre-1993 period, the importation of bananas from third countries into the French market was possible only under one scenario: the failure of a preferential supplier to replace the banana volume that a

---

[3] When Madagascar stopped exporting bananas, its quota was redistributed between the two other former French colonies.

DOM or ACP exporter could not supply. Under such circumstances, the state agency Groupement d'Intérêt Economique Bananier (GIEB) was requested to purchase bananas on the world market, i.e. to import bananas from the dollar zone (subject to the 20% CET), in order to meet the estimated import demand. These complementary volumes of imported dollar bananas were then distributed to the French importers in proportion to their market shares. In effect, the GIEB enjoyed a monopolistic position in the French market with respect to dollar banana imports. While purchasing bananas from the dollar zone at the relatively low international price and reselling them at the border to domestic importers at the higher price level of ACP and eurobananas, the GIEB generated large rents that accrued to the French treasury. However, in most years the quantity of bananas imported into France from non-DOM and non-ACP sources was minimal.

The main characteristic of the structure of the French banana market is the existence of a large number of operators at the various stages of the distribution chain, in relation to the volume of bananas traded. Before 1993, more than 30 companies were registered as importers. However, the five largest ones shared more than 70% of banana imports. In the pre-1993 period, most of the bananas imported by French companies were ripened by the importers themselves, and then sold at the retail level, hence French importers performed the function of wholesalers as well. Moreover, most of the importers had held large shares in the producer associations and the exporting companies. Thus, a vertical integration of the marketing activities was a common feature of the French distribution system for bananas. This vertical integration as well as a lower degree of firm concentration were the main differences between the structure and conduct of the French and the German banana markets before 1993.

Italy did not have 'domestic' banana production, but maintained close links with its former colony Somalia, whose banana production it wanted to protect. Until the end of 1964, Italy maintained a state monopoly for bananas that completely controlled all import and marketing activities, including the fixing of prices.[4] After the elimination of the monopoly and privatization of domestic trade, import quotas were set and a tax on banana consumption was introduced. The purpose of the quota was to provide continued protection to bananas from Somalia, while the banana tax originally was supposed to compensate for the loss of revenues from the former monopoly. Later, though, the tax proved to be a convenient source of fiscal revenue, and it was raised significantly (from 60 Lit kg^{-1} in 1965 to 525 Lit kg^{-1} in 1982).

---

[4] The following description of the situation in Italy is largely based on Behr and Ellinger (1993).

Moreover, a welcome side effect of the resulting higher price of bananas was the indirect protection it provided to other domestic fruit.

Italian imports from ACP countries since 1974 were exempted from the overall quota on banana imports, but continued to require an import permit. Imports from the rest of the world were regulated through a quota and subject to a CET of 20%. The quota was originally 205,000 t and grew gradually to 330,000 t in 1991. In addition, there was a 10% quota for 'free practice' imports, i.e. bananas that had been subject to a tariff already in a third country. The import requirement for dollar bananas was determined depending on the supply situation for EU and ACP bananas, and allocated to importing companies on the basis of quantities 'presented'. These were the quantities companies had shipped to Italian ports and registered there. This 'presented' quantity usually well-exceeded the quota. The excess quantities were then sold to other markets, mainly in the eastern Mediterranean Basin.

The resulting price for bananas on the Italian market was the highest among all EU member states (with the exception, later, of Greece). The Italian banana tax had to be abolished in 1991 due to a ruling of the European Court of Justice. However, because of the continued existence of the quota regime, the consumer price did not fall accordingly. Instead, the already rather large quota rent earned by Italian importers rose even more.

The Benelux countries, rather like Germany, did not have any producer interests in the banana sector. On the contrary, because of the importance for EU banana imports of the large ports, mainly in Belgium (Antwerp and Zeebrugge), and to a lesser extent in the Netherlands, these countries were interested in a liberal import regime. However, unlike Germany, they applied a CET of 20% to banana imports, with the exception of imports from the ACP. However, as with Germany, their imports came nearly exclusively from countries in the dollar zone.

Further Diversity Resulting from EU Enlargement

With the first enlargement of the EU in 1973, two 'liberal' countries without invested interests in the banana sector, Denmark and Ireland,[5] and one country with close links to banana-producing developing countries, the UK, entered the scene. Thus both types of banana camps

---

[5] The position of Ireland, though, was not always considered 'liberal' by other EU member countries, as it was also influenced by the commercial interest of Fyffes, a company strongly involved in ACP banana trade and interested in expanding business in other parts of the EU. See following section.

in the EU, the liberals and the protectionists, gained new members. Moreover, with the entry of the UK another very specific arrangement for the importation and marketing of bananas was added to the particular regime already existing in France.

Denmark and Ireland, after having joined the EU, applied the same regime as the Benelux countries, i.e. a 20% CET and duty-free access for ACP bananas. As in the other 'liberal' countries, their banana imports continued to be sourced nearly exclusively from the dollar zone, with the minor exception of a 5% share of ACP bananas in the Danish market, mainly from the Dominican Republic, an ACP country lacking a protector in the EU and therefore left to having to compete with dollar bananas.

The UK, on the other hand, when it became a member state of the EU, had behind it a 40-year history of preferential imports from its former colonies in the Caribbean region.[6] The Caribbean countries concerned, the Windward Islands, Jamaica, Belize and Suriname, exported bananas almost exclusively to the UK. Among these countries, the Windward Islands held about half of the UK market, with rapidly growing export volumes.

With entry of the UK, and hence with the addition of another set of former colonies to those developing countries with special relations to the EU, the EU needed to put its relationships with these countries on a new and more permanent footing. This was done through the Lomé Convention, first concluded in 1975. The manifold political, economic and assistance arrangements between the EU and the ACP countries that were established by the Lomé Convention included free access of bananas from ACP countries to the EU market, enshrined in a specific banana Protocol annexed to the Convention (for details, see below). As far as the UK was concerned, this arrangement allowed for continued banana trade relations with the Caribbean countries that had long used to supply the UK market. In theory, all ACP and DOM suppliers had unconstrained and duty-free access to the UK market. However, because of specific relations of the major companies importing bananas into the British market (tight contractual arrangements in the cases of Geest and Fyffes, capital links in the case of Jamaican Producers), in practice the Windward Islands, Jamaica, Belize and Suriname continued to have priority over other ACP/DOM producers on the UK market. As a matter of fact, all imports from the Windward Islands were affected, on the basis of contractual arrangements, by Geest. Imports from Jamaica were split in a 2 to 1 ratio between Jamaican Producers and Fyffes. Shipments from Belize and Suriname came exclusively

---

[6] The following accounts of the situation in the UK, Greece, Spain and Portugal are largely based on Behr and Ellinger (1993).

through Fyffes. Other companies did not have access to supplies from these countries.

After UK accession to the EU, administration of the UK banana market was handed over, in 1973, to the Banana Trade Advisory Committee (BTAC). Members of the BTAC were the major market participants, i.e. two marketing organizations of producers from the Windward Islands, and the three largest importing companies, namely Geest, Fyffes and Jamaican Producers. The Committee was chaired by a representative of the Ministry of Agriculture, Fisheries and Food. One of the major functions of the BTAC was to determine the quantity of dollar bananas that was allowed on the UK market, in addition to the imports coming from the Caribbean region. Legally, licences for imports of dollar bananas were issued by the Department of Trade and Industry, which however tended to follow the recommendations of the BTAC.

The quota for dollar banana imports into the UK, on which the 20% CET was charged, was set in accordance with domestic 'demand'. However, in reality the most important criterion for determining the amount of Latin American bananas allowed on the UK market was the price level aimed at for bananas from the Caribbean region, so that they could cover their production costs. At the same time, because the world market price for dollar bananas was significantly below the domestic price on the protected UK market, comfortable rents could be earned on imports from Latin America. In contrast to the situation in France, this rent was not skimmed off by the government, but accrued to the private importers. Licences for the quota for dollar bananas originally were shared by the three large importing companies. Later, in 1989, a second quota for dollar bananas was added to be allocated to independent ripeners. Under the tight regime for imports and domestic marketing, the consumer price for bananas on the UK market was high, in 1991 almost 80% above that in Germany.

The following two rounds of EU enlargement brought countries into the Union that had significant producer interests in their own territories. Greece, joining the EU in 1981, originally reserved its banana market exclusively for supplies from its domestic production in Crete. In 1988, however, the European Court of Justice ruled that under the provisions for free trade among EU member states, Greece had to provide access for bananas from other sources as well. Yet, for a transition period Greece was allowed to apply protective measures under Article 115 of the Treaty of Rome, providing for the possibility of regulating imports from other EU member states if they threaten the sustainability of national regimes that are in accordance with the Treaty obligations and cause economic difficulties. Preference for bananas from Crete was, under this provision, secured by a rather high import tax, in the case of dollar bananas levied in addition to the 20%

CET. Though this made dollar bananas significantly more expensive on the Greek market than bananas from Crete, it did not prevent Greek consumers from buying dollar bananas in growing quantities.

Spain and Portugal joined the EU in 1986 and both also brought domestic banana production into the Union. In Spain, legislation from 1972 had reserved the domestic market exclusively for bananas from the Canary Islands. After accession to the EU, this regime was allowed to continue under the transition regime for agricultural products, originally until the end of 1995, though the 1993 COMB then set an end to the national Spanish arrangement.

Portugal had maintained a closed market for exclusive supplies from Madeira until 1984. In 1985, a national market organization was established. Among its various elements, it also opened up the Portuguese market to imports, though under a tight quota regime. After EU accession, the regime was modified, but was allowed to continue under the transitional arrangements regulating Portugal's EU accession. A global quota was established, with a minimum share reserved for Madeira. The quota was increased rapidly on an annual basis, to four times its 1987 level by 1991. Price and margins along the whole marketing chain were fixed under the market regime. The quota rent was skimmed off by the state through an auctioning system. However, because of the rapid increase of the overall quota volume, not all licences were actually bought by the trade in some years, which tends to show that improved delivery of the market was a more decisive criterion than maximization of rents or protection of producers from Madeira. Portuguese per capita consumption of bananas grew quickly, and ranked second to that of Germany.

The last round of EU 'enlargement' before introduction of the COMB was German reunification in 1990. Strange as it may sound, bananas played some role in this process. In a way, bananas were one of the symbols of access to modern Western products in the former GDR. The ability, or lack of it, of the GDR government to make bananas available to GDR consumers tended to be taken as an indication of the economic (if not political) strength of the socialist regime. In his book on the dramatic events forcing the collapse of the GDR, Honecker, in effect head of state of the GDR until shortly before its final breakdown, has cited the inability of the GDR government to always import a sufficient quantity of bananas as one of the reasons for the eventual failure of the regime (Leeb and Lipper, 1995: 34). Such was the desire of GDR consumers for bananas that Otto Schily of the West German Social Democratic Party (SPD), when asked to explain the election victory of Helmut Kohl's Christian Democratic Union (CDU) after German reunification, pulled a banana out of his pocket in front of the TV cameras (Wessels, 1995: 11). After German reunification, per capita consumption of bananas in the New Bundesländer jumped from 3.1 kg in 1987/88 to 22.5 kg in 1991, more than 50% above the level in western Germany (Behr and Ellinger, 1993: 13). There is little doubt that this situation in the New Bundesländer only reinforced Germany's preference for an unrestricted access to banana supplies.

In summary, the various regimes for the importation and marketing of bananas in the individual member states of the EU that existed in the early 1990s can be grouped into three categories (Read, 1994: 222).

- Type I: Imports completely free of tariffs and quotas in Germany, irrespective of their origin. Bananas came nearly exclusively from the dollar zone. Unrestricted competition among trading companies, with a mix of US-based multinationals, suppliers from exporting countries and domestic companies.
- Type II: Imports subject only to 20% CET, but unrestricted by quotas in the Benelux countries, Denmark and Ireland. Though ACP (and DOM) bananas could enter duty-free, dollar bananas also dominated these markets. Company structure differed among countries.
- Type III: Quota restrictions on dollar bananas, in addition to the 20% CET, with free access to ACP and DOM bananas, in France, the UK, Italy, Greece, Spain and Portugal. Depending on the particular regime, domestic, ACP and DOM dominated these markets more or less significantly. Company structures differed, with a tendency of the state to provide special treatment to specific companies.

Of course, the different national regimes as well as the resulting divergent structure of marketing in the individual member states strongly shaped economic conditions on their markets. One indication was the pronounced differences in levels of per capita consumption among the three groups of member states, as shown in Fig. 3.1.

Emergence of the Common Market Organization for Bananas

Given the widely varying interests of the EU's member states in the banana sector, and the corresponding large differences between their national banana policies, it required a major exogenous factor to put an end to the prevalence of this highly diversified market structure among the EU member states. This factor was the resolve to put into practice what the EU had always striven for, i.e. a truly open regime for intra-EU trade under the Single Market initiative, to be completed by the end of 1992.

At this point one may ask why it was possible at all that some highly restrictive banana regimes in some member states, grossly interfering with intra-EU trade, could survive so long in a Union that was

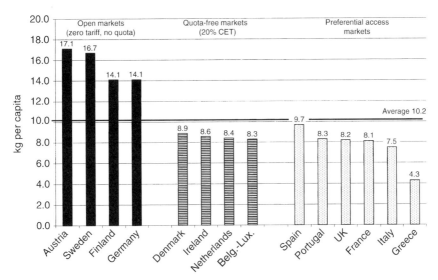

Fig. 3.1. Per capita consumption (kg) of bananas in different EU member states, 1990. Adapted from Verissimo (2001).

supposed to provide free internal trade.[7] The political reasons and economic interests behind that situation have been outlined above. But what about the legal situation? The essential legal provision that allowed this regime to exist was Article 115 of the Treaty of Rome. This Article in effect responded to the fact that, in spite of the EU principle of a common European market and a common external trade policy, in some areas national trade regimes had been allowed to survive, originally only for a transition period, but eventually for a much longer time. Examples of such cases were trade arrangements with (socialist) state trading countries, restrictions to trade in textiles under the MFA, trading arrangements regarding lamb and bananas (Kretschmer, 1983: 1970 ff.). Under Article 115, the European Commission could authorize national protective measures restricting intra-EU trade if: (i) trade measures implemented by member states, in accordance with EU law, threatened to be undermined by re-routed trade flows, or (ii) differences between such national measures caused economic difficulties in one or more member states. Though this Article did not provide *carte blanche* for all national restrictions (see above, partial opening up of the Greek market in 1988), it was used to safeguard most of the restrictive national banana regimes that existed in the EU until the

---

[7] Another important question is whether the existing national regimes were consistent with the provisions of the GATT. That they were not was found in the first GATT banana panel of 1993. For an account of that GATT dispute, see Chapter 9 on the GATT/WTO.

early 1990s. Under this provision, the right to restrict intra-EU trade in bananas was granted to France, Italy, the UK and Greece (Becker-Çelik, 1996: 45). Spain and Portugal did not need to rely on this provision, as their national banana regimes had been sanctioned under the provisions for a transitional arrangement in their treaties of accession to the EU.

When the Single Market was established in the EU, this provision should have been eliminated, and this was what the European Parliament proposed (Krüger, 1994: 7). However, Article 115 survived the amendments made in the Maastricht Treaty in 1992, and is still part (after renumbering, now as Article 134) of the 1997 Treaty of Amsterdam.[8] However, what really forced an end to the national regimes was the elimination of border controls in the EU under the Single Market initiative. In the absence of controls on trading activities at the borders between member states, it was simply technically impossible to restrict the flow of goods among member states. Hence, in the absence of a new common regime, the dollar bananas freely imported into Germany could have been cross-traded to all other member states. This would have completely undermined the preferential treatment that so many member states used to grant to bananas imported from sources outside Latin America.

At this point, the significant economic interests of various participants in the banana play were threatened: producers inside the EU, from the DOM and ACP countries, but also the trading companies that had benefited from the old national regimes. Moreover, there was a legal commitment that the EU had to honour. This commitment was laid down in the successive Lomé Conventions and obliged the EU to continue to provide preferential treatment to ACP banana exporters. Article 168 of the Lomé Convention[9] provides that (among other products for which the EU's import regime foresees no more than tariffs) bananas have to be given duty-free access to the EU market. However, more important, there is also a Banana Protocol annexed to the Lomé Convention (Protocol 5 under Lomé IV). Articles 2 and 3 of that Protocol provide for EU assistance for improving competitiveness of the ACP banana sector, and EU support for financial and technical assistance, mainly through measures targeted at stabilizing export

---

[8] In Maastricht, one part of the Article was slightly revised so that member states can no longer directly use safeguard measures in urgent cases, but have to apply to the European Commission. The Commission, though, could already, under the original provision, decide that such measures had to be changed or abolished.

[9] The same Article was part of all four Lomé Conventions, Lomé IV having been signed in March 1990. The Banana Protocol (see below) also was a nearly identical element of all Lomé Conventions.

revenues (STABEX). For trading relations, Article 1 of the Banana Protocol is decisive. It stipulates that 'In respect of its banana exports to the Community markets, no ACP State shall be placed, as regards access to its traditional markets and its advantages on those markets, in a less favourable situation than in the past or at present'.

The importance of this commitment always has been emphasized very strongly, in both the ACP countries and among their allies in the EU. For example, in 1987 Prime Minister Thatcher said in Kingston, Jamaica, 'we shall continue to fight hard in the European Community to make sure that Jamaica and other Caribbean countries go on enjoying the preferential arrangements for bananas under the Lomé Convention' (Hallam and Peston, 1997: 7).

Among the EU member states that used to import bananas from the ACP countries, the legal commitment embodied in the Lomé Convention was interpreted as requiring that the EU's trade policies, rather than other measures, continued to provide the 'advantages' enjoyed by the banana-exporting ACP countries. It is then logical that they argued for trade restrictions against imports from other third countries, because in the realm of trade policies the only form of advantage that one gives to one group of countries is to treat them better than others, or more relevant here, to treat others less favourably than those that are supposed to receive advantages. Moreover, with zero tariffs for the preferred countries, the intended size of the advantage (no 'less favourable . . . than in the past or at present') can only come from a sufficiently high barrier against access from non-preferred sources. After all, it was exactly such high barriers against banana imports from Latin America that had provided the advantage for ACP producers in the past. From this perspective, it could not come as a surprise that the EU member states concerned should favour a new EU-wide regime that was to constrain access to the EU market from Latin American countries. That a regime of that sort would, at the same time, also benefit producers in EU and DOM territories like the respective national regimes had done in the past was, by the member states concerned, seen as a positive side-effect. As a matter of fact, even that protective effect for EU/DOM producers could be said to have some legal basis, in Article 39 of the Rome Treaty requiring the EU to provide an adequate standard of living to its farmers. Moreover, it was in line with one of the 'pillars' of the CAP, which requested the maintenance of 'Community preference'.

The difficulty, though, with this strand of argument was that the 20% CET was not considered sufficient, or at least not always sufficient depending on the market situation, to grant the required 'advantages' to the ACP countries, nor (always) enough to provide what was considered the necessary protection to EU/DOM producers. However, raising that tariff was not a directly viable option either, because that tariff had been bound in the GATT in 1963. Moreover, because of that earlier tariff binding, bananas in the EU did not qualify for the process of tariffication as pursued in the Uruguay Round negotiations of the GATT going on at the same time.[10] A proposal put forward by the French government, to charge a variable levy on imports of dollar bananas (Hallam and Peston, 1997: 8), was not only inconsistent with the EU's tariff binding, but also ran counter to the aim of tariffication.

If the EU wanted to establish a trade regime that did not simply rely on the 20% CET, it had to renegotiate this concession in the GATT. In the course of events, the EU did indeed notify the contracting parties of its intention to renegotiate the 1963 concession on bananas in accordance with the provisions of GATT Article XXVIII: 5, and Brazil, as the country holding initial negotiating rights, was to be a prime negotiating partner.[11] However, these negotiations were never concluded, but overtaken by later events in the EU and the GATT. In any case, the EU could not simply erect arbitrary high barriers against the importation of bananas from non-ACP sources.

In this situation, a number of options could be considered by the EU. Most of them were suggested and analysed by various parties, not least from the economics profession.[12] As a matter of fact, some of these options already had been suggested long before. For example, in 1967, Armengaud, Member of the Parliamentary Association Conference and one of the most energetic proponents of the economic interests of the former colonies, had already proposed that revenue from EU tariffs on third-country imports could be used to pay subsidies to imports from preferred countries, or that EU importing companies should be forced to purchase certain shares of their imports from preferred countries and thereby transfer to them part of their profits made on imports from third countries.[13] The complex 'solution' finally adopted, in the form of the 1993 COMB, included several of the elements that had been suggested by various participants in the debate, though certainly not the ones and not in a structure that economists had identified as the least distortionary.

---

[10] From this perspective, the analysis of the 'appropriate' tariff equivalent for EU bananas provided, with reference to tariffication in the Uruguay Round, by Raboy *et al.* (1995) (and estimated to have been 47% in the pre-COMB period) is not quite to the point.

[11] GATT document DS32/R, 3 June 1993.

[12] Some of the best-known economic analyses of the options at the time were Borrell and Yang (1990), Borrell and Cuthbertson (1991), Fitzpatrick & Associates (1990) and Matthews (1992).

[13] For references to these suggestions in the so-called Armengaud Report, see Biskup *et al.* (1968), pp. 29, 44–45.

When the EU banana regime was designed, the widely diverging interests of different groups of actors and member states were very obvious.[14] Heavy lobbying was a central ingredient in the process (Pedler, 1996). The EU Commission was a central player, but different Directorates General also had diverging views, as shown in Table 3.1. The Directorate General for Agriculture (DG VI) had prime responsibility for formulating a new banana regime. Its principal interest was to establish a COMB in line with the principles of the EU's Common Agricultural Policy, and particularly to respect Community preference. DG VIII (Development), in charge, among others, of the Lomé Convention, felt responsible for ensuring effective implementation of the Banana Protocol under any new regime. Finally, DG I (External Relations) had to look after the GATT and the Uruguay Round negotiations that were in progress at that time, but also after EU relations with Latin America through its North–South committee (Stevens, 1996).

An inter-service working party had been set up as early as 1988 to prepare for a banana regime under the CAP, but little progress had been made until the EU came close to establishing the Single Market, requiring a common policy on bananas. In August 1992, 1 month after

Table 3.1.   Interest groups in the COMB negotiations. Source: Stevens (1996).

Main types	Sub-divisions	Interests
European Commission	DG VI	Support for EU producers
	DG VIII	Support for ACP
	DG I	Support for GATT negotiations
European Parliament	Development and External Affairs Committees	Support for ACP
Member states	UK, France, Italy	Continuation of preferential links
	Belgium, Germany	Unrestricted imports (most via Antwerp)
	Netherlands	As Belgium/Germany, but balanced with development concerns for Caribbean and Suriname
Companies	Geest, Fyffes	Protection for high-cost trade (plus access to other markets)
	Chiquita, Dole, EU importers and ripeners	Unrestricted imports, maintenance of dominant position in dollar banana trade
Supplying states	Caribbean	Strong protection in traditional markets
	Africa	Protection in traditional markets
	Latin America	Unrestricted imports

---

[14] A good account of the emergence of the COMB is provided by Stevens (1996).

the UK took over the Presidency of the EU council from Portugal, the European Commission issued a quota-based proposal (favourable to the cause of the domestic and ACP producers) to introduce a CAP regime for bananas under Article 43 of the Treaty of Rome.[15] This meant that the matter would be decided in the Council of Ministers of Agriculture, by qualified majority vote. In December 1992, the Agriculture Council voted on the principles of the COMB, and specifically the trade-related aspects of the new banana regime, leaving the internal implementation for the following meeting.[16] While the details of the proposed solution were changed significantly from the Commission's initial proposal, it remained fundamentally geared towards the preservation of protected markets for ACP and eurobananas.

A quick review of the Council votes of the major EU member countries at the time would have suggested that the defendants of a 'liberal' regime would have had sufficient votes to form a blocking minority. Yet the regime was adopted by a qualified majority in the December 1992 meeting of the Agriculture Council (see details in Table 3.2). As in many other difficult cases, the banana issue had not been put up for vote as a single issue, but rather was part of a larger package of as many as 17 agricultural policy measures (Pedler, 1996). Several states voted in a way that was contrary to what might have been expected, based on what appeared to be their obvious economic interest. Ireland, an open banana market, had been exposed to intensive lobbying from the Dublin-based company Fyffes, a key player in ACP banana trade seeking to expand business across the EU, and voted in favour of the regime. While expected to vote against the proposed regime, Belgium and the Netherlands supported it, probably driven by their tradition-ally pro-ACP foreign trade policies.[17] Finally, Portugal, a preferential market expected to be in favour of the proposed regime, voted against the agricultural package for reasons unconnected with the banana issue.

At the following Agricultural Council, in February 1993, the banana issue came up for vote again, regarding the internal implemen-tation of the new regime. This time, banana regulations were dealt with as a separate issue. Thus, Portugal reverted to the expected vote, as did Belgium and the Netherlands, whose request for changes to the regime was rejected by the Commission. However, in order to avoid being part of the exact minimum for a blocking minority, Denmark, which had succeeded the UK in January in the Council Presidency and worked

---

[15] The details of the proposal can be found in the Commission document COM(92) 0359.

[16] AGRA-EUROPE, Bonn, 52/92.

[17] The Netherlands actually shifted position during the Council debate (Wessels, 1995). Later, the Belgian and Netherlands' governments claimed that they had been misled over the exact effects of voting for the package (Stevens, 1996).

Table 3.2. EU Council vote distribution on the banana trade regime. Source: Stevens (1996).

In favour	Votes	Against	Votes
The first vote in Agricultural Council, December 1992. The COMB was adopted by qualified majority (needing 54 votes).			
Spain	8	Denmark	3
France	10	Germany	10
UK	10	Portugal	5
Ireland	3		
Italy	10		
Netherlands	5		
Belgium	5		
Greece	5		
Luxembourg	2		
Total	58	Total	18
The second vote in Agricultural Council, February 1993. The COMB was adopted by qualified majority (needing 54 votes).			
Spain	8	Germany	10
France	10	Netherlands	5
UK	10	Belgium	5
Ireland	3		
Italy	10		
Greece	5		
Luxembourg	2		
Portugal	5		
Denmark	3		
Total	56	Total	20

towards a qualified majority, voted in favour of the banana regime (see Table 3.2). Thus, the implementing provisions were adopted and the common organization of the market for bananas (COMB) was called into life.

The complex new banana regime became effective on 1 July 1993. Though the basic structure of the regime survived for nearly 8 years, the measures were changed frequently, and the numerical parameters were adjusted time and again. The regime described here is that originally established in 1993. The COMB contained measures for the domestic EU market as well as for international trade. These measures, summarized in Fig. 3.2, can be outlined here in only rough form, with an emphasis on the instruments regulating imports from third countries.[18]

---

[18] For a detailed account, see, for example, Verissimo (2001). The original EU Regulation establishing the regime was 404/93.

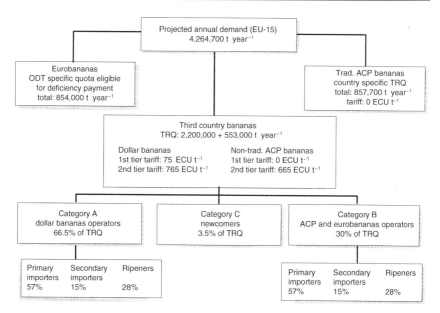

Fig. 3.2. Basic structure of the EU banana regime established in 1993. Adapted from Verissimo (2001). The quota quantities and tariffs (in 'commercial' ECU) shown are those applicable in January 1998.

As far as the domestic EU market is concerned, the COMB regulations provided for quality and marketing standards, the promotion of producer organizations, the compensation to producers for loss of income up to certain levels of production, and other payments. EU banana producers were entitled to deficiency payments, calculated as the difference between a 'flat rate reference income' in the pre-COMB period (annual price for 1991) and the 'average production income' earned on domestic bananas in the current COMB year. Thus the deficiency payments were designed to protect EU banana producers against any price decline resulting from the policy changes made after the introduction of the Single Market. Deficiency payments were limited to a maximum quantity of 854,000 t per annum. This quantity exceeded the average production of the 3-year period preceding the establishment of the COMB by 7%, and was never fully utilized after introduction of the COMB (Verissimo, 2001).

The core of the COMB, though, was the measures regulating the quantities supplied to the EU market. As a base of the quotas to be set for bananas from different origins, 'a forecast supply balance [was to] be prepared on production and consumption in the Community and of imports and exports'. As far as economics go, this was of course a red herring, because expected consumption in the EU depends on expected price, which again is determined by the supply allowed on the EU market. In the end, the 'forecast supply balance' boiled down to a statement on the quantities of bananas from different sources that EU policy was prepared to accept on the EU market. For imports from third countries, the 1993 COMB was based on a tariff rate quota (TRQ) approach, with two different quotas.

The first TRQ was set aside for traditional ACP suppliers, amounting to 857,700 t overall, with specific quantities allocated to 12 individual ACP countries. This quantity of bananas entered duty-free. The second quota was available for 'non-traditional' ACP bananas and dollar bananas. This quota was set at 2 million t originally, and could (in theory) be adjusted based on the projected supply balance. 'Non-traditional' ACP bananas were those from newer suppliers among the ACP countries and sales above traditional ACP quantities. As far as tariff treatment was concerned, a distinction was made between 'non-traditional' ACP bananas and dollar bananas, reflecting the 'advantages' to which the ACP countries were considered to be entitled. These 'advantages' were thought to require a tariff preference for ACP countries of 100 ECU per t *vis-à-vis* dollar bananas. Thus, 'non-traditional' ACP bananas entered duty-free within the 2 million t quota, while dollar bananas within the quota were charged a tariff of 100 ECU per tonne. On shipments above the TRQ, ACP bananas paid 750 ECU per tonne and dollar bananas 850 ECU per tonne. These 'normal' tariffs were prohibitive, and hence in terms of its economic effects, the TRQ regime essentially amounted to a quantitative limit on banana imports, with a tariff preference for ACP bananas.

Making the import regime more complex was the allocation of licences for the quotas. The traditional ACP quota was allocated to the various ACP countries on a broadly historical basis. Importing companies in the EU had free access to licences for these ACP bananas, and these licences did not carry any economic value as the quota on traditional ACP bananas was large enough not to be restrictive. The situation was completely different for the quota on third-country bananas, i.e. mainly dollar bananas. This quota was very restrictive, and hence licences for imports under it carried significant economic value. The allocation of the third-country quota to individual importers was, therefore, a highly controversial matter. The regime chosen was a rather complex two-level approach. At the first level, the allocation of licences was done by operator categories. Licences for 66.5% of the profitable third-country TRQ were allocated to operators who had marketed third-country and/or 'non-traditional' ACP bananas in the past (Category A). Thirty per cent of the licences to the third-country banana imports were available to firms that had imported traditional ACP bananas and/or sold eurobananas in the past (Category B). The remaining 3.5% was kept for companies that started marketing bananas other than EU and/or traditional ACP bananas from 1992 (Category C).

Operators in Categories A and B could obtain licences based on the average quantities of bananas that they had sold in the three most recent years for which figures were available.

At the second level, firms were grouped by their functions, and imports reserved for operators in Categories A and B were subdivided accordingly. Licences to 57% of the Category A and B imports were reserved for 'primary importers', i.e. those that produced or purchased from the producer, consigned and sold bananas in the EU. A further quantity of 15% went to 'secondary' importers, owning, supplying and releasing bananas for free circulation in the EU. The remaining 28% was allocated to companies acting further down in the marketing chain as ripeners.

It is interesting to see how the particular approach adopted by the EU in the form of the COMB was hoped to 'solve' the problem of having to honour the various largely inconsistent commitments the EU had to respect and the major economic interests it wanted to cater for. The GATT commitment not to raise access barriers for dollar bananas beyond the bound CET of 20% was honoured, it was believed, by set-ting a within-quota tariff that, though specific rather than *ad valorem*, in the eyes of the EU was no higher than the original tariff binding. Moreover, the quota for dollar bananas was, as argued by the EU, sufficiently large so as to provide continued access for dollar bananas, at levels equivalent to those that had been shipped in the past. The above-quota tariff, though certainly much higher than the previous bound level, was considered by the EU to have 'no actual or potential effects on the trade opportunities' of the countries concerned as the quota volume was sufficiently large to allow continued access.[19]

As far as the interests of ACP and EU/DOM producers are con-cerned, it was felt that the new trade regime, though maintaining 'Community Preference' for EU/DOM producers and helping to achieve a price significantly above the world market, would not suffice to bring about a price level as desired for these producers. For this reason, deficiency payments to both EU/DOM and ACP producers were added to the regime. However, even that was not considered to be sufficient. This is why a novel element was added to the regime (though it was not quite so novel, see reference to the Armengaud Report above). This element was to link company allocation of licences for imports of dollar bananas to the volume of ACP and EU/DOM bananas imported by the company concerned.

The arguments advanced by the proponents of that particular device were: (i) that importers of dollar bananas were to be integrated in the process of fostering structural adjustment of ACP and EU/DOM

---

[19] The phrase quoted was the EU's argument in the second GATT banana panel (GATT, 1994: 11).

producers; (ii) that it was desirable to promote an increased feeling of responsibility by all trade participants in the administration of the market; (iii) that marketers of dollar bananas on the one hand and EU/DOM/ACP bananas on the other hand should be induced to co-operate in joint ventures; and (iv) that EU/DOM/ACP bananas and dollar bananas should be mixed in the marketing process (Leeb and Lipper, 1995: 23). However, what sounded like a story of creating harmony between conflicting interests in essence amounted to cross-subsidization of bananas from ACP and EU/DOM producers from quota rents earned on restricted imports of dollar bananas. Licences for dollar banana imports were expected to have a value, and in order to reap as much as possible of that quota rent by getting access to a larger volume of licences, companies are prepared to import more bananas from ACP/EU/DOM sources than they would otherwise do. The resulting expansion of demand for these preferred bananas drives up their price – and this is the cross-subsidization implicit in the regime.

Making licences tradable enhanced the process further. As it turned out, most of the trade in licences was from importers of traditional ACP/EU/DOM bananas (Category B operators) to importers of dollar bananas (Category A operators) (Verissimo, 2001). This was because the licences allocated to dollar banana importers were for quantities significantly less than they wanted to import, and often for less than the volume of longer-term trading contracts they had agreed with suppliers. Hence the importers of dollar bananas were keen to buy licences from importers of traditional ACP/EU/DOM bananas. As a matter of fact, licence prices turned out to be rather high, showing the extent to which the quota on dollar bananas was restrictive. Given that licence prices are sensitive business information, there is little public knowledge of their level and development. For the first 12 months of the COMB, the European Commission reported a licence price between US$3 and US$5 per 18 kg box (US$165–265 t^{-1}) (European Commission, 1994). In the following period until the summer of 1995, licences reportedly changed hands for a price ranging uniformly across the EU from US$4 to US$7 per box (US$220–385 t^{-1}) (CIRAD/NRI, cited in Verissimo, 2001). Verissimo has estimated a time series of licence values, adapted in Fig. 3.3, which is well in line with that sporadic information. At the level of licence prices estimated, their value was equivalent to between one-quarter and one-third of the importer's selling price in the EU.

As a side-remark, the fact that licences for dollar banana imports have indeed attracted such a high value in the EU is indicative of a situation in which, contrary to statements of the EU made in the second GATT banana panel, the quota is very much restrictive.

Another notable feature of the new regime was the way in which it responded to the complex structure of the companies that were

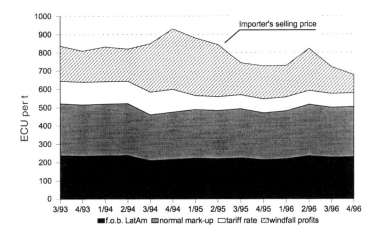

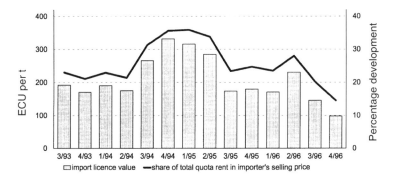

Fig. 3.3. Quarterly development of import margin components and import licence value under the COMB. Adapted from Verissimo (2001).

involved in marketing bananas in the EU and that had, of course, lobbied intensively during the process of deciding on the new regime (Pedler, 1996). Given the company-specific trading relations with different sources of bananas, the new regime, interfering directly with banana imports from different origins, was bound to affect the commercial operations of banana marketers. The TRQ on dollar bananas constrained the volume of business of the companies concerned, or at least plans for expansion. Most important, the licences issued under the TRQs were bound to carry rents, and hence to have a very direct impact on company profits. The complex structure of the regime finally established for allocating licences reflects the difficulties in finding an 'appropriate' solution to these issues at the company level. Of course, different companies belonged to different elements in the classification of different types of banana marketers, and determining the regime for the specific allocation of licences to the different classes was a complicated political game of balancing their respective interests. On the other hand, there is no doubt that the new regime had far-reaching consequences for the structure and conduct of the industry, which became obvious in the years following its establishment.[20]

Given that the COMB necessarily affected some parties in the EU negatively (in addition to causing trouble at the international level), it could not come as a surprise that these parties tried to pull all conceivable strings in order to avoid it while it was being discussed, and to change or eliminate it after it had been established. Among the strings pulled, legal actions were particularly prominent. In the EU, legal actions were taken at both the European level, i.e. before the European Court of Justice (ECJ), and at the level of national jurisdiction.

The ECJ has long been kept busy with banana issues. Between 1974 and 1992, before the introduction of the COMB, the ECJ took 18 decisions on banana issues (Cascante and Sander, 1999: 185–187). After the COMB had been established in 1993, the number of cases brought before the ECJ increased even more. Between June 1993 and March 1998, 37 decisions on banana cases were taken by the ECJ (Cascante and Sander, 1999: 180–185). The series of complaints against the COMB brought before the ECJ started immediately after the Council of Ministers had decided on the COMB in February 1993, and even before it entered into force on 1 July 1993. A number of banana-importing companies in the EU initiated proceedings against the new COMB in May 1993, arguing that the new arrangements for trade with third countries impaired their economic fate. However, their complaint was considered inadmissible by the ECJ in June 1993, because the complainants were, in the view of the ECJ, not directly and individually affected by the new regime. Though this decision appeared rather debatable to some legal observers (Cascante and Sander, 1999: 44–46), it remained in force.

A day after the banana importers had approached the ECJ, the German government, supported by the governments of the Netherlands and Belgium, also complained against the COMB. This complaint, politically linked to the proceedings initiated by the companies (Wessels, 1995: 72–80), targeted several issues. It argued, amongst other things, that: (i) the procedure by which the decision had been taken in the EU was deficient in several regards; (ii) the COMB was inconsistent with the objectives of the CAP as laid down in Article 39 of the Rome Treaty (Article 33 after renumbering in the Treaty of Amsterdam); (iii) the allocation of licences was inconsistent with EU

---

[20] For an analysis of the implications of the COMB for the structure and conduct of the industry, see Verissimo (2001).

competition rules under Article 42 (36 new) of the Treaty; (iv) the
COMB conflicted with the basic rights of property and freedom to
pursue an economic activity and with the principles of proportionality;
(v) it violated the rules on non-discrimination (Article 40; 34
new Treaty); (vi) it did away, without sufficient legal basis, with
the banana protocol that Adenauer had managed to get annexed to
the Treaty of Rome; (vii) the regulations on non-traditional ACP
bananas violated Article 168 of the Lomé Convention; and (viii) the
COMB conflicted with the EU's obligations under the GATT (Cascante
and Sander, 1999: 47–71). However, after having first decided that an
interim order against the entering into force of the COMB, sought by
Germany, was not justified, the ECJ finally ruled against Germany
in October 1994 and upheld the COMB. Here again, legal observers
were not completely convinced of all elements of the ECJ's decisions
(Cascante and Sander, 1999). One of the resulting problems was the fact
that the ECJ decision essentially gave EU legislation priority over GATT
obligations, creating a legal conflict for EU member states. Member
countries of the EU are also members of the GATT/WTO, and thus
legally bound by GATT rules. At the same time, however, as EU
members they have to live up to EU law, as interpreted by the ECJ. In
effect the decision by the ECJ meant that EU member countries were
forced to violate their obligations under the GATT. Later legal proceedings against central elements of the COMB, against the Framework
Agreement (see below) and against rules for allocating licences,
brought before the ECJ by Germany, the Netherlands and Belgium as
well as by trading companies, were equally unsuccessful.

Legal actions against the implications of the COMB were also
initiated at national courts, mainly in Germany. For example, a German
importing company lodged a complaint against the allocation of
licences at the Administrative Court of Frankfurt/Main in 1994, which
then asked the ECJ to decide on the legality of the COMB. Yet, as was to
be expected, the ECJ confirmed its decision of October 1994 in the case
brought by the German government (Cascante and Sander, 1999: 91).
The Fiscal Court at Hamburg, when asked by an importing company to
rule against the imposition of the high above-quota tariff, requested the
German customs authority to grant that company a certain quantity of
bananas duty-free outside the quota, as an interim order while the ECJ
was asked to rule in this matter. The German Federal Fiscal Court,
when requested to overrule the action taken by the Hamburg Fiscal
Court, refused to do so. It argued that the COMB was inconsistent with
the GATT, as demonstrated in the GATT panel, and that international
legal obligations had priority over EU legislation. Though in the end
this did not change the COMB, the legal issue remained whether EU
legislation has priority over international obligations and national law.
The latter issue, i.e. the consistency between basic national law and

EU legislation, remains unresolved in a number of regards, and the German Constitutional Court, which had, among others, looked into the consistency of the Maastricht Treaty with the German constitution, still has to decide on a number of issues in this context (Becker-Çelik, 1996: 154 ff.; Cascante and Sander, 1999: 92 ff.).

References

Agra Europe, Bonn, German edition, various issues.

Agra Europe, London, English edition, various issues.

Becker-Çelik, A. (1996) EG-Marktordnungsrecht im Konflikt mit den GATT-Vorschriften und deutschem Verfassungsrecht: Eine Untersuchung am Beispiel der EG-Verordnung Nr. 404/93 des Rates vom 13. Februar 1993 über die gemeinsame Marktorganisation für Bananen. [EC law on market regimes in conflict with GATT rules and German constitutional law: a study of the example of EC Council regulation no. 404/93 of 13 February 1993 on the common market organization for bananas.] Europäische Hochschulschriften, Reihe II: Rechtswissenschaft, Vol. 2000, Peter Lang, Frankfurt am Main.

Behr, H.-C. and Ellinger, W. (1993) *Die Bananenmarktordnung und ihre Folgen*. ZMP, Bonn.

Biskup, R., Clapham, R. and Starbatty, J. (1968) *Dirigismus versus Marktwirtschaft in der EWG: Das Beispiel der europäischen Bananeneinfuhr.* Untersuchungen Nr. 19. Institut für Wirtschaftspolitik an der Universität zu Köln, Köln.

Borrell, B. and Cuthbertson, S. (1991) *EC Banana Policy 1992: Picking the Best Option.* Centre for International Economics, Canberra.

Borrell, B. and Yang, M.-C. (1990) *EC Bananarama 1992*. Working paper 523, International Economics Department, The World Bank, Washington, DC.

Cascante, J.C. and Sander, G.G. (1999) *Der Streit um die EG-Bananenmarktordnung.* Tübinger Schriften zum internationalen und europäischen Recht, Band 46. Duncker & Humblot, Berlin.

European Commission (1994) *Report on the EC Banana Regime.* Document DGVI/5671/94. European Commission, Brussels.

Fitzpatrick, J. & Associates (1990) *Trade Policy and the EC Banana Market, An Economic Analysis.* Fitzpatrick & Associates, Dublin.

GATT (1994) *EEC-Import Regime for Bananas.* Report of the Panel, GATT document DS38/R. GATT, Geneva, 11 February.

Hallam, D. and Lord Peston (1997) *The Political Economy of Europe's Banana Trade.* Occasional Paper 5, Department of Agricultural and Food Economics, University of Reading.

Kretschmer, H. (1983) Artikel 115. In: von der Groeben, H., von Beck, H., Thiesing, J. and Ehlermann, C.-D. (eds) *Kommentar zum EWG-Vertrag.* Band 1, Artikel 1-136, 3rd edn. Nomos Verlag, Baden-Baden.

Krüger, J. (1994) *Eine polit-ökonomische Betrachtung der EG-Handelspolitik Beispiel: Bananen.* Arbeitspapiere des Fachbereichs

Wirtschaftswissenschaften der Universität-Gesamthochschule Paderborn, Neue Folge Nr. 40. Fachbereich Wirtschaftswissenschaften, Paderborn.

Leeb, F. and Lipper, H. (1995) *Das krumme Ding: Von Bananen, Multis und Märkten*. Schmetterling Verlag, Stuttgart.

Matthews, A. (1992) The European Community's Banana Policy after 1992. *Discussion Papers in Agricultural Economics* 13. Institut für Agrarpolitik und Marktforschung, University of Giessen.

Pedler, R.H. (1996) The fruit companies and the banana trade regime. In: Pedler, R.H. and Van Schendelen, M.P. (eds) *Lobbying the European Union: Companies, Trade Associations and Issue Groups*. Dartmouth, Aldershot, UK.

Raboy, D.G., Simpson, T.L. and Xu, B. (1995) A transition proposal for Lomé Convention trade preferences: the case of the EU Banana Regime. *The World Economy* 18, 565–581.

Read, R. (1994) The EC internal banana market: the issues and the dilemma. *The World Economy* 19, 217–235.

Stevens, C. (1996) EU policy for the banana market: the external impact of external policies. In: Wallace, H. and Wallace, W. (eds) *Policy-Making in the European Union*. Oxford University Press, Oxford.

Verissimo, P. (2001) Implications of the EU banana trade regime for selected import markets: economic analysis and political dimension. PhD dissertation, Institute of Agricultural Economics, University of Göttingen, published by Dissertation.com, USA.

Wessels, B.-A. (1995) *Das Bananendiktat: Plädoyer für einen freien Aussenhandel Europas*. Campus Verlag, Frankfurt.

The European Common Banana Policy

4

Stefan Tangermann[1]

Introduction

The domestic legal proceedings against the EU's new common banana regime were not the only threat for the sustainability of that policy. Legal action was of course also taken against the EU banana policy at the international level in the GATT/WTO. While the developments in the GATT are discussed in a separate chapter, they were time and again reflected in repeated changes made to its regime by the EU. These developments in the EU after the original establishment of the common banana regime are the subject of this chapter. It starts with a section on the relationships between EU banana policy and the Uruguay Round negotiations, and continues with the EU response in 1998 to the third WTO banana panel. As that response again proved not to satisfy the EU's trading partners, another round of WTO proceedings against the EU was triggered and required further changes to the EU's banana policy. However, before the respective changes were made, and at a moment when they were already far progressed in the pipeline of the EU legislative process, in April 2001 the EU and the USA suddenly

[1] The author is grateful to Patrick Verissimo for his assistance in the analysis of developments in the EU banana sector. Parts of this chapter are adapted from his doctoral dissertation, Verissimo (2001). Thanks are also due to Thomas Jürgensen for helpful comments on an earlier draft.

struck a deal which, as they said, resolved the long-standing dispute over the EU's banana import regime. This last episode in the banana saga is reported in the final section of the chapter.

EU Banana Policy and the Uruguay Round

As previously mentioned, the EU's banana policy was not directly an element of the Uruguay Round of negotiations in agriculture, as the EU had a bound tariff on bananas before the Uruguay Round, and hence tariffication was not relevant in that case. Deficiency payments to EU banana producers are included in the EU's domestic support commitment (and the relevant WTO notifications since the beginning of the Uruguay Round implementation period). However, there was no particular problem involved in the negotiations on that part of the EU's commitments. The EU's banana policies entered the Uruguay Round through the back door. It was the negotiation of the Framework Agreement between the EU and four Latin American banana exporters while the Uruguay Round went on, and inclusion of that Agreement in the EU's Schedule at Marrakesh, which established some links between the COMB and the Uruguay Round.

In January 1993, Colombia, Costa Rica, Guatemala, Nicaragua and Venezuela requested the EU in the GATT to hold consultations on the draft COMB on which the EU Council of Ministers had voted in December 1992. When these consultations failed, the five Latin American countries initiated a formal dispute in the GATT, which led to the second banana panel.[2] The subject of that dispute is discussed in the Chapter on GATT/WTO issues. Soon after the panel report on that second GATT banana dispute was issued in January 1994, the EU persuaded four of the five complaining countries (all except Guatemala) to drop their multilateral efforts to obtain a GATT-consistent EU regime by offering them, in an arrangement known as the Framework Agreement on bananas, specific benefits on a bilateral basis. As part of the Framework Agreement, the four Latin American countries agreed that they would 'not pursue the adoption of the GATT panel report on this issue'. The EU subsequently blocked the efforts by Guatemala to have the second panel report adopted in the GATT Council.

The Framework Agreement was a peculiar mix of some liberalization, country-specific reward for those Latin American exporters that had agreed to drop the GATT challenge, and even more complexity added to the COMB. One element of apparent liberalization came in the

---

[2] The same five Latin American countries had requested the first GATT banana panel in 1992.

form of a reduction of the in-quota tariff, from 100 'green' ECU to 75 'commercial' ECU per t, an effective reduction by 38% considering that one 'green' ECU was equivalent to 1.21 'commercial' ECU. However, by itself this tariff cut did not liberalize trade, but rather resulted in larger rents to the holder of licences to dollar banana imports (see Fig. 3.3). The more relevant element of liberalization was an increase of the TRQ on dollar bananas, from 2 million t to 2.1 million t in 1994 and 2.2 million t for 1995 (later to be further expanded because of EU enlargement). This factor tended to depress quota rents (see Fig. 3.3 above).

Reward to the four Latin American signatories of the Framework Agreement came in two forms, both also adding to the complexity of the regime. First, the previous aggregate TRQ for third country bananas was now split up among different origins. One country-specific part (49.4% of the total TRQ) was to be allocated, on a country-by-country basis, to the four Latin American countries that had signed the Framework Agreement. Ninety thousand tons were reserved for non-traditional African Caribbean and Pacific (ACP) bananas, and only the residual (46.5% of the 1995 quota) was available on an MFN basis. The quotas allocated to the four 'well-behaved' Latin American countries provided them with market access significantly above their past exports to the EU. In addition, these four signatories of the Framework Agreement received the further benefit that they were now allowed to issue export licences for 70% of their country-specific quotas. Though the motivation for this new element in the COMB was, according to the text of the Framework Agreement, 'to make it possible to improve regular and stable trade relations between producers and importers', the economics of this device clearly were that the exporting countries concerned were in this way enabled to attract part of the quota rent that used to flow to importing companies in the EU.

The Framework Agreement was an attempt at solving the EU's banana problem in the GATT, unsuccessfully as it later turned out. At the same time it was hoped that the Agreement would help to reduce disharmony among some participants in the banana game. However, in effect, it was a divisive act in several regards. In Latin America, it caused a split in the association of banana-exporting countries (UPEB), because it offered benefits to only some of its member countries, while others, such as Ecuador and Panama, were left at the fringe (Leeb and Lipper, 1995: 29).

Inside the EU, member states had widely diverging views on the Agreement. Germany, in particular, was opposed to the Agreement, because it feared that this type of accord might undermine the possibility that the COMB, which was against German interests, could be attacked in the GATT, and the EU then be forced to liberalize its banana policy. The German government was also opposed to discrimination among Latin American countries (i.e. between signatories and non-signatories of the Framework Agreement). Moreover, some German companies had lobbied forcefully against the addition of export licences to the regime. Their argument was that this would raise the prices they had to pay to banana producers, and hence both reduce their profits and result in higher consumer prices (Wessels, 1995: 102 ff.). However, in reality the companies concerned feared that they would lose quota rents.[3]

The European Commission wanted both to solve the GATT problem and to counteract criticism from inside the EU. It appeared to the Commission that an ideal way of attaining these aims was to fold the Framework Agreement into the conclusion of the Uruguay Round by making it an integral part of the EU Schedule.[4] In a way this procedure lacked logic, because bananas, with a bound EU tariff, had not been included in the process of tariffication. The only thing that the EU Schedule should have said about bananas was that the old bound tariff was maintained.[5] However, inclusion of the Agreement (including the paragraph saying that it represented a settlement of the dispute between the EU and the four Latin American countries) in the EU Schedule was hoped to give it full status in international law. The adjusted COMB would thus, it was thought, become safe against further complaints in the WTO, not only from the four Latin American countries involved, but also from all other WTO members which, after all, would finally accept everything that was included in any Uruguay Round Schedule. How and why this assumption proved to be wrong will be outlined below in the Chapter on the GATT/WTO.

The EU Commission hoped that opposition from inside the EU, in particular from Germany, would be overcome because all member

---

[3] Export licences established under the Framework Agreement applied only to Category A and C operators, but not to Category B operators (importers of ACP/EU/DOM bananas). Thus a further element of discrimination among different categories of trading companies was introduced, as also found by the ECJ in dealing with a complaint brought by Germany in 1998. This appears to have been the only case in which the ECJ found an element of the COMB inconsistent with EU law (Jürgensen, 1998).

[4] In the EU Schedule that resulted from the Uruguay Round, the tariff rate and TRQ volume negotiated in the Framework Agreement are listed under 'current access', with an Annex containing the full text of the Agreement.

[5] Instead, the EU Schedule from the Uruguay Round lists the above-quota tariff of 850 ECU t^{-1}, to be reduced to 680 ECU t^{-1} by 2000. Strange enough for a commodity that had not undergone the usual process of tariffication, the EU Schedule also foresees the option of applying the Special Safeguard provision to bananas.

states finally had to vote on the overall outcome of the Uruguay Round, but could not pick individual elements (Cascante and Sander, 1999: 38). In the end this tactic was successful. However, for a while the situation looked difficult. On the first day of the Marrakesh meeting in April 1994, German Chancellor Kohl wrote a letter to Delors, President of the European Commission, warning that conclusion of the Framework Agreement in the context of the Final Act of the Uruguay Round could result in 'significant risks for the Marrakesh Ministerial Meeting', and asking Delors to make sure that 'a solution that is acceptable also from the German perspective' was found to the banana problem (Wessels, 1995: 119). Günter Rexrodt, then German minister of economic affairs, responsible for trade matters in the German government, wrote a letter of similar substance to EU Trade Commissioner Sir Leon Brittan (Wessels, 1995: 119). France, on the other hand, strongly favoured inclusion of the Framework Agreement in the EU Schedule. In order to find a solution, the presidency of the European Council met individually with each member state. In the struggle between France and Germany, France threatened not to sign the (plurilateral) Agreement on Government Procurement, and to stop its investment in Germany's New Bundesländer (Wessels, 1995: 129). At the last minute, a compromise was found in the form of a declaration of the EU member states, in which the legal and political reservations of some member states, in particular Germany, were acknowledged (Wessels, 1995: 128). Thus the Framework Agreement, and the EU's banana policy based on it, found its way into the Final Act agreed at Marrakesh.

Soon after Marrakesh, another round of EU enlargement took place on 1 January 1995, with the accession of Austria, Finland and Sweden. All three countries previously had followed a free-trade policy with respect to bananas and imported exclusively from the dollar zone. After joining the EU, they now had to adopt the COMB. Consequently, to accommodate the additional import demand resulting from its enlargement, the EU opened a second TRQ set at 353,000 t, to complement the TRQ set in the Framework Agreement. This additional TRQ was to be administered in the same way as the original TRQ resulting from the Framework Agreement.[6]

---

[6] From January to October 1995, though, the distinction between operator functions (primary importers, secondary importers and ripeners) did not apply to the three new member states. Licences were, instead, simply allocated to companies located in the three new member states, which in the past had often bought bananas from primary importers located in other EU member countries (mostly Germany). Had these companies been treated as secondary importers or ripeners right away, they would have received much smaller numbers of licences.

EU Response to the Third Banana Panel

Hopes that inclusion of the Framework Agreement in the EU's Uruguay Round Schedule would make it immune against criticism in the newly founded WTO soon proved futile. In September 1995, Guatemala, Honduras, Mexico and the USA requested consultations with the EU, and, in February 1996, Ecuador joined them. Soon a third banana dispute was initiated, this time under the new dispute settlement procedures of the WTO (see Chapter on GATT/WTO issues). The panel report, issued in May 1997, again found the EU to be in breach of its international obligations. The EU appealed against the panel decision, but the report of the Appellate Body ended no better for the EU. The EU was given until January 1999 to bring its banana regime in line with its WTO obligations.

In response to the third banana panel, the EU modified the COMB again in the second half of 1998.[7] The new regime has been in place since January 1999 and is essentially still applied at the time of writing.[8] With respect to traditional ACP bananas, although the quota ceiling remained unchanged at 857,700 t year^{-1}, the EU shifted from an allocated to an unallocated quota. In other words, the country-specific allocations previously existing for the 12 traditional ACP banana-supplying countries have been removed. This implies that traditional ACP exporting countries, who under the previous regime had filled their national quota and were either forced to limit their traditionally EU-oriented export production accordingly, or to export their above-quota volumes to non-EU markets,[9] could take advantage of the lack of supplies from those ACP countries who had previously regularly under-filled their quota. Therefore, the new regime enhanced competition among the group of traditional ACP exporting countries.

Far more significant in the new banana regime of the EU were the provisions regarding trade with dollar and non-traditional ACP bananas. In particular, the EU eliminated all regulations related to the Framework Agreement and reviewed the management of its

---

[7] The principles of the new EU banana regime were adopted, by the EU Council of farm ministers, as part of a package of reform measures in the agricultural sector. Denmark and the Netherlands voted against the package, which also included measures on the olive oil regime, as well as the EU farm price package for 1998/99.

[8] The text of the rest of this section is largely adapted from Verissimo (2001).

[9] It can be assumed that even with a preferential tariff margin of 100 ECU t^{-1} over dollar bananas, the importation under the former COMB of above-quota traditional ACP bananas (per definition, non-traditional ACP imports) was prohibited by the high second-tier tariff rate.

TRQ for third-country bananas. The EU maintained the TRQ of 2.2 million t year^{-1} bound in its GATT Schedule, as well as the autonomous TRQ of 353,000 t year^{-1} introduced to account for the EU enlargement to 15 countries. However, following the failed negotiations with third countries having a 'substantial interest' (i.e. a 10% minimum share in previous imports) in the supply of bananas to the EU, the EU allocated the bound and autonomous third-country TRQs on the basis of the 1994–1996 period. As a result, Ecuador, Costa Rica, Colombia and Panama obtained individual shares, amounting to over 90% of the total TRQ, while the residual was allocated to the remaining exporting countries, i.e. non-traditional ACP and other dollar-zone countries.

In terms of trade flows, the new allocation of the TRQ for third-country bananas implied that the four dollar-zone countries could, on aggregate, ship a higher share of bananas to the EU than ever before. In addition, each of these four countries could export a higher volume of dollar bananas to the EU than under previous COMB regulations, including Costa Rica and Colombia who had already obtained a larger TRQ share under the Framework Agreement than their previous export performance. Bananas from the dollar zone imported within the TRQ continued to be subject to a first-tier tariff rate of €75 t^{-1}.[10] Above-quota imports of dollar bananas faced the bound second-tier tariff rate of €737 t^{-1}.[11]

Under the COMB established in 1999, the regulations for the importation of non-traditional ACP bananas were changed dramatically. Their access to the EU banana market was improved by replacing their duty-free quota of 90,000 t allocated under the Framework Agreement by a share in the bound and autonomous TRQ of 9.43%, i.e. 240,748 t.[12] However, this share in the overall quota was not allocated to individual countries, and could also be used by exporters from the dollar zone, a potentially attractive opportunity for dollar-zone countries such as Honduras, fifth largest single pre-COMB supplier to the EU, who have not been allocated a national share of the third-country TRQ.

---

[10] In an initial proposal that had been rejected, the EU Commission intended to set the in-quota tariff rate for the autonomous TRQ at ECU 300 t^{-1}.

[11] In January 1999, the EU replaced the ECU with its new currency, the euro (currency symbol €), on a one-to-one basis (€1 = ECU 1). The above-quota tariff was to be reduced in annual steps according to the EU Schedule established in the Uruguay Round.

[12] Also, non-traditional ACP bananas enjoyed an increase in the margin of preference for above-quota supply to the EU from €100 to 200 t^{-1}. In other words, they were subject to an above-quota tariff of only €537 t^{-1}. However, even this tariff was likely to be prohibitive.

Finally, with the COMB regulations implemented since January 1999, the EU reformed the administrative aspects of its TRQs, addressing some of the most controversial elements of its previous banana regime. Unlike under preceding regulations, the distribution of import licences to EU-based banana marketers was managed in common for all TRQs, that is for the aggregate of the traditional ACP, the bound and the autonomous TRQ (in total 3,410,700 t).[13] Furthermore, abolishing the operator categories (A, B and C) as well as the distinction by activity functions (primary importer, secondary importer, ripener), the EU made the aggregate TRQ volume available to only two categories of operators – traditional operators (92% of the TRQ) and newcomers (8%). As a result, the controversial allocation of 30% of the market share for dollar bananas to traditional traders of ACP and eurobananas (formerly category B operators) was eliminated. Most important, licence allocation to operators was based on the quantities imported in a fixed reference period, namely the 3-year period 1994–1996, and independent of their source. This fundamental change, while continuing to discriminate against traditional importers of dollar bananas relative to their situation before introduction of the COMB, eliminated the incentive to import more ACP and EU/DOM bananas in order to obtain a larger volume of licences. As a result, cross-subsidization of ACP bananas from rents on dollar bananas disappeared. Eventually, EU import demand for ACP and eurobananas was bound to decline under the new COMB.[14]

Furthermore, the redefinition of operator categories implied that, whether established or newcomers, licences were distributed solely to those who actually physically ship bananas and release them for circulation in the EU. In effect, this implied a transfer of rents from former category B operators to former category A importers, since the corresponding volume of B-licences previously purchased by category A operators was no longer attributed to the former category B operators. Thus, in contrast with the old licence system, the new regime favoured importers in countries whose markets had been dominated by dollar bananas prior to 1993, at the expense of operators in formerly protected markets. Data show that, relative to 1998, the import licence volume allocated to Spain and France for 1999 corresponded to a loss of approximately 41 and 20% respectively, while Austria had gained

---

[13] This followed a model put forward by the Netherlands and backed by all EU countries that had open-market trade policies for bananas before 1993 (*Agra Europe*, 25/98; Agra Europe, Bonn).

[14] In anticipation of the economy losses, the EU increased the deficiency payments for its domestic producers and agreed to direct aid for ACP producers.

around 118%, Sweden 114%, Finland 85% and Germany 12% (WTO, 1999).[15]

In addition, banana importers could, under the new COMB, apply for licences to import bananas regardless of the fruit's country of origin. This gave traditional importers of dollar bananas the opportunity to access the supply from ACP countries. With regard to the considerable strategic investments made by the US transnational corporations in the past, it was likely that this could lead to a restructuring (and possibly concentration) in the lower links of the banana distribution chain (i.e. producer–exporter/shipper–importer). Overall, it appeared that under the new regime traditional traders of ACP and eurobananas had lost some of the benefits enjoyed under the pre-1999 COMB, while marketing and transaction costs for traditional dollar banana importers were reduced, thus enhancing competition between the different EU-based importers.

The Policy Changes Go On: Developments After 1998

The most important outcome of the new regime in place since January 1999 was that it failed to meet the demands of the countries that had confronted the EU in the third banana panel. Therefore, in December 1998, these countries requested the WTO Dispute Settlement Body to examine whether the envisaged new COMB was compatible with WTO rules. As was widely expected, the Panel found that several elements of the revised regime, too, were not consistent with WTO rules. As a result, the EU was once again requested to bring its COMB into conformity with the WTO provisions. Moreover, the Panel, for the first time in the history of the banana dispute, suggested how this could be achieved (see chapter on GATT/WTO issues). In this situation, it became clear to the EU that it could no longer sustain a banana regime that did not meet the EU's obligations in the WTO. This conclusion was reinforced through the ensuing retaliations by the US, the threats from Ecuador to join the US and impose further trade sanctions against the EU, and the increasing burden on the EU budget resulting from the financial aid to ACP and eurobanana producers. There was also no prospect of a successful appeal of the WTO ruling. Against this background, the EU promptly worked on a proposal to once again reform its import regime for bananas.

---

[15] The significant gains of the three new EU member states (Austria, Finland and Sweden) have to be seen in the context of the specific rules applying in these countries from January to October 1995, which generated a larger reference quantity for them. See footnote 6.

In addition to meeting the same diverging interests and commitments as when it designed the initial COMB in 1993, the EU faced a situation where interested parties could look back at their experience of several years of common EU banana market policies. Views as to how the next regime should operate continued to differ widely. Ecuador and Panama were opposed to a country allocation between the principal dollar-zone suppliers. Costa Rica and Colombia felt that the Framework Agreement had appropriately set their share of the third-country TRQ. The US preferred a tariff-only regime, possibly after a transitional period in which TRQ would continue to apply. However, the USA considered that allocation of licences in a TRQ should be based on a pre-1993 period, while Ecuador favoured the 1995–1997 period in which it had a particularly high share of EU imports. Among ACP suppliers, the majority continued to favour a TRQ system with duty-free access for ACP bananas, arguing that aid cannot replace trade. Some more competitive ACP suppliers, on the other hand, might also have accepted transition from a TRQ-based regime towards simple tariffs.

In trying to deal with these ever-divergent interests, the European Commission issued a proposal in November 1999 to modify the current regime in a two-step approach. After a first period, with a transitional system still based on TRQs, the EU would then move to a tariffs-only system by 2006 (European Commission, 1999). For the transition period, the EU was to retain the existing bound and autonomous TRQs of 2,200,000 and 353,000 t, at the old reduced tariff rate of €75 t^{-1}. ACP countries were to have access to this quota at zero duty. In addition, a new third TRQ of 850,000 t would be opened for which the reduction of the bound tariff would be determined using a bidding system. All these three TRQs would be open to bananas from all non-EU sources.

Regarding country allocation of the TRQs, the Commission argued that they should remain unallocated, unless an agreement with the supplying countries could be reached, which at the time looked unlikely. With respect to the company allocation of licences under the bound and the autonomous TRQ, the preferred option remained a system based on a reference period, though the Commission envisaged an 'appropriate form' of a first-come, first-served system as an alternative solution. To most observers it was completely unclear how a first-come, first-served regime might ever work efficiently in the banana sector. The European Commission anticipated such doubts and conceded that 'the practical administration of the . . . system could present a number of technical and administrative difficulties which would need to be overcome in such a way that the scheme is both physically practical and demonstrably non-discriminatory'.

For the additional TRQ of 850,000 t, the Commission proposed the allocation of licences under a new auctioning system open to all operators, referred to as 'striking price'. Operators requesting import licences would bid a certain amount of quasi-tariff they were prepared to pay, for parts of the quantity made available by the EU for the respective period (e.g. for each quarter). Bids would be ranked starting with the highest, until the overall quantity was filled. The lowest bid within the overall quantity would determine the fee operators had to pay for the licences to import under this TRQ. In effect this fee would have been equivalent to a tariff paid on those imports. This approach would have implied that if the total volume for operators' bids was less than the lot available (i.e. the TRQ is not filled), the effective tariff was zero.

The Commission suggested that ACP bananas should be granted a preference of €275 t^{-1} in this TRQ of 850,000 t, i.e. operators importing ACP bananas would pay a quasi-tariff of €275 t^{-1} less than the one resulting from the auction. This would imply a zero duty on ACP bananas within this third TRQ as long as the resulting quasi-tariff did not exceed €275 t^{-1}.

At the time one could only speculate whether that EU proposal might have induced the EU's counterparts to drop their complaints in the WTO, particularly with respect to the proposed transitional measures. A number of issues were less than fully clear, in particular the allocation of the first two TRQs, and the implications of a first-come, first-served licence distribution system. The proposed transitional regime raised some important questions.

Why a 6-year transition period? The European Commission argued for the need to give ACP and domestic suppliers enough time to pre-pare for a tariffs-only system. However, it can be argued that since the GATT panel ruled against the COMB back in 1994, it must have been obvious to all parties involved that in order to be consistent with the international legal framework, the COMB would sooner or later have to be changed fundamentally. Thus, it can also be argued that suppliers of ACP and eurobananas should, since then, have had enough time to adjust to a future regime that necessarily involved less regulation and market interference. On the other hand, the time horizon of 2006 must also be seen in relation to the efforts to find a new WTO-compatible successor for the Lomé Convention's arrangements for preferential trade relations between the EU and the ACP countries.

Why a new licence allocation system only for the third TRQ? The striking price auctioning system for licences under the third quota would have represented a distinct novelty. Auctioning is arguably the fairest and economically most efficient way to allocate licences, as it ensures that all importers are given equal opportunities to supply their marketing services. Furthermore, unlike the systems based on a historical reference period which tend to freeze the market, the auctioning of licences would have allowed for open competition between operators and have provided scope for market dynamics to prevail. Hence, the EU should have shown greater willingness to actually reform its regime by expanding the licence auctioning system to all three TRQs.

The real innovation in the Commission's approach to the EU import regime for bananas was the COMB envisaged after the transition period. A tariffs-only regime with a preferential margin for ACP bananas has the potential of bringing an end to the banana dispute, if the EU can negotiate an appropriate tariff level in the WTO.[16] Moreover, it can greatly enhance market performance through coupling the EU landed price for bananas to the world banana price, and by doing away with the constraints to competition among marketers which resulted from the licensing regime. At the same time, a tariffs-only regime can generate sufficient revenue in the EU budget for financing the direct aid to domestic and ACP suppliers. The concept of a self-financing tariff has long been advocated by economists as the first-best option to the EU's banana problem (Fitzpatrick & Associates, 1990; Borrell and Cuthbertson, 1992; Matthews, 1992).

Although no particular tariff rate was mentioned in the Commission's proposal, there were indications that a rate of €275 t^{-1} for dollar bananas was considered when the proposal was made in November 1999. With zero duty access for ACP bananas, it may be thought, a tariff of that level could provide an 'appropriate' margin of preference for ACP bananas, and a price level sufficient for EU/DOM producers. However, it is more than doubtful whether a tariff of that order of magnitude is negotiable with most suppliers from the dollar zone. Moreover, this level of tariff may be far above that which would suffice to generate the extra budget revenue that the EU may need to compensate ACP and EU/DOM producers for their losses when the EU market is made more accessible to supplies from the dollar zone.[17]

In any case, it seems that with its November 1999 proposal the EU had finally begun to realize the necessity of bringing its banana regime in line with WTO rules. However, the EU had to find out whether its trading partners could also be convinced that this was the proper way towards a WTO-compatible EU import regime for bananas, and whether the proposal was also acceptable among key players inside the EU. As a matter of fact, after having issued its November 1999 proposal, the Commission began intensive negotiations with the third countries concerned, and internally in the EU. As it turned out, unsurprisingly, interests of the various parties continued to diverge widely. The

---

[16] At the same time, the EU needs to find a WTO-compatible approach to providing preferential access to ACP bananas. However, this will have to be an element of the anyhow unavoidable general overhaul of the preferential trading regime that was maintained under the Lomé Convention.

[17] Tangermann and Verissimo (1999) have estimated that a tariff of around €125 t^{-1} would be sufficient to raise that revenue.

auctioning regime proposed by the EU Commission did not go down well with the third countries concerned. Hence negotiations returned to the issue of how to allocate the third-country TRQ to supplying countries and operators. However, in talks mainly with the USA and Ecuador, no agreement could be found on the appropriate reference period for allocating licences under a regime that would continue to be based on given shares for exporting countries – either the pre-1993 period or a more recent period after the establishment of the COMB.

Pressure on the EU mounted when the WTO authorized Ecuador, in May 2000, to impose new sanctions on the EU. As a novel approach in the WTO, Ecuador was allowed to engage in 'cross-retaliation', imposing sanctions on intellectual property rights under the TRIPS agreement (see Chapter on GATT/WTO matters). Also, the USA threatened to apply 'carousel' sanctions, i.e. to impose punitive tariffs on a periodically shifting list of products imported from the EU.

Internally, in the EU, the Commission's November 1999 proposal met with opposition from various sides, including the European Parliament. In particular, the Parliament disliked the proposal to establish a flat-rate tariff regime for bananas in 2006, and instead argued for maintaining a TRQ regime for at least 10 more years, and for a tariff preference of €300 t^{-1} for imports from ACP countries.[18] In a move to force an agreement, EU trade Commissioner Lamy threatened, in May 2000, to move to a tariffs-only approach directly. He referred to the negotiations over quota allocations to third-country exporters by using the metaphor of 'kids fighting over jam', where the jam was the quota rent, and suggested that a tariffs-only regime was equivalent to 'taking the jam off the table'.[19] However, one of the problems the Commission had to face was that those member states of the EU that had an interest in banana production (France, Spain, Portugal, Italy and Greece), backed by the UK, were opposed to giving up on a TRQ-based regime.[20] On a side track of developments, in June 2000 it turned out that 160,000 t of bananas from Ecuador had been imported illegally into the Italian port of Catania over the last 3 years with falsified import certificates, entering the EU under the lower within-quota tariff, though in effect these quantities were imported outside the quota, thus adding to legal imports under the annual 2.2 million t TRQ.[21]

Tired by the lack of success in negotiating an agreeable solution, on 5 July the EU Commission moved in a new direction. In a press release, it made the following statement:

---

[18] European Commission (2000a).
[19] *Agra Europe*, 26 May 2000, p. EP/8.
[20] *Agra Europe*, 26 May 2000, p. EP/8.
[21] *Agra Europe*, 16 June 2000, p. EP/10.

Following eight months of intensive discussions and despite the Commission's strenuous efforts to resolve the banana dispute, it has not proved
possible to reach a compromise with third countries at this stage. Since
the negotiations on maintaining a tariff quota regime on the basis of
managing import licenses on a historical basis have reached an impasse,
and taking into consideration the discussions within Council and
Parliament, the Commission has today proposed the following strategy:
It will continue to study a transitional system of tariff quotas, but at
this stage on a 'first come, first served' basis for the three tariff quotas
(a tariff preference of 275 euro/t for the ACP countries would apply). The
Commission retains its proposal for an automatic transition, on 1 January
2006, to a system based on tariffs only. In addition, the Commission
asks the Council to give its authority to begin negotiations under Article
XXVIII of the GATT with the relevant suppliers in order to implement a
flat tariff system, in case no solution can be found on the tariff quota
basis.[22]

In what was considered by some observers to be conceived as a pincer
movement strategy, the first-come, first-served approach, coupled with
the threat to move to a tariffs-only regime as the immediate alternative,
may have been designed mainly as a tactical move, not necessarily
as an approach really favoured by the Commission. If it was, some of
its persuasive power was undermined, though, by the EU Council of
foreign ministers soon after the Commission had suggested its new
plan, when the Council backed the first-come, first-served idea, but
rejected the option of moving straight to a tariffs-only regime should
negotiations on the new proposal fail.[23]

At the time it appeared that the Commission itself was not quite
convinced of the feasibility and benefits of a 'first-come, first-served
regime'. However, in the months following July 2000, it kept negotiating with the parties concerned inside and outside of the EU, and
obviously came to the conclusion that no alternative approach proved
universally acceptable. On 5 October 2000, it therefore tabled a
communication to the Council, outlining in somewhat more detail its
'first-come, first-served' proposal. As the Commission argued, 'being
WTO compatible, transparent and flexible, this system provides a
viable alternative to a system based on "historic references" on which
negotiations have reached an impasse'.[24] Under this proposal, the three
TRQs contained in the November 1999 proposal would have been
maintained. Under the 2.2 million t quota as well as the 353,000 t
quota, dollar bananas would continue to pay a €75 t[-1] tariff, while ACP
bananas would enter duty free. For the additional TRQ of 850,000 t, the

---

[22] European Commission (2000a).
[23] *Agra Europe*, 14 July 2000, p. EP/5.
[24] European Commission (2000b).

new proposal envisaged a tariff of €300 t⁻¹, while ACP countries would have duty free access to this quota as well. The proposal still envisaged a switch to a tariffs-only regime in 2006.

Allocation of all three quotas to countries of origin (including the ACP countries) and trading companies would be implemented on a first-come, first-served basis, sometimes referred to as a 'boat race'. The quotas would be managed on a fortnightly or weekly basis 'to ensure a regular import flow of the EU market'. Traders would be required 'to commit bananas to the vessel before submitting the declaration of intent to import and to lodge a sufficiently high security'. This measure is aimed at deterring speculation.

> There would also be a pre-allocation procedure based on operators declaring their intention to import a specified quantity. The pre-allocation would be decided when vessels are a sailing distance from Europe to avoid discrimination against countries that are further away.[25]

On that basis, licences would be issued on a 'first-come, first-served' basis until the quantity available for the current period was exhausted. Quantities already on vessels but not receiving an import licence under the proposed regime would have to be reshipped to alternative destinations (presumably mainly Central and Eastern Europe), or to be imported into the EU at the (economically prohibitive) beyond-quota tariff.

As usual, responses to the 'first-come, first-served' proposal were mixed. Among EU member states, opinions diverged, with countries such as Germany, and surprisingly also Italy, being opposed, while countries with their own banana interests went along with the Commission. The European Parliament signalled agreement. ACP countries were rather sceptical, as was the USA originally. The ACP feared that dollar bananas might fare better under the regime, while the USA felt it might give an effective advantage to ACP bananas. However, when Dole – contrary to the position taken by Chiquita – indicated that it could live with a 'first-come, first-served' approach, it appeared that Washington dropped its opposition. Latin American producer countries adopted varying positions. Panama, Honduras, Costa Rica, Guatemala and Nicaragua considered that a first-come, first-served regime was not WTO-compatible and perpetuated discrimination. Mexico, Colombia and Ecuador said they were studying the implications.[26] As far as different types of trading companies are concerned, the first-come, first-served approach would have favoured larger companies with their superior logistical options, while smaller companies, having only one consignment of bananas on a ship at a time, would

---

[25] European Commission (2000b).
[26] *Agra Europe*, 22 December 2000, p. EP/3.

have been in difficulties had they not received an import allocation, with the consequence that they would have had to re-direct their whole banana supply to non-EU destinations. Without having reached comprehensive agreement with all third countries concerned, the EU farm Council of Ministers adopted the regime on 19 December 2000, and the 'first-come, first-served' system was supposed to enter into force on 1 April 2001, a date that later was postponed to 1 July 2001.[27]

The Surprise Understandings of 2001: the End of the Banana Problem?

Yet, as if to demonstrate that the 'first-come, first-served' proposal had indeed only been a threat, suddenly another new turn was made in the banana saga. In a surprise move, the European Commission and the US Administration announced on 11 April 2001 that they had agreed a different solution, no longer involving the 'boat race' approach. Instead, for the transitional period before switching to a tariffs-only regime in 2006, the EU would return to a regime under which licence allocation to companies was based on historic trade. According to the press release by the EU Commission, EU Commissioners for trade and for agriculture, Lamy and Fischler, as well as US Trade Representative Zoellick and US Secretary of Commerce Evans praised the agreement saying:

> Today's step marks a significant breakthrough. It demonstrates the commitment of the Bush Administration and the European Commission to work together closely and effectively on trade issues. The banana disputes of the past nine years have been disruptive for all the parties involved – traders, Latin American, African and Caribbean producers, and consumers. We are confident that today's agreement will end the past friction and move us toward a better basis for the banana trade.[28]

The EU press release also said that:

> both parties recognized that they had shared objectives: to reach agreement on a WTO-compliant system, to ensure fair and satisfactory access to the European market for bananas from all origins and all operators, and to protect the vulnerable African Caribbean Pacific (ACP) producers. Most important, both parties agreed the time had come to end a dispute which had led to prolonged conflict in the world trading system.

Under the accord, the USA promised to end the trade sanctions imposed on the EU as a result of the WTO disputes. The EU notified the

---

[27] Rules for the first-come, first-served regime are laid down in Council Regulation 216/2001.
[28] European Commission (2001a).

WTO about the Understanding, as a mutually agreed solution to the banana dispute.

To most observers, and even to people closely involved in the EU banana regime, the background to the sudden agreement between the EU and the USA was and still is something of a mystery. The negotiations obviously took place behind tightly closed doors, in an extremely small circle. On the EU side, the member states were not involved. The so-called 113 Committee of member states' trade officials, acting as a substitute to the Council of trade ministers on a day-to-day basis, is usually consulted by the Commission during international negotiations on serious trade matters. In this case it appears the 113 Committee was only informed after the fact. What made the impasse on bananas, that had existed for such a long time, break in April 2001 awaits the research of historians. One factor may have been an attempt on both the EU and the US side to demonstrate, in the context of a highly visible (but economically limited) trade dispute, that the new US Administration and the European Commission can fruitfully cooperate. Along similar lines, it appears that US Trade Representative Zoellick and EU Trade Commissioner Lamy get along well with each other, and were interested to show that this was effective even in difficult cases.

The text of the Understanding on Bananas starts by saying that 'the European Commission and the USA have identified the means by which the long-standing dispute over the EC's banana import regime can be resolved'.[29] It then confirms that the EU will introduce a tariffs-only regime no later than 1 January 2006, though nothing is said about the tariff rate to apply under that regime. The main content of the Understanding, though, is the agreement on administration of the TRQ regime during the transitional period. The EU commits itself to implementing in Phase I, to start on 1 July 2001, an import regime on the basis of historical licensing. The three types of TRQs set in the most recent EU regulation of February 2001 (thought to establish the first-come, first-served regime) are maintained, i.e. the WTO-bound quota of 2.2 million t (quota 'A'), the autonomous quota of 353,000 t (quota 'B') dating back to EU Northern enlargement, and an additional autonomous quota of 850,000 t (quota 'C'). Like before, the tariff is €75 t^{-1} on imports within quotas A and B, and €300 t^{-1} on imports within quota C. Imports from ACP countries are granted a preference of €300 t^{-1}, meaning that they enter duty-free under all three quotas. Given the high non-ACP tariff on quota C, this quota is essentially reserved for ACP supplies, though the tariff on non-ACP imports within that quota can be reduced if ACP supplies don't fill the quota.

---

[29] Internal Commission document containing the text of the Understanding on Bananas.

As far as TRQ administration is concerned, quotas A and B are to be managed as one, and according to the Understanding,

> there is no expectation of allocations of shares of either of these TRQs among country suppliers, and the Commission will not seek to convene a meeting to that effect of the principal supplying countries except upon the joint request of all such countries.

Quota allocation, then, relies wholly on the distribution of licences to importing companies. As a new element, licences for no less than 83% of the A and B quotas are to be distributed to 'traditional operators A/B', based on their average imports in the 1994–1996 period. The definition of these importers is such that companies that had actually imported dollar bananas or non-traditional ACP bananas in the 1994–1996 period are covered. Licences for the remaining 17% of the A and B quantity go to 'non-traditional' operators that did not import the bananas concerned in the 1994–1996 period. Licences for quota C are equally allocated on an 83/17 basis to traditional and non-traditional operators, where imports of traditional ACP bananas during the reference period determine whether operators are traditional or non-traditional for the purposes of quota C.

The Understanding also provides that in Phase II, to begin 'as soon as possible', the EU will shift 100,000 t from quota C to quota B, with the remaining 750,000 t in quota C then reserved for ACP bananas. Licence allocation will continue to be managed as in Phase I until 31 December 2003, but after that date will be based only on usage of licences under Phase II. The start of Phase II will be subject to the adoption of the WTO waiver that the EU needs in order to continue to provide preferential treatment, for bananas and other goods, to imports from the ACP countries. In this regard, the Understanding provides that the USA will support EU efforts in the WTO to obtain that waiver. Regarding US punitive tariffs on imports from the EU, introduced in April 1999 as part of the banana dispute, the Understanding commits the USA to suspend them provisionally during Phase I, and to terminate them under Phase II, though they may be reimposed if Phase II does not enter into force by 1 January 2002.

The intended move to a tariffs-only regime in 2006, confirmed again by the Understanding, has also to be seen in the context of another development in the EU's trade policy that took place in early 2001. It was the EU's decision to provide duty and quota free access to all imports from the least-developed countries, except imports of arms. This 'Everything but Arms' (EBA) initiative, adopted by the EU Council of Ministers on 26 February 2001, aims, among other things, at replacing the EU's preferential trade arrangement for the ACP countries under the Lomé Convention (now Cotonou Agreement) by a WTO-consistent regime for those ACP countries that belong to the category of least-developed countries. To the surprise and opposition of many in the EU, the EBA regime also foresees duty- and quota-free access for three 'sensitive' agricultural products, namely sugar, rice and bananas. In the case of bananas, imports will be liberalized through a process of five annual steps of reducing the full EU tariff by 20% every year, starting on 1 January 2002. In other words, from 1 January 2006 all least-developed countries will have completely free access to the EU's banana market. According to a document prepared by the EU Commission, it is not yet clear what effect that policy change will have on the EU banana market and trade.[30]

When the surprising bilateral deal between the USA and the EU was struck in April 2001, it was not yet clear whether all other countries involved in the dispute, in particular Ecuador, would go along. The text of the US/EU Understanding said that 'the EC and the United States have informed Ecuador and will cooperate in seeking the agreement of all parties'. However, it appears that at that time Ecuador was not yet really on board. The Ecuadorian Ambassador to the EU was on record having commented, after the US/EU Understanding was presented to the surprised public, that 'the "banana war" cannot end without an agreement which includes the world's largest exporter of this fruit . . . and which does not exclusively satisfy the interests of a country which is not even a banana producer'.[31] Ecuador's ministers of external affairs and agriculture issued a statement to the effect that 'it is disconcerting that the US and EU . . . while preparing for a new Round at the WTO, think that their will can override the principles of the multilateral trading system'.[32] EU officials, on the other hand, commented that the accord struck with the US 'is not a bad deal for Ecuador. It is very close to the Ecuadorian position.'[33] However, a little later even Ecuador gave the green light to the new accord, after the EU had promised to formulate the definition of 'non-traditional operators' under quotas A/B such that native firms from the exporting countries got a better chance to access this quota in competition with the big multinational companies.[34] The EU and Ecuador also concluded a formal understanding, also notified to the WTO, in which the provisions for the EU's future banana measures are specified in exactly the same way as in the EU/US understanding.

From then on, things appeared to move smoothly. The EU acted quickly to implement Phase I of the Understanding, by adopting a new

---

[30] European Commission (2001b).
[31] *Agra Europe*, 20 April 2001, p. EP/2.
[32] *Agra Europe*, 20 April 2001, p. EP/2.
[33] *Agra Europe*, 20 April 2001, p. EP/2.
[34] *Agra Europe*, 4 May 2001, pp. EP/3–4.

banana regulation on 7 May 2001, to be applied from 1 July 2001.[35] The
new regime implemented, in a one-to-one fashion, the content of
the US/EU understanding. The US also kept its promise and lifted the
trade sanctions on 1 July 2001. These sanctions, in the form of 100% *ad
valorem* duties on EU exports to the US worth US$191.4 million, had
been in place since 19 April 1999. Trading companies were reasonably
happy with the new banana regime. Most of them preferred it over
a boat race approach, though the exact degree of happiness of each
individual company of course depended on how it fared in the
new allocation regime for licences, based on its imports during the
1994–1996 reference period. In August 2001, the EU Commission also
tabled a new draft Council Regulation that would implement Phase II of
the Understanding, i.e. a transfer of 100,000 t from quota C to quota B,
with the remaining 750,000 t in quota being exclusively reserved for
ACP countries, at zero duty. There were only two minor irritations in
the summer of 2001. First, it turned out that the French administration
had given out licences for more than 50,000 t of dollar bananas under
the reduced tariff, though French importers had, according to the
Commission, rights to no more than 4000 t a year (European Commission, 2001c). The Commission immediately initiated infringement
proceedings against France.

Second, four Central American countries (Panama, Honduras,
Guatemala and Nicaragua) made noises to the effect that they might
block the WTO waiver from GATT Article XIII that the EU was seeking
to obtain in order to be able to administer quota C for ACP bananas
in conformity with the understandings reached with the US and
Ecuador.[36] Their argument was that the EU suggestion for a waiver
until the end of 2007 was not in line with the promise to switch to a
tariffs-only regime in 2006. Ecuador had made the same point, but the
four countries went further by threatening not even to participate in the
WTO talks on the waiver should the EU not agree to the 2005 deadline
before consultations begin. For the EU, this was a somewhat difficult
point because it wanted this waiver to extend over the same period
as the waiver thought to cover the general preferences for the ACP,
including the banana protocol. As the timetable built into the Cotonou
Agreement (successor of the Lomé Convention) was such that a new
WTO-compatible regime was to be negotiated before 2008, the EU felt it
needed the waiver until the end of 2007. The Central American banana
exporters, though, obviously with tacit support from the US, were keen
to get another timely lever over the EU that they could use should it
turn out that they encountered difficulties in negotiations with the EU

---

[35] Commission Regulation 896/2001.
[36] *Agra Europe*, 3 August 2001, pp. EP/3–4.

on the level of tariff in the eventual tariffs-only regime to be established in 2006.

At the time of finishing this chapter (September 2001), it was not yet clear how this irritant was to be removed. More fundamentally, it was not eventually clear whether the new regime agreed in 2001 would turn out to be a durable solution to the banana conflict. Most important, there were not yet any signs regarding the level of tariff for the final regime in 2006 that might be agreed, in GATT Article XXVIII negotiations, between the EU and the major banana exporters. The only thing that was easy to predict was that negotiations on that tariff level were likely to be very difficult, both between the EU and the banana suppliers and inside the EU between the member states with different interests in the banana economy. Hence, even though the Understandings reached in 2001 opened up the way towards an eventual solution to the long-standing banana dispute, and to the EU's banana saga, all experience of this extremely difficult story suggested that it was far too early to declare the end of that story.

References

Agra Europe, German edition, Bonn, various issues.

Agra Europe, English edition, London, various issues.

Borrell, B. and Cuthbertson, S. (1991) *EC Banana Policy 1992: Picking the Best Option*. Centre for International Economics, Canberra.

Cascante, J.C. and Sander, G.G. (1999) *Der Streit um die EG-Bananenmarktordnung*. Tübinger Schriften zum internationalen und europäischen Recht. Band 46. Duncker & Humblot, Berlin.

European Commission (1999) *Commission proposes to modify the EU's banana regime*. Brussels, 10 November. Available at: europa.eu.int/comm/dg01/0911banen.htm

European Commission (2000a) Commission gives new impetus to resolve banana dispute. Press release DN: IP/00/707, 5 July.

European Commission (2000b) Commission proposes solution to end banana dispute. Press release DN: IP/00/1110, 4 October.

European Commission (2001a) U.S. Government and European Commission reach agreement to resolve long-standing banana dispute. Brussels, 10 April. Available at: europa.eu.int/comm/agriculture/newsroom/en/84.htm

European Commission (2001b) EU trade concession to least developed countries: everything but arms proposal. Possible impacts on the agricultural sector. Available at: europa.eu.int/comm/commissioners/fischler/eba_en.pdf

European Commission (2001c) Commission initiates infringement proceedings against France over banana imports. Press release DN: IP/01/11092, 25 July. Available at: europa.eu.int/rapid/start/cgi/

Fitzpatrick, J. & Associates (1990) *Trade Policy and the EC Banana Market, an Economic Analysis*. Fitzpatrick & Associates, Dublin.

Jürgensen, T. (1998) Gemeinschaftsrechtliche Grenzen der Bananenmarktordnung. *Europäisches Wirtschafts- und Steuerrecht* 9, 357–365.

Leeb, F. and Lipper, H. (1995) *Das krumme Ding: Von Bananen, Multis und
Märkten.* Schmetterling Verlag, Stuttgart.

Matthews, A. (1992) *The European Community's Banana Policy After 1992.*
Discussion Papers in Agricultural Economics, 13. Institut für Agrarpolitik
und Marktforschung, University of Giessen.

Tangermann, S. and Verissimo, P. (1999) The sensible solution to the EU's
banana problem. *Agra Europe*, English edition, 8 October, p. A/1–4.

Verissimo, P. (2001) Implications of the EU banana trade regime for selected
import markets: economic analysis and political dimension. PhD dissertation, Institute of Agricultural Economics, University of Göttingen,
published by Dissertation.com, USA.

Wessels, B.-A. (1995) *Das Bananendiktat: Plädoyer für einen freien
Aussenhandel Europas.* Campus Verlag, Frankfurt.

WTO (1999) *Report of the Panel: European Communities – Regime for the
Importation, Sale and Distribution of Bananas – Recourse to Article 21.5
by Ecuador.* WTO document WT/DS27/RW/ECU, WTO, Geneva, 12 April.

Evolution of the Banana Multinationals

5

Tim Taylor

Introduction

The banana is a rather simple and unassuming fruit. It may thus seem a bit surprising that the industry that has evolved around it is character- ized by large multinationals and an oligopolistic market structure. Moreover, it also surprising that bananas have become the centre of one of the most notable trade disputes placed before the fledgling WTO. However, analysis of the industry's evolution from the standpoint of technology innovation, economic forces and business strategy provides an understanding of how and why the industry evolved as it did, as well as insight into the actions of the banana multinationals in the current banana dispute. It also provides a foundation for investigating the likely structure and competitive dynamics of the industry in the future.

At present, the bulk of world trade in bananas is controlled by the three major multinationals engaged in the industry. According to van de Kasteele (1998), in 1996 Chiquita Brands International, Dole and Fresh Del Monte accounted for 65% of total world exports. The Irish company Fyffes accounted for an additional 6–7% of total exports.[1] Though these companies are independent and engaged in intense com- petition in the world market, they share much common history. Indeed,

---

[1] In addition to these multinationals, the parastatal Noboa accounts for about 10% of total exports.

©CAB International 2003. Banana Wars: the Anatomy of a Trade Dispute (eds T.E. Josling and T.G. Taylor)

to a large extent they are all related and their common ancestor is the United Fruit Company.

There is perhaps no agricultural industry that has a more complex or interesting history than that associated with bananas. To adapt a phrase from Charles Dickens, the evolution of the banana industry is really 'a tale of two industries'. The tale of one industry centres on the American banana multinationals and the story of the United Fruit Company (UFCO). Perhaps no single company in US corporate history has been more dominant than the UFCO during the first half of the 20th century, nor have there been many companies more controversial.

The tale of the second industry begins with the evolution of export banana production in the Windward Islands. This industry has also been at the centre of the banana dispute. The development of the Windward Islands banana industry was a microcosm of British colonialism. The Windward Islands banana industry grew out of the decline of sugar, the desire of the British government to break the UFCO monopoly on its banana supply and the need to address key development issues facing its colonial islands. As a result, the industry was born, and has continuously been nurtured under a variety of protective regimes.

Whether the future will bring 'the best of times or the worst of times' for each of these industries remains a matter of conjecture. To a large extent, policy actions over the next few years, especially the way in which the resolution of the banana dispute is implemented, will be the determining factor. Understanding how policy decisions will impact upon participants in the banana industry is greatly enriched by an understanding of their history.

This chapter provides a concise history of the banana multinationals. In presenting this history, evolution of the multinationals is broken down into six distinct time periods: 1870–1899; 1900–1929; 1930–mid-1960s; late-1960s–1992; 1993–2000; and the post-resolution period beginning in May 2001. Concluding comments comprise the final section of the chapter.

Formation of the United Fruit Company, 1870–1899

The beginnings of the banana industry go back to at least 1835, when bananas were brought to the US as occasional deck cargo. Due to its proximity to producing areas, the main port of entry was New Orleans. By 1870, regular shipments of bananas were arriving in New Orleans and in ports along the US eastern seaboard. According to Read (1983), over the 1870–1899 period, as many as 114 banana-trading companies were registered in the US. However, intense competition and logistical difficulties thinned this number to 22 by 1899, and only four firms were of any appreciable size. Of these, the United Fruit Company grew to dominate the industry for almost half a century.

The origins of the UFCO are found in the confluence of the activities of three individuals: Lorenzo Baker, Andrew Preston and Minor Keith. Lorenzo Baker, a sailing captain from Boston, began shipping bananas from Jamaica on a regular basis in 1871. Finding the venture very profitable, he obtained a purchase contract for bananas produced on 2000 acres of former sugar land and developed a fleet of dedicated ships to support this trade. The bulk of his bananas were marketed through the Seavern's & Company commission merchants, who were headquartered in Boston.

Over the next three decades, there was substantial growth in the banana trade. The market was very competitive and prices were volatile. In this environment, Andrew Preston, the sales clerk at Seaverns's & Co. handling Baker's shipments, developed considerable skill in marketing bananas. Seeking to capitalize on their expertise in the rapidly expanding banana market, Baker, Preston and others joined forces to create the Boston Fruit Company (BFC) in 1885.

As the market continued to grow, the BFC increased its land holdings in Jamaica to supplement its purchase contracts and gain some control over supply. Land was also acquired in Cuba and the present Dominican Republic as a means of managing production risk. The switch to steamships in the 1880s increased the volume and reliability of supply, and extended the marketing season, and soon supply was outstripping demand. In response, the BFC acquired several marketing firms in the northeastern US and set up the Fruit Dispatch Company in the late 1890s to develop the marketing infrastructure needed to begin supplying interior markets.[2] By 1898, the BFC and its subsidiaries controlled an estimated 35% of the US market.

Concurrent with these developments, Minor Keith went to Costa Rica in 1871 to join his family business in building a railroad from San José to Puerto Limon. However, midway through the project, Keith ran out of money. To remedy this situation Keith began growing bananas on some of the 800,000 acres of land conceded by the Costa Rican government, and exported them to New Orleans. The bananas not only provided freight income, but also yielded sizeable profits.[3] As a result, Keith formed the Tropical Trading and Transport Co., and expanded banana shipments to New York. To support the expanded trade, Keith acquired additional land in Colombia.

---

[2] Due to their perishability, bananas were initially marketed in port cities along the eastern seaboard and Gulf coast. The advent of rail transportation and refrigeration facilitated the development of inland markets.

[3] Bananas also provided a staple food for workers constructing the railroad.

In 1890, the companies marketing Keith's bananas went bankrupt and the Boston Fruit Co. became the exclusive marketing agent for Tropical Trading and Transport Co. in northeastern US markets. Keith continued to expand his land holdings through acquisitions in Panama. However, the combination of bad weather and unfortunate circumstances left Keith near bankruptcy. Indeed, by 1898, Keith had control of over 200,000 acres of land, but had no liquidity. The merger of Keith's interests with those of the BFC remedied this situation and brought into existence the UFCO.

With its creation, the UFCO embodied one of the first and largest vertically integrated multinationals of its time. As seen in Table 5.1, the holdings of UFCO included companies spanning the bulk of the supply chain. The company's assets included 250,000 acres of land in Colombia, Costa Rica, Cuba, Honduras, the Dominican Republic, Jamaica and Nicaragua, of which 66,000 acres were in crop production, including 44,000 acres of bananas, 11 steamships, 12 chartered vessels, 112 miles of railway linking production areas to ports and an extensive marketing network in the US. It is estimated that in the early 1900s, UFCO controlled 80–90% of all US imports and exercised control over prices

Table 5.1. United Fruit Company corporate holdings, 1899–1906. Source: Read (1983: 193).

Company	Holding (%)
Boston Fruit Co. & Fruit Dispatch Co.	100
Banes Fruit Co.	n.a.
Dominican Fruit Co.	100
American Fruit Co.	> 50
Quaker City Fruit Co.	50
Buckman Fruit Co.	50
Sama Fruit Co.	50
Tropical Trading and Transport Co.	> 50
Colombia Land Co.	> 50
Snyder Banana Company	> 50
Belize Royal Mail and Central American Steamship Co.	100
Santo Oteri & Son	100
Camors-McConnell & Co.	86
Orr & Laubenheimer	50
Bluefields Steamship Co.	50
Camors-Weinberger Banana Co.	50
Monumental Trading Co.	50.4
Atlantic Fruit Co.	50.4
Vaccaro Brothers Co.	50
Hubbard-Zemurray Co.	60
Thatcher Brothers Steamship Co.	60

n.a., not available.

through exclusive marketing contracts and control of supply (Roche, 1998).

Bananas are highly perishable, and the early development of the industry was geared towards the efficient movement of the product to the retail consumer. Indeed, the primary driving forces influencing the early structural evolution were associated with scale economies and coordination along the vertical supply chain. As seen in Fig. 5.1, there are six basic stages in the supply chain: (i) provision of production inputs; (ii) production; (iii) assembly (which includes the post-harvest activities of boxing and shipping); (iv) ripening; (v) wholesale; and (vi) retail distribution.

Initially, the banana industry was organized loosely. Coordination along the supply chain was poor and haphazard. Bananas were considered as occasional deck cargo with high risks, but also high potential returns. There were numerous firms involved in the banana trade. The lack of information along the supply chain resulted in very high transaction costs, as well as high levels of risk. As noted, the number of firms engaged in the banana trade declined dramatically during the later part of the 19th century.

In response to the high transaction costs associated with coordination, the structure of the banana trade began to evolve in several

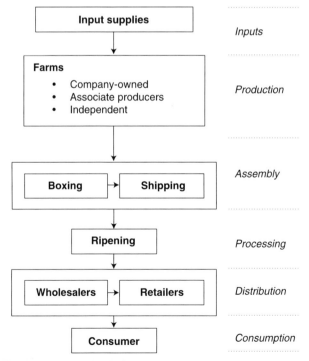

Fig. 5.1.   The banana supply chain.

directions. First, in order to develop more consistent volumes and control over quality, shippers began developing company-owned plantations as well as utilizing long-term purchase contracts. Additionally, some specialization in the movement of bananas from specific production locations to markets evolved. To some extent this matching of markets and production areas was driven by the desire to minimize shipping times (e.g. New Orleans was the closest port and population centre to many early production areas). However, in other cases, it seems to have evolved on the basis of personal relationships (e.g. Lorenzo Baker was from Boston).

As the industry began to evolve, four factors can be argued to have influenced its development: (i) technological innovations; (ii) land and railway concessions; (iii) internalization; and, as always, (iv) chance. Several significant technological innovations occurred in the latter part of the 19th century and first decade of the 20th century. The conversion from sailing vessels to steamships dramatically altered the competitive dynamics on several fronts. Ships had increased shipping capacity and much faster shipping times. This extended the length of the shipping season, resulted in improved product quality and expanded the number of ports reachable. The ability to supply increasing quantities of bananas also placed downward pressure on market prices as coastal market demand reached saturation.[4]

The development of inland rail transportation links and refrigerated rail transport, in combination with excess supplies in coastal consuming markets spawned the development of interior markets for bananas. The Fruit Dispatch Company was created by the BFC specifically to develop the necessary marketing infrastructure to increase effective demand through the development of inland markets.

Improvements in communications technology, especially the development of telephone and radio, which provided direct and rapid communication links with Central America,[5] greatly improved the ability of companies to coordinate harvesting and shipping activities. As the information provided by these technologies was mainly available to the banana companies, it created information asymmetries that conveyed significant market power to them in their dealings with independent producers.

Land concessions were significant in their relationship to the development of infrastructure to facilitate the movement of bananas from production areas to ports, and in providing access to large tracts of

---

[4] The prolific nature of bananas has created difficulties of excess supply throughout the industry's history.

[5] Read (1983) noted that UFCO was the first company to establish reliable communication links with Latin American countries. Indeed, UFCO formed the Tropical Radio Telegraph Co. (which still exists) in 1913 as a subsidiary.

land. One characteristic shared by the three major banana-producing companies during the 1900–1930 period was that all acquired land concessions to construct railways and, in some cases, port facilities in Central America. The experience of Minor Keith demonstrated the complementarity that existed between banana production and railway construction in Central America. Bananas not only provided freight income, but also significant profits. Concessions provided the opportunity for certain companies to replicate the activities of Minor Keith, thereby providing the opportunity to achieve the required minimum efficient scale of operation. In so doing, production areas and transportation linking them to port facilities evolved in an integrated fashion.

The need for efficient and timely product movement, scale economies and high transaction costs along the supply chain provided a strong incentive for internalization. The formation of the BFC internalized the production and shipping assets of Lorenzo Baker with the marketing expertise of Andrew Preston. The need to develop new markets inland led companies like BFC to pursue the acquisition of marketing assets and develop transportation linkages to inland markets. Minor Keith internalized production activities, shipment to ports and transportation of bananas to US markets. He also undertook geographic diversification of production as a means of risk management and disease control. The evolution of the Standard Fruit and Steamship and Cuyamel Fruit Companies followed similar patterns of internalization.

Despite the internalization of the supply chain, the ultimate formation of UFCO was to a considerable extent the result of chance. The confluence of events largely beyond the control of any of the major parties led to the formation of UFCO. Indeed, the formation of UFCO not only internalized virtually the entire banana supply chain (see Fig. 5.2), but did so on an unprecedented scale. As noted previously, with its formation, UFCO controlled 80–90% of the US market.

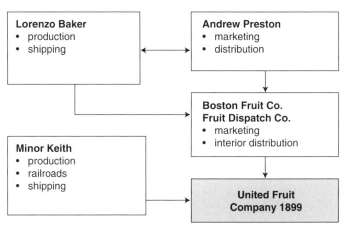

Fig. 5.2. The United Fruit Company, established 1899.

The internalization of activities along the supply chain on such a large scale conveyed considerable competitive advantages to UFCO. The magnitude of its size not only enabled the company to manage its supply chain efficiently, in effect it enabled UFCO to control the entire industry supply chain. It did so through the use of exclusive supply contracts with producers, in addition to its own large land holdings, and its control over shipping assets affording the company considerable control over banana supplies. Additionally, the company's use of exclusive marketing contracts provided considerable control over market access. The combination of scale and first-mover advantage enabled UFCO to effectively control the US market during the first two decades of the 20th century.

Growth, Competition and Consolidation, 1900–1929

From 1900 to 1929, UFCO dominated the US banana market. The company also expanded its sphere of operation in 1903, when it entered the European market with the purchase of a 50% interest in Elders & Fyffes Company. Elders & Fyffes, which was itself the outgrowth of the merger of two competitors in the EU market, Elders-Dempster and Fyffes-Hudson, sourced its bananas from Jamaica. In 1910, UFCO acquired the remaining 50% of Elders & Fyffes and essentially replicated its US operations in Europe. Although UFCO had 100% ownership, Elders & Fyffes operated autonomously, remaining in control of all production, shipping and marketing decisions. Notable actions by Elders & Fyffes during this period included the introduction of the first refrigerated steamships dedicated to bananas and the introduction of Fyffes 'Blue Label' in 1929. This was, of course, the first attempt at product differentiation in the banana trade.

Though UFCO remained the dominant banana company in the world market over the 1900–1929 period, the company experienced a decline of its market share. It is estimated that its world market share declined from about 77% in the first decade of the 20th century to about 60% by 1930. The major reason for this decline was the emergence of two significant competitors in the North American market, the Cuyamel Fruit Company and the Standard Fruit and Steamship Company.

Cuyamel Fruit Company

The origins of the Cuyamel Fruit Company are in the Hubbard-Zemurray Co., founded by Samuel Zemurray in 1903. The UFCO held 60% of the initial stock. After some acquisitions (primarily shipping assets) and failures, UFCO withdrew its holdings and the company reorganized, forming the Cuyamel Fruit Company in 1911. Cuyamel Fruit Company purchased fruit from Mexico and established the La Lima Division in Honduras, which soon became the leading banana division in Central America, producing fruit of extremely high quality. The La Lima Division was notable for its innovative production techniques and efficiency. In 1920, the company was awarded the Antichresis Concession by the Honduran government, giving it control over the National Railway.

The success of Cuyamel Fruit Company spawned a price war in the North American market that ended in 1929, when UFCO purchased the company for US$32 million. Assets acquired included about 250,000 acres of banana land in Honduras, 15 steamships, port facilities and the Antichresis Concession to the National Railway. With the purchase of Cuyamel Fruit Company, Samuel Zemurray became the largest shareholder in UFCO and gained a place on its Board of Directors. When UFCO experienced financial difficulties during the depression years, Zemurray became Chairman and undertook a major reorganization of the company, replacing UFCO tropical managers with former Cuyamel Fruit Company employees. In the final analysis, though UFCO purchased the assets of the Cuyamel Fruit Company, in essence Cuyamel Fruit Company took over the operation of UFCO.

Standard Fruit and Steamship Company

The origins of Standard Fruit and Steamship Company (SFSC) are with Vaccaro Brothers Company, founded by Salvador d'Antoni and Joseph Vaccaro in 1898 as a distributor of fruits and other foodstuffs in the New Orleans area. In 1903 Vaccaro Brothers Company acquired a concession to build a railway in Honduras to facilitate the shipment of bananas to the port at La Ceiba. A portion of the financing for these projects was obtained from UFCO, which acquired a 50% stake in the company.

Over the next few years, the company was incorporated, and through numerous acquisitions acquired an estimated 10–15% market share in New Orleans, which was second only to UFCO. From 1908 to 1919, Vaccaro Brothers garnered exclusive concessions for the construction of additional railways and wharf facilities in Honduras, expanded operations in Honduras and began diversifying into other crops. In 1923, the company forged a strategic alliance with several companies and began sourcing from Cuba, Mexico and Panama to geographically diversify the sources of its banana supply. To finance this expansion, Vaccaro Brothers reorganized as the SFSC with a market capitalization of US$50 million.

From 1926 to 1929, SFSC entered into a marketing alliance with the Cuyamel Fruit Company in an effort to compete more effectively with UFCO. This ended with UFCO's acquisition of Cuyamel Fruit Company. In 1930, the company acquired land holdings in Jamaica, including a US marketing contract with the Jamaica Banana Producers Association.

Competitive Dynamics

From 1900 to 1929, the US banana market was dominated by UFCO. Its only major competitors were the SFSC and the Cuyamel Fruit Company (which it eventually purchased). Though other independent banana companies operated, they did so mainly under a price umbrella allowed by UFCO. Given the control over access to production and marketing assets, as well as control over shipping by UFCO, these firms were not truly independent. Though this period was characterized by intense price competition as supplies were consistently creating downward pressure on prices, the dominance of UFCO was evidenced by two major events, the acquisition of Elders & Fyffes in 1904 and the acquisition of Cuyamel Fruit Company in 1929.

As UFCO and its major competitors were evolving in the North American market, Elders & Fyffes was developing a viable banana trade between Jamaica and the UK. The precise reason for UFCO's acquisition of Elders & Fyffes (hereafter Fyffes) is unclear. However, there are several factors that played a significant role.

First, Fyffes was a significant competitor with UFCO for bananas supplied by Jamaican producers. The acquisition of Fyffes not only removed this competition for banana supplies, but created a monopsony giving the company a strong position from which to deal with local producers. A second motive may have been to prevent the possible entry of Fyffes into the US market. Given the control UFCO exercised over the US distribution system, it is not clear how serious the threat of Fyffes' entry into the US was. However, one could conjecture that Fyffes may have sought to enter via some sort of alliance with either SFSC or Cuyamel. The resulting entity would have represented a formidable competitor to UFCO.

A third motivation was the desire of UFCO to diversify its operations into the European market. The development of refrigerated shipping and Fyffes' active involvement in developing refrigerated vessels dedicated to bananas greatly facilitated development of this market. Though Fyffes was operated autonomously after its acquisition, the company's evolution in Europe mimicked that of UFCO in the US. By 1920, Fyffes had a near monopoly in the UK and was the dominant banana company in Europe.

United Fruit Company's acquisition of Cuyamel Fruit Company in 1929 appears to be motivated by the desire to forestall competition. Through its La Lima Division, Cuyamel Fruit Company was able to produce and market large fruit of very high quality. By acquiring Cuyamel, UFCO was able to segment its markets on a geographic basis to prevent direct competition with UFCO bananas, which were considered to be of lower quality. Read (1983) quotes Samuel Zemurray as supporting the acquisition, since UFCO had 'built up a demand for quality fruit in excess of its present supply and can market and distribute to great advantage the increased Cuyamel production'. Though it may seem strange that Zemurray would embrace his company's acquisition by UFCO, it should be remembered that a few years later, Zemurray assumed control of UFCO and undertook a significant corporate reorganization.

Maturation and Duopoly, 1930–mid-1960s

With the acquisition of Cuyamel Fruit Company by UFCO, the US market essentially became a duopoly. For the period from 1930 to the mid-1960s, the relationship between the two companies has been described as cooperative rather than competitive (Read, 1983). As noted, though other 'independent' banana firms existed, they were not truly independent, as the two dominant firms held considerable control over access to production and port facilities, shipping and distribution networks. The major influences on the competitive dynamics of the industry during this period were technological innovations and government antitrust actions. Both had significant impacts on the nature of organization along the supply chain and competition.

In the 1930s, the incidence of Panama disease and black sigatoka became a significant problem. Though Panama disease could be controlled through land rotation and flood fallow, the latter was not economical. In the case of black sigatoka, a treatment was quickly found. However, it was extremely expensive. In response to the need to rotate lands, the companies began moving away from ownership of land to using independent producers under long-term contract. These associate producers worked closely with the companies in order to maintain acceptable levels of technical efficiency and product quality. The companies also began diversifying into other crops in order to use land no longer suitable for banana production.

The seriousness of these disease problems also spawned research directed at finding disease-resistant varieties. The SFSC was especially effective in this pursuit and in the early-1950s began experimenting with Cavendish varieties that demonstrated the desired resistance. By the late-1950s, all of SFSC's planting was of Cavendish varieties.

In addition to their disease resistance, Cavendish varieties were higher yielding, produced high-quality fruit and were less susceptible to blow downs than the traditional Gros Michel varieties. However, Cavendish varieties were also extremely fragile, and required boxing to ensure the necessary quality at final markets. Though the use of boxing was expensive, it was quickly determined that the extra cost incurred at the shipping point was more than offset by cost savings in other segments of the supply chain.

The switch to boxing gave rise to agglomeration effects, as factories to produce boxes developed in banana-production areas. It should be noted that the switch to boxing created competitive difficulties for the emerging banana industry in the Windward Islands. Unlike the Central American producing countries, where the demand for boxes was sufficiently large to allow the development of an economically viable support industry, such was not the case for the Windward Islands. Additionally, the adoption of boxing altered the relative labour intensity along the supply chain away from the distribution end toward post-harvest handling. This also worked against Windward Islands producers.

By the late 1960s, the switch to Cavendish varieties was universal. Interestingly, UFCO was one of the last to convert to Cavendish varieties. The precise reason for this is unclear. Organizational friction in combination with the company's dominant market position is one possible explanation. Regardless of the reason, it is certain that their delay in adopting the Cavendish varieties conveyed some competitive advantage to SFSC.

A final aspect of the switch to the Cavendish varieties and the adoption of boxing is that it brought about increased attention to quality control and stimulated the first attempts at branding by the US firms. Though Fyffes introduced their 'Blue Label' in 1929, the US multinationals did not follow suit. By the mid-1960s, however, increased attention to quality brought about the introduction of the 'Chiquita' brand for UFCO bananas and 'Cabana' brand by SFSC.

The US government significantly influenced the structure of the banana industry in the 1950s, when the dominance of UFCO was investigated and action was taken under the Sherman Anti-Trust and Wilson Acts. The complaint against UFCO contended that the 'company had contracted, combined and conspired to restrain interstate and foreign trade in bananas and had monopolized such trade over a number of years' (United Nations Conference on Trade and Development, 1974). The final consent degree required UFCO to divest itself of a complete banana division, capable of producing 9 million stems, and agreeing to make no further purchases of banana-producing companies. UFCO met this condition in 1972 with the sale of its Guatemalan division Compania Agricola de Guatemala to the West Indies Fruit Company, a wholly owned subsidiary of Del Monte.

Mergers and Diversification, mid-1960s–1992

From the mid-1960s until 1992, the banana industry experienced some fundamental changes. While the industry remained highly concentrated, the structure of ownership changed dramatically as mergers and acquisitions altered the competitive landscape. Additionally, the rise of Noboa in Ecuador and the Union de Paises Exportadores de Banano (UPEB), as well as other national companies, brought additional players into the international banana market

The beginnings of these changes occurred in 1968, when Castle & Cook completed its acquisition of SFSC. This was followed in 1970 by the merger of UFCO with AMK Corporation to form the food conglomerate, United Brands International. Del Monte Corporation, after having acquired a small banana company, West Indies Fruit Company in 1967 to forestall a potential UFCO takeover, became a significant competitor in the banana industry, when it purchased UFCO's Guatemalan banana division in 1972. Indeed, Del Monte became the first major entrant into the banana industry in over 70 years.

United Fruit Company becomes Chiquita Brand International

The period from the mid-1960s to 1992 was one of turbulence, financial difficulties and change for the UFCO. A combination of factors, including poor corporate management, resulted in UFCO losing its dominance in the world banana market. Indeed, the person charged with reorganizing UFCO in the 1960s stated that 'no longer was United Fruit the major source of quality bananas. No longer was the "Great White Fleet" . . . the only dependable furnisher of refrigerated transport of fruit from the tropics' (Gale Business Resources, 2000).

In an effort to remedy its financial difficulties, new management was brought in to better integrate coordination along the supply chain. The company also began pursuing a strategy of corporate diversification, purchasing a number of companies including A&W Root Beer, Baskin-Robbins and Foster Grant. This process eventually led to a merger with the conglomerate AMK Corporation. With this merger, the existence of UFCO as a distinct entity came to an end and United Brands International was born.

The strategy of conglomeration in combination with Hurricane Fifi, which devastated most of the company's banana operations in

Honduras, and the 'banana war' initiated by the export taxes levied by Central American government in 1974, led to significant losses in the mid-1970s. From the mid-1970s to the early-1980s, the company experienced a number of changes in corporate leadership. Though some progress was made in returning the company to profitability, United Brands was described as 'a case study in corporate calamity' (Gale Business Resources, 2000).

In 1982, Carl Lindner began acquiring shares in United Brands, and in 1984 became the majority stockholder and appointed himself as CEO. Under Lindner's leadership the company made some significant divestitures, sold several subsidiaries and began to refocus on core business activities. Perhaps the most significant divestiture was the sale of Elders & Fyffes to Fruit Importers of Ireland (FII) in 1986. Since its purchase by FII, Fyffes has exhibited significant growth in the EU banana market and its competitive relationship with Chiquita has been especially contentious. Indeed, Fyffes' attempt to establish long-term supply contracts with producers in Honduras in 1989 triggered what Roche (1998) called the second banana war.

In 1990, seeking to build on the strength and name recognition of the Chiquita Brand, the company changed its name from United Brands to Chiquita Brands International. Using funds raised from public offerings, Chiquita made a number of key acquisitions, including Frupac, an importer, packer and exporter of fresh fruits produced mainly in Chile. While the company pursued a more focused strategy of acquisitions, it remained highly dependent on bananas.

Standard Fruit and Steamship Company Becomes Part of Dole

From the 1930s to the early 1950s, SFSC's management was family dominated. According to Read (1983), a combination of factors, including poor strategic decision making and accumulated debt resulted in poor performance, leaving the company on the verge of bankruptcy. In 1953, Joseph d'Antoni assumed control of the company and undertook a major reorganization, placing emphasis on research and marketing. Perhaps the most notable event in this regard was the company's decision to switch from the Gros Michel to Cavendish varieties. The switch to Cavendish varieties dramatically altered the nature of the banana supply chain. In addition, the hesitancy of UFCO to switch to these varieties provided SFSC a slight competitive advantage for almost a decade.

The impacts of the restructuring of SFSC are seen in Table 5.2, which presents US market shares for the three major banana multinationals over the 1950–1974 period. As can be seen, the market share

Table 5.2. US market share of the major banana multinationals, 1950–1974. Source: Arthur *et al.* (1968).

	United Fruit/ United Brand	Standard Fruit/ Castle & Cooke	Del Monte	Independents
1950	80.0	8.9	–	11.1
1965	51.5	31.4	3.8	13.1
1966	56.4	31.2	3.1	9.3
1967	57.4	30.1	2.0	10.5
1968	55.7	33.3	1.7	9.3
1969	52.3	35.8	4.4	7.6
1970	46.2	36.6	8.5	8.7
1971	46.8	36.6	8.6	7.9
1972	44.5	37.2	9.6	8.7
1973	34.7	43.4	13.1	8.8

of SFSC jumped from a mere 8.9% in 1950 to over 31% in 1965. Castle & Cook, a conglomerate with large holdings in numerous fresh and processed food activities, acquired a 55% stake in SFSC in 1964, and acquired all remaining shares in 1968. The effect of Castle & Cook's acquisition of SFSC is clearly demonstrated in Table 5.2. From 1965 to 1973, Castle & Cook's share of the US market rose from 31.4 to 43.4%.

In 1972, Castle & Cook discontinued the use the 'Cabana' label that had been used by SFSC and introduced the 'Dole' label in its place. The company also expanded its production activities in Central America with the development of two large plantations in Costa Rica and Nicaragua. As shown in Table 5.1, these activities resulted in Castle & Cook assuming the US market-share leadership in 1973.

From 1972 to 1992, Castle & Cook made numerous acquisitions and divestitures. Of significance to banana operations, the company terminated banana operation in Nicaragua in 1982. The company also increased its holding in shipping assets and containers. In a key strategic move, the company also established a division of Dole Foods in London in 1989 in anticipation of policy changes in the EU.

In 1991, Castle & Cook changed its corporate name to Dole Food Company, Inc. Commensurate with this change, the company reorganized, placing all fruit and vegetable operations under the name of Dole Food Company and all real estate operations under the name of Castle & Cook.

Del Monte Enters the Banana Market

The Del Monte Corporation has long been one of the largest global suppliers of fresh and processed fruit and vegetable products. Its corporate origins date back to 1875 and the California Fruit Packing Company started by James Dawson. The name 'Del Monte' was first used on the label for a premium coffee specially packaged for the Hotel Del Monte in Monterey, California. In 1916, several producer associations, including the California Fruit Packing Company, joined forces to create the California Packing Corporation (CALPAK), headquartered in San Francisco. Using strict quality control, all of CALPAK premium products were marketed under the Del Monte label. In 1967, seeking to take advantage of its brand image, CALPAK changed its name to Del Monte.

Like Dole, Del Monte entered the banana industry through diversification. In contrast, however, its initial entry in the banana trade was a defensive act taken to stem a possible takeover by the UFCO. In 1967, UFCO acquired a 6% interest in Del Monte, an action that was viewed by many as a precursor to a takeover attempt. To stem the possible takeover, Del Monte acquired the West Indies Fruit Company, a small company importing bananas from Ecuador. Under the terms of its anti-trust settlement, UFCO was prohibited from acquiring additional banana companies. Thus, Del Monte's acquisition of the West Indies Fruit Company effectively blocked UFCO's apparent takeover attempt.

In 1972, Del Monte expanded its banana activities with the purchase of the United Brand's Compania Agricola de Guatemala by its subsidiary, West Indies Fruit Company. With this purchase, Del Monte became the first major entrant to the banana industry in 70 years. As one of the world's largest food processing companies, Del Monte was able to overcome the structural entry barriers through a strategy of diversified entry. Of course, this was facilitated by the forced sale of UFCO's Guatemala division under the terms of the US anti-trust action. As seen in Table 5.2, with the acquisition of UFCO's Guatemala division, Del Monte's market share reached 13.1% in 1973.

Since the mid-1970s, Del Monte has been a party to considerable merger activity and ownership has changed hands numerous times. In 1979, R.J. Reynolds Industries purchased the company as part of its diversification strategy. In 1989, Kohlberg Kravis and Roberts acquired R.J. Reynolds. As part of the acquisition, the company was split into three distinct units: fresh fruits, processed food, and international foods and beverages. The fresh fruits unit was organized as Fresh Del Monte Produce Company.

Fyffes

The sale of Fyffes to Fruit Importers of Ireland by United Brands in 1986 added a fourth major multinational competitor to the banana market. After its separation from United Brands, Fyffes expanded rapidly. The basic strategy the company followed was to buy from independent producers and strengthen its position in downstream segments of the supply chain.

Historically, Fyffes sourced bananas from Jamaica, Belize and Suriname. The company's initial effort to expand its banana sourcing to Honduras initiated what has been described by some (Roche, 1998) as the second banana war. Fyffes offered producers long-term supply contracts at substantially higher prices than United Brands. United Brands (Chiquita) quickly responded using legal manoeuvres to block Fyffes and a rather contentious dispute began. Diplomatic efforts on the part of the EU and intervention by the Honduran President were required to bring the dispute to an end. Since this encounter, competition between Fyffes and Chiquita has remained contentious.

Competitive Dynamics

With these mergers and acquisitions, the foundation of the current competitive landscape for the multinational banana companies was cast. Banana activities became tied to the corporate strategies of large diversified companies. In the case of United Brands International, bananas remained the major source of revenues and profits. In the case of Castle & Cook (Dole) and Del Monte, this was less so. Additionally, many of the long-time influences of family on the corporate culture of the banana multinationals were replaced by differing corporate management styles and cultures. The strategic activities of the banana industry evolved accordingly.

Although the motivation behind the creation of United Brands was the creation of a dominant and diversified food company, success was never realized as the company never performed to expectations. In response, Carl Lindner acquired a controlling interest in 1984 and began a process of restructuring and rationalization, selling off numerous subsidiaries.[6] One of the most notable actions was the sale of Fyffes to FII in 1986. Through this restructuring, bananas remained the focal point of company activities. In 1990, seeking to build on brand name recognition, United Brands changed its name to Chiquita Brands International.

Castle & Cook's purchase of SFSC brought UFCO's long-time competitor into the fold of a highly diversified fresh produce company. Although Castle & Cook's origins were in pineapples, with its acquisition of SFSC, bananas became its principal business. In a similar fashion to Chiquita, in 1991 Castle & Cook changed the company name to Dole in an effort to use its brand name more effectively.

---

[6] An argument can be made that Lindner's takeover is a textbook example of the market for corporate control.

Interestingly, the strategic influence of Castle & Cook (hereafter Dole) began to move banana activities in a somewhat different direction than that pursued by Chiquita Brands International. Indeed, as noted by Roche (1998) and van de Kasteele (1998), in contrast to Chiquita Brands International, which continued to function along traditional lines regarding the vertical chain, Dole placed increased emphasis on shipping, distribution and marketing. This divergence in strategic focus has had significant impacts on the competitive landscape since 1992 and the imposition of the new banana regime.

From the mid-1960s to 1992, there were no technological innovations that affected the conduct and performance of the industry on a par with earlier epochs. However, general improvements in transportation and communication technology served to reduce transaction costs along the supply chain. As a result, there was some movement by the multinationals from vertical integration to vertical coordination. This was manifest in the increased reliance on independent producers under long-term contract for banana supplies in lieu of company-owned plantations and on the use of leased as opposed to owned shipping assets. The degree to which this occurred varied across firms.

This period also witnessed the rise of branding and attempts at product differentiation. As previously noted, Fyffes originated labelling bananas with its 'Blue Label' in 1929. However, widespread labelling in the US market did not begin in earnest until the introduction of Cavendish varieties. United Brands began marketing their bananas under the Chiquita label, with strict quality requirements. Castle & Cook soon followed with their Cabana label, which was subsequently changed to Dole.

The multinationals' attempts to differentiate bananas using labelling are quite interesting. There is no doubt that the multinational trademarks have very high consumer recognition and an association with quality. However, there is much research (van de Kasteele, 1998) that suggests that this recognition has translated into relatively minor, if any, product differentiation in the eyes of consumers. Despite this research, Chiquita continues to pursue product differentiation-associated pricing differentials as a competitive strategy.

The Single European Market and the New Banana Regime, 1993–2001

The creation of the Single European Market (SEM) and the imposition of the New Banana Regime[7] (NBR) brought enormous change to the

---

[7] See Tangermann (Chapter 4) for a discussion of the New Banana Regime and subsequent policy developments.

competitive environment facing the banana multinationals. The trade dispute that resulted from the imposition of the NBR has been widely documented and studied (e.g. Borrell, 1994). It also resulted in the imposition of hundreds of millions of dollars in punitive tariffs on EU products by the US, and more recently Ecuador. From the standpoint of the banana multinationals, the NBR also created difficulties in terms of oversupply and low prices. This has had negative impacts on the banana business of all participants in the banana market. The NBR initially resulted in some clear winners and losers among the multinationals. The initial winners appear to have been Dole and Fyffes, while the clear loser was Chiquita Brands International. The company's active involvement in the trade dispute is evidence of this. The effect of the NBR on Fresh Del Monte Produce is rather difficult to gauge.

The effects of the NBR on the multinationals are evidenced in Tables 5.3 and 5.4. As can be seen in Table 5.3, the impact of the NBR on Chiquita Brands in terms of market share was devastating. Its world market share dropped from 34% in 1992 to about 26% in 1997, and its EU market share dropped from more than 30% to about 19% over the same period. In Germany, Chiquita Brands' largest EU market, the company's market share is estimated to have dropped from 40% prior to the NBR to a current level of about 20%. In contrast, over the same period Dole increased both its world market share from 20 to 25% and its EU market share from 12 to 16%. Fresh Del Monte's world market

Table 5.3. US market share of the major banana multinationals, 1950–1974. Source: van de Kasteele (1998).

Company	1992		1995		1997	
	World	EU	World	EU	World	EU
Chiquita Brands	34	> 30	> 25	19	25–26	18–19
Dole Food	20	12	22–23	15–16	24–25	15–16
Fresh Del Monte	15	7–8	15–16	8	16	10–11
Fyffes	2–3	4–5	7–8	17–18	6–7	16–17
Geest	3–4	5–6				
Noboa			12		13	

Table 5.4. Net income for the US multinationals, 1991–1999 (US$million). Sources: Company annual reports.

Company	1991	1992	1993	1994	1995	1996	1997	1998	1999
Chiquita Brands International	128	–284	–51	–72	9	–51	0.3	–18	–58
Dole Food Company	134	16	78	68	23	89	160	12	49
Fresh Del Monte Produce		–63	–58	–64	–72	–134	44	59	57

share remained relatively constant (about 15–16%) over the 1992–1997 period, while its EU market share increased.

Table 5.4 also brings attention to the fact that the NBR was beneficial to Fyffes. Indeed, even after accounting for the purchase of Geest by the joint venture between Fyffes and the Windward Islands Banana Export Development Company (WIBDECO) in 1995, the company's EU market share increased significantly between 1992 and 1997. There is no doubt that this is at least partly a result of the preferences the NBR granted to EU firms.

The net income of the US banana multinationals is depicted in Table 5.4. It is clear that the NBR had a significant negative impact on the net income of Chiquita. In only 2 years since 1992, Chiquita had realized positive net income. The positive returns in these 2 years are attributable to divestitures and the reorganization of transportation logistics. Fresh Del Monte also experienced negative returns from 1992 to 1996. While Dole has maintained positive net income in every year since 1992, its earnings per share have been below par when compared to other companies in its industry segment. This underperformance is directly related to difficulties in world banana markets.

The differential corporate performance of the banana multinationals since the imposition of the NBR is the result of both the corporate structure of the companies and their corporate strategy. Table 5.5 presents various measures of corporate structure for the US banana multinationals as of 1999. Dole Food is clearly the largest of the three companies, with net sales in 1999 of over US$4.5 billion and 59,000 employees. It is also the most diversified, with 71% of its sales coming from fresh produce, 20% from processed products and almost 10% from other sources (mainly cut flowers). Only about 30% of Dole's net sales come from bananas. Dole is also the least dependent on foreign sales, with only about 21% of its sales outside the US. The EU and other international markets (mainly Asia-Pacific) account for only 10% of total sales.

Chiquita is considerably smaller and is less diversified than Dole. In 1999, Chiquita had net sales of US$2.6 billion and 36,000 employees. Fresh produce accounted for 80% of Chiquita Brands' net sales, of which bananas accounted for about 67%. While Chiquita markets processed products under its own labels, it is also among the largest private-label food processors in the US. As seen in Table 5.5, about 39% of net sales originate in the EU and other international markets.

Fresh Del Monte, with 1999 sales of US$1.7 billion and 20,000 employees, is the smallest of the three US multinationals. The company is almost solely involved in the production and distribution of fresh produce.[8] About 54% of net sales come from bananas. Of the three

---

[8] Recall that Fresh Del Monte was formed from the Fresh Produce Division of Del Monte Food Company in 1989.

Table 5.5. Comparative corporate structure of the US banana multinationals, 1999. Sources: Company annual reports.

	Chiquita Brands		Dole Foods		Fresh Del Monte	
	US$1000	%	US$1000	%	US$1000	%
Net sales by product type						
Fresh	2,044,788	80.0	3,184,324	70.7	1,652,600	94.8
Processed	511,011	20.0	882,823	19.6		
Other			439,370	9.7	90,600	5.2
Total	2,555,799		4,506,517		1,743,200	
Net sales by region						
North America	1,552,320	60.7	2,100,555	79.2	830,400	47.6
Latin America	8,124	0.3	283,565	10.7		
EU and other international	995,355	38.9	267,463	10.1	912,800	52.4
Total	2,555,799		2,651,583		1,743,200	
Assets by region						
North America	427,542	33.8	390,651	53.2	219,800	22.1
Latin America	532,504	42.1	339,955	46.3	529,200	53.1
EU and other international	285,082	22.5	323,073	44.0	382,100	38.3
Shipping	448,132	35.4	71,710	9.8	85,100	8.5
Total	1,265,718		734,738		996,400	
Owned and leased land by country (acres)						
Costa Rica			28,100		24,200	
Guatemala			9,600		18,700	
Honduras	130,000		18,420			
Panama						
Colombia			7,200			
Ecuador			1,730			
Mexico					1,800	
Philippines						
Shipping assets						
Number owned	16		6		17	
Number under long-term lease	8		20		26	
Employees	36,000		59,000		20,000	

companies, Fresh Del Monte is the most dependent on EU and other international markets. In 1999, the company received about 36% of total net sales from EU markets and 16% from markets in the Asia-Pacific region.

These data suggest that Dole's corporate performance can at least partially be explained by the highly diversified nature of the company and lesser dependence on the EU and other international markets for sales. That it has the largest market share in the EU attests to the size of the company. Though Dole has had difficulties in banana markets, it has been able to offset any losses with returns from other profit centres. In contrast, Chiquita's, and to a lesser extent Fresh Del Monte's, corporate performance is much more dependent on conditions in the banana market. As such, it has been more difficult for it to offset losses since 1993 with returns from other corporate profit centres.

While the corporate performance of the US multinationals since 1993 can be explained partially by their corporate structure, it can be argued that their corporate strategies have played an even greater role. Indeed, Chiquita, Dole and Fresh Del Monte have pursued very different corporate strategies in response to the NBR.

The roots of Chiquita's difficulties date to the late 1980s, when the company began expanding production in anticipation of the EU single market. This strategy was based on the belief that the creation of the EU single market would bring about an essentially free market for bananas.

As the dominant supplier in the German market, Chiquita believed it could build on its experience and brand name in Germany to expand rapidly in the newly liberalized EU market. Not only did this strategic vision not come to fruition, the NBR (and the subsequent banana framework agreement) resulted in a more protected market and increased preferences for EU importing and distribution firms.

In the immediate post-NBR period, Chiquita found itself in the position of having to divert its expanded production to other markets, driving down world prices. Additionally, the company's lack of liquidity hampered its ability to compete with Fresh Del Monte, Dole and Fyffes by making strategic acquisitions.[9] The most visible corporate response has been associated with the banana dispute put before the WTO. Given the history of Chiquita Brands International and current management, such a corporate response is not all that surprising.

In addition to pursuing a political remedy, the company took other steps in response to the NBR. Most notably, Chiquita began a process of diversification, through a number of acquisitions in food processing (Box 5.1). Indeed, fresh produce as a percentage of net sales dropped from 90% of total sales in 1997 to its present level of 80%. Additionally, the company paid increased attention to supply chain management and logistics (1999 Chiquita Annual Report). Despite these efforts, the company announced in January 2001 that it would be unable to meet its debt payment and asked bondholders to swap US$862 million in debt for equity.

---

[9] Chiquita had an interest in buying Geest, but could not find sufficient funds to consummate an acceptable deal.

Box 5.1. Selected acquisitions and divestments by Chiquita Brands International.

1993 Compagnie des Bananes (CDB), 49% owned by Chiquita Brands, takes 33% of Societe Bananiere Caraibe (Sobaca), with option for the remainder, from Fabre-Domergue group (Martinique). A distribution agreement is also signed.

1994 Joint venture with Eurobrands, Italy to market fruit juice on the European market.

1995 Sale of last part of its meat division to Smithfield, the other parts being sold in 1992–1994.

1995 Sale of Numar edible oils in Costa Rica.

1997 Acquired Friday Canning Corporation (Wisconsin), American Fine Foods (Idaho), Owatonna canning (Minnesota) in a combined US$77 million deal.

1997 Acquired 83% in Blueberries Farms of Australia.

1998 Acquired Stokely, USA, a vegetable canning company.

1998 Direct Fruit Marketing GmbH, joint venture Chiquita's European Frupac operations and Atlanta.

1999 Acquired certain canning assets of Agripac Inc.

Dole pursued a corporate strategy considerably different from Chiquita's. In contrast to Chiquita Brands, which foresaw a liberalized and expanded EU banana market, Dole took a more cautious approach. The company placed increased attention on strengthening its marketing and distribution network in the EU and in developing partnerships with retail buyers. Dole's response to the NBR was to gain access to the EU market through the acquisition of EU and ACP firms (Box 5.2). Notable strategic moves included a joint venture with Compagnie Fruitier for distribution in France and Spain, and acquisition of a minority stake in Jamaica Fruit Producers Ltd. At present, Dole operates distribution and ripening facilities in France (12), Italy (2), Germany, Spain (7) and Belgium. It also has supply arrangements with producers in the French colonies of Martinique and Guadeloupe, the Canary Islands and the ACP countries of Jamaica, Cameroon and Côte d'Ivoire. It is also notable that Dole has an arrangement to supply dollar bananas to Fyffes.

As evidenced by Dole's gains in EU market share, the company's strategy was clearly successful in negotiating the policy minefield created by the NBR. Dole did not, however, escape the resulting downturn in the world banana market. The company is streamlining its banana business and downsizing some of its operations in Nicaragua and Venezuela. However, the company is also looking to expand in the Asia-Pacific market.

Since 1992, Fresh Del Monte has been through an extensive series of ownership changes. Upon the bankruptcy of the company's owner,

---

Box 5.2. Selected acquisitions and divestments of the Dole Food Company.

–   Joint venture Compagnie Fruitiere for distribution in France and Spain. Common investment in Cameroon and Côte d'Ivoire.

1993   Acquired Saman-Micasar, a leading dried fruit company in France.

1994   Acquired 35% in Jamaica Producers Fruit Distributors Ltd, Dartford, Kent, UK. 1993 sales US$225 million. Combination has 20% of the UK market.

1994   Acquired D&C, Agrofruta, Chile's ninth fresh fruit exporter.

1995   Disposed of part of juice business and dried fruit business, USA.

1995   Acquired the New Zealand operations of Chiquita Brands. Until then Dole had no financial interests in New Zealand excepting the markets through Market Gardners. In late 1994, Chiquita had 39% of the market and Dole 18%.

1996   Acquired 90.8% in Pascual Hermanos, the largest fruit and vegetable firm in Spain.

1996   Acquired a major stake in Paul Kempowski & Co., Germany, a large banana ripener and distributor (25,000 boxes week^{-1}).

1996   Joint venture with BAMA Group, Norway, forming Dole-BAMA Fresh Salads.

1997   Acquired SCB plantations, Côte d'Ivoire through Comp. Fruitiere.

1998   Acquired Sunburst Farms, Inc., Fours Farmers, Inc., Finesse Farms and Colombian Carnations, Inc. and affiliated companies.

1998   Acquired 60% interest in Saba Trading AB.

1999   Invested in banana operation production in South America, and banana production and distribution operations in Latin America and Asia.

Polly Peck, in 1992, Fresh Del Monte was sold to Grupo Empresarial Agricola Mexicano (GEAM), a Mexican investor group led by Carlos Cabal. In 1994, GEAM made an offer of US$1 billion for Del Monte Foods, with the intention of rejoining fresh and processed operations, thereby obtaining full rights over the Del Monte brand name. However, in 1995 Cabal was found to have made illegal loans to himself, and the Mexican government moved against Cabal to prevent the purchase. Cabal disappeared and the company was placed under state administration by the government of Mexico. The government urged GEAM to sell Fresh Del Monte, and in 1996 Grupo IAT, owned by the Abu-Ghazeleh family, purchased the company.[10] In 1997, Fresh Del Monte made a public offering with the Abu-Ghazeleh family retaining a majority interest in the company.

Given the turmoil surrounding the ownership of Fresh Del Monte and the difficulties created in the world banana market by the NBR, the financial performance of the company over the 1992–1996 period (Table 5.4) is not surprising. The turnaround of the company since its

---

[10] Noboa also expressed an interest in purchasing the company.

purchase by Grupo IAT suggests that many of Fresh Del Monte's difficulties were directly tied to corporate management, or a lack thereof.

From a strategic standpoint, it can be argued that the management
difficulties at Fresh Del Monte prevented, or at least inhibited, the company's corporate response to the NBR. Since its purchase by Grupo
IAT, Fresh Del Monte has adopted numerous cost-cutting measures,
and has adopted a strategy of growth by acquisition (van de Kasteele,
1998). As can be seen by some of the company's acquisitions since
1996, it has expanded and diversified into fresh produce operations
(Box 5.3).

Fresh Del Monte has expanded its banana operations and, as seen
in Table 5.3, has gained market share globally, and especially in the EU.
The company has invested in ACP countries such as Cameroon and has
acquired marketing and distribution assets in the EU. Fresh Del Monte
is also the clear market leader in the Asia-Pacific region.

It cannot be argued that Fresh Del Monte was a clear winner since
the imposition of the NBR. However, an argument can be made that the
current management of the company has been successful in crafting a
corporate strategy for overcoming the market distortions created by the
EU banana regime. It is interesting that Fresh Del Monte's strategy
essentially mimicked the 'EU strategy' of Dole, which centred on the
acquisition of EU marketing and distribution assets.

The fourth major player in the banana market is Fyffes. The com-
pany is the largest EU importer of fruits and vegetables, and is the main
EU banana company. In 1999, Fyffes had net sales of €1.89 billion
(US$1.81 billion at current exchange rates). As evidenced by the fact
that sales have almost tripled since 1992, the NBR clearly benefited
Fyffes. This is no doubt in part due the licensing preferences given to
EU operators under the NBR. Indeed, a recent *Wall Street Journal*
(Jenkins, 1999) article has questioned the degree to which Fyffes
influenced EU policy towards bananas.

Box 5.3.   Selected acquisitions of Fresh Del Monte.

1994   Joint venture with four Brazilian companies from Pernambuco, Interfruit,
       to produce 200,000 t of Del Monte bananas per year.
1994   Investment in Mexican agricultural lands to expand non-banana fruit
       production.
1996   Control over UTC, Chilean fruit exporter, due to the acquisition of FDMP
       by the IAT group.
1997   Nusantara Tropical Fruit, Indonesia. Joint venture with Umas Jaya Agro
       Industri for the development of a plantation on Sumatra.
1999   Acquired all outstanding shares of BMB, a European marketing
       company.
2000   Acquired Red Rose International, Ltd, fruit import distributor in the UK.

The company sources banana from the EU (Canary Islands, Guadeloupe and Martinique), ACP countries (Windward Islands, Jamaica, Belize and Suriname) and the dollar zone (Colombia, Honduras, Guatemala and Costa Rica).[11] About 50% of Fyffes' bananas are sourced from EU–ACP countries and the remaining 50% from the dollar zone. In contrast to the three US banana multinationals, Fyffes is not involved in the production portion of the supply chain. Fyffes also functions as a marketer and distributor for major international marketing boards, including Capespan, Carmel, Zespri and Maroc (Fresh Del Monte Produce 1999 Annual Report). In 1999, it also launched its World of Fruit website, which is intended to become a major business to business extranet for international buying and selling of fresh fruits and vegetables (www.Worldoffruit.com). To date, this effort has brought disappointing results (EIU, 2000).

Fyffes' corporate strategy appears to have been based on expanding through various types of marketing alliances, joint ventures and acquisitions. Fyffes has been especially active in forging various types of strategic alliances with leading EU distribution and marketing firms. In 1995, Fyffes, in a joint venture with WIBDECO, purchased Geest Bananas. Through this joint venture, Fyffes became the sole marketer of Windward Island bananas.

Resolution of the Banana Dispute

Despite resolution of the banana dispute in July 2001, several legal battles remain. In January 2001, Chiquita was unable to meet its debt obligations and was forced to seek an alternative remedy to this situation. One action taken by Chiquita was to file a lawsuit against the European Commission for the amount of €564 million for damages suffered as a result of the NBR. Chiquita also filed suit against Dole in August 2001 for failing to transfer import licences to Chiquita's European distributor. The suit alleges Dole's intentional interference with contractual relations, interference with prospective economic advantage and unfair competition (HonoluluAdvertiser.com). The suit seeks US$50 million in damages.

The agreed-upon resolution to the banana dispute seems to be a clear victory for Chiquita. The chosen reference period should enable the company to regain a significant market share. The situation for Dole is less clear. While the EU market will be liberalized, Dole's current imports of bananas are larger than those it had during the chosen reference period. This explains why Dole strongly supported the first-come first-served proposals for ending the dispute.

---

[11] Its dollar zone bananas are sourced through a marketing alliance with Dole.

According to DePalma (2001), Fyffes is expected to gain some market share as a result of the banana accord. However, the company recently has experienced significant financial difficulties. Indeed, it has been suggested that all or part of the company might look for a buyer.

The impact of the agreement on Fresh Del Monte remains unclear. The company has been diversifying its activities, especially in the areas of melons and pineapples, as well as taking major positions in the Asian banana markets. It reported strong financial results for the first half of 2001.

Concluding Comments

Examining the evolution of the major banana multinational over the past 100 years of multinationals is an exercise in corporate genealogy. The common ancestor was the United Fruit Company. As through a family's generations, marriage, divorce, procreation and family values led to diversity; so too have mergers, acquisitions, new business creation and innovation, and corporate culture led to diversity among the banana multinationals. This diversity is no more apparent than in the various corporate responses to the NBR and its eventual outcome.

The NBR placed a premium on the acquisition of licences and provided an incentive for companies to participate in various levels of the supply chain. Dole's and Fyffes' response was to acquire the requisite assets in distribution, ripening and wholesaling to provide access to the EU market. Fyffes was also active in establishing strategic alliances with banana producers in the ACP and other EU countries (e.g. Canary Islands, Guadeloupe, Martinique). Dole and Fyffes were initially the clear 'winners' in terms of making the appropriate strategic responses to the NBR.

The corporate leadership difficulties experienced by Fresh Del Monte during the first half of the 1990s more or less paralysed strategic responses to the NBR. Since being purchased by IAT, the company has begun an impressive turnaround. To some extent, Fresh Del Monte has emulated the Dole strategy of accessing EU markets via acquisition of EU marketing and distributions assets. Del Monte has also placed emphasis on developing markets in the Asia-Pacific region, and is currently the clear leader in these markets.

Chiquita Brands International was the initial loser to the NBR. It appears that the company clearly misread the EU policy situation by assuming the market would essentially become open. The NBR hit Chiquita with a double blow. Not only did the EU market not open up, the complex system of licensing (the 'B' licences) worked against the existing structure of Chiquita's supply chain. Caught with inadequate liquidity, Chiquita was unable to follow the Dole strategy of accessing the EU market via acquisition. In light of this situation, the company's pursuit of a remedy via trade policy is understandable. Eventually this strategy appears to have paid off. The final terms of the resolution are beneficial to Chiquita.

While the corporate strategies for dealing with the NBR differed, there are also evolving strategies that share some commonalities. Dole is by far the most diversified of the banana multinationals. It continues to reduce its dependence on bananas, announcing in 1999 its intentions to downsize global production by about 17% (25 million boxes). In spite of this downsizing, Dole is expanding its banana activities in the Asia-Pacific region. The company is also placing greater emphasis on increasing profits through the efficient coordination of the transportation and distribution activities of its supply chains. In the EU, Dole is also integrating forward in the food retail sector.

Since coming under the control of the Abu-Ghazeleh family, Fresh Del Monte has pursued a strategy of growth and diversification via acquisition. A part of this strategy, Fresh Del Monte is attempting to reduce its dependence on bananas. Despite this, the company is expanding it banana operations in the Asia-Pacific region, where it presently enjoys a dominant position. Fresh Del Monte has also entered into banana production in the ACPO countries of Cameroon and Côte d'Ivoire. The company is also attempting to move into value-added fresh produce. This would bring Fresh Del Monte into direct competition with Dole in this product segment.

Chiquita Brands International has also pursued a corporate strategy designed to reduce its dependence on bananas, as well as concentrating on core business activities. Chiquita has acquired some major food-processing assets. In March 2000, the company announced major organizational realignment. This realignment separated the company into two divisions. Chiquita Fresh consolidated all banana and fresh produce activities in North America and the EU into one division. All processing activities were consolidated into the Chiquita Processed Foods division. The importance of fresh produce dropped from 90% of total sales in 1997 to its present level of about 80%. Additionally, the company paid increased attention to supply-chain management and logistics (Chiquita Brands International 1999 Annual Report). Despite these efforts, the company announced in January 2001 that it would be unable to meet its debt payment and asked bondholders to swap US$862 million in debt for equity. Chiquita still has to resolve its financial difficulties and it continues to pursue strategies based on litigation.

Fyffes continues to pursue a strategy of growth by acquisition. However, the company recently has been plagued by financial difficulties, apparently stemming from its involvement in what has been termed a 'mafia racket' involving illegal shipments of bananas and use of falsified import licences (Brown, 2001).

References

Arthur, H., Houck, J.P. and Beckford, G. (1968) *Tropical Agribusiness Structures and Adjustments: Bananas.* Division of Research, Graduate School of Business Administration, Harvard University, Cambridge, Massachusetts.

Borrell, B. (1994) *EU Bananarama III.* Policy Research Working Paper 1386, The World Bank, New York.

Brown, J. (2001) Mafia Racket Blamed for Fyffes Fall. *Financial Times,* 21 March.

Chiquita Brands International (1999) *1999 Annual Report.* Available at: www.chiquita.com/bottomline/annual.pdf

DePalma, A. (2001) U.S. and Europeans Agree on Deal to End Banana Trade War. *New York Times,* 12 April.

Dole Food Company (1999) *1999 Annual Report.* Available at: www.dole.com/pdfs/annuals/99annrpt.pdf

EIU (2000) *Regional Developments: Disputes Plague the Banana Industry.* The Economist Intelligence Unit Country Report for the Windward and Leeward Islands, 28 January.

Fresh Del Monte Produce (1999) *1999 Annual Report.* Available at: media.corporate-ir.net/media_files/NYS/FDP/reports/FDP_ar99.pdf

Gale Business Resources (2000) *Chiquita Brands International – History.* Available via search at: www.galenet.com

Jenkins, H. (1999) Yes we have no banana policy (can we borrow yours?). *The Wall Street Journal,* 10 February, p. A23.

Read, R. (1983) The growth and structure of multinationals in the banana export trade. In: Casson, M. (ed.) *The Growth of International Business.* Allen & Unwin, London.

Roche, J. (1998) *The International Banana Trade.* Woodhead Publishing Limited, Cambridge.

United Nations Conference on Trade and Development (1974) *The Marketing and Distribution System for Bananas.* Committee on Commodities Report TD/B/C.1, p. 162.

van de Kasteele, A. (1998) The banana chain: the macroeconomics of the banana trade. Paper presented at the International Banana Conference, Brussels, May 1998.

Banana Trade in Latin America

6

Esteban R. Brenes and Kryssia Madrigal

Introduction

Latin America plays a significant role in the international production and trade of bananas, accounting for 80–85% of world banana exports, with Ecuador, Costa Rica and Colombia as the major exporting countries. Currently 18 Latin American countries produce bananas, accounting for approximately 75% of worldwide production (UPEB, 1992). Nine countries produce about 88% of world bananas. In order of their importance, they include Ecuador, Brazil, Costa Rica, Mexico, Colombia, Venezuela, Honduras, Guatemala and Panama. Banana trade is a significant source of employment and foreign exchange in Latin American economies, primarily in countries where banana production and exports have significant weight. In the 1980s, most Latin American countries began pursuing non-traditional export promotion strategies, leading to a decrease in the importance of traditional exports, such as coffee, bananas, tobacco and grains. However, the impact of traditional exports continues to be significant.

The 'banana wars', initiated by the 1993 EU banana regime, highlight the differing and often conflicting interests of regional trading blocs, individual states, national and multinational corporations. International banana trade issues and policies have placed these key actors in often unexpected adversarial negotiating positions. Latin American states confront the EU; Latin American growers are set against Caribbean growers; Guatemala finds itself with interests differing from those of Costa Rica, Venezuela, Colombia and Nicaragua; Ecuador is set

©CAB *International* 2003. *Banana Wars: the Anatomy of a Trade Dispute* (eds T.E. Josling and T.G. Taylor)

against the other Latin American exporting countries; and Dole vies with Chiquita.

The different positions of countries in the region in relation to the banana trade options proposed by the EU over the years are influenced by production structures and costs, hiring systems, labour and environmental management. The key issues of labour and environmental management are increasing in importance with the spread of environmental certification and international labour standards. Differences in production costs in Latin America are strongly influenced by differences in environmental and labour standards. The relative share of bananas in external trade, agricultural GDP and employment provides a potential for conflicts between the interests of states and multinational corporations (MNCs).

Banana Republics and Previous Banana Wars

The economic structures in Latin America in the 21st century are closely tied to the colonial influences of the 20th century. After gaining their independence in the first half of the 19th century, the colonial pattern of exporting raw materials and agricultural products and importing manufactured and processed goods continued to define Latin American trade patterns. In the period from independence up until the 1960s, the economies of most Latin American countries were dependent primarily on income earned through the export of one or at most two commodities. This was the case with coffee in Brazil, Colombia, El Salvador and Guatemala, and bananas in Panama and Honduras. The reliance of some Latin American countries on banana production and exports during the first part of the 20th century led to their description as 'banana republics'.[1] Honduras was the first Latin American country to be known as a 'banana republic' due to the more than 60% share of bananas in Honduran exports and the increasingly influential role of the banana companies at the beginning of the 20th century. The role of bananas in Honduras dates back to 1899 with the granting of the first banana concession, which led to the establishment of the predecessor to the United Fruit Company.

As foreign direct investment (FDI) stimulated rapid industrialization and an increasingly strong manufacturing sector, the role of the agricultural sector in per cent of GDP and exports has declined in the last

---

[1] The term has both economic and political implications. In an economic context, 'banana republic' was generally used to refer to any poor developing country that relied on a single export commodity. Although this term is also used in a political sense to refer to corruption in the governments of these countries, this usage is not implied here.

half of the 20th century. Although crop diversification has increased, as more and more countries make this a declared goal of economic policy, banana production remains a significant factor in the economies and international trade of several Latin American countries. The increases in the price of petroleum since 1973, combined with the global recession and fluctuations in petroleum prices in the early 1980s, have led to a resurgence of the importance placed on bananas by Latin American governments in the context of national and international policy issues.

The history of bananas in Latin America is tightly intertwined with the history of the United Fruit Company. The United Fruit Company, which was incorporated in 1899, owned or leased 3.5 million acres in Guatemala, Honduras, Costa Rica, Nicaragua, Panama, Cuba, Jamaica, the Dominican Republic, Colombia and Ecuador. The United Fruit Company employed over 90,000 Latin Americans in the 1930s. The rise of bananas as an export crop ended Guatemalan dependency on coffee. The growth of the banana industry resulted in the clearing of jungle for farmland, which eliminated malaria in the region. United Fruit was a dominant economic force and influenced politics in Guatemala from 1906 until 1972, when it sold out to Del Monte. The influence of United Fruit in the political arena gave rise to a 'black legend', which depicts United Fruit as interfering in national politics, exploiting workers, reaping high profits and not contributing to Guatemala's development (Stanley, 1994).

The period from 1970 to 1984 saw many changes and significant developments in the role of bananas in Latin American countries (FAO, 1986). This was a period of declining import growth rates, increased competition and rising production costs. Prices tended to remain stable or increase after 1974. Latin American countries exported 4,297,000 t in 1983, comprising 69% of the world's banana exports. The primary destinations of Latin American bananas were North America and Western Europe. North America imported 2,684,000 t and Western Europe 1,373,000 t, accounting for 62% and 32% of Latin American exports, respectively.

During 1970s and 1980s, there were three main banana exporting countries located in Central America (Costa Rica, Honduras and Panama) and two in South America (Colombia and Ecuador).[2] Technological changes were introduced in Central America by corporate plantations. Their use spread to associated producers in Central America and the changes were later adopted in Colombia and Ecuador by independent producers (FAO, 1986). Producers also switched from growing the Gros Michel variety of banana to the Cavendish. This had a positive impact on banana yields. At the same time, Central American

---

[2] Guatemala is not included in this history because its percentage share of total Latin American exports from 1973 to 1983 never went above 8.1%.

countries began to apply export taxes on bananas, which changed the landscape of Latin American banana exports fundamentally. The two main South American exporters thus moved into a better position in the market. Ecuadorian bananas became the least expensive in the Latin American area and Colombia substantially increased its market share. Country-specific analysis is covered in more detail in the country sections in this chapter.

The decades preceding the 'banana wars' saw the continuing influence of colonial structures and multinational banana companies, as well as the shifting of influences and interests and the creation of new polarities. The Union of Banana Exporting Countries (UPEB) was established in 1974 by Colombia, Costa Rica, Guatemala, Honduras and Panama, in part as a policy response to the changes in banana production costs, prices and export markets (FAO, 1986).[3] The UPEB had a strong influence on transforming the role of multinational corporations in the region.[4] One side effect was the increase in state intervention in the banana export sector. The influence of the UPEB led to new legislation in Central America in the mid-1970s that fundamentally changed the institutional and regulatory framework for bananas in Costa Rica, Honduras and Panama (FAO, 1986). As a result, contracts with multinationals were cancelled and their concessions were revoked.[5] The UPEB countries, with the exception of Colombia, instituted export taxes that became an important source of revenue for the respective governments. The UPEB also set up special banana policy agencies in Costa Rica, Honduras and Panama. As a result of the changes that took place during the 1970s and 1980s, the price of Ecuadorian bananas was 20% below that of bananas from Colombia, Costa Rica, Honduras and Panama, a reversal of the situation in the early 1970s. In addition, the export taxes imposed by Central American countries tended to reduce their potential for competitiveness in the increasingly competitive world market for bananas.

Bananas in Latin America

Bananas are a key element of the economy in many Latin American countries in terms of GNP, export earnings and employment, and

[3] Ecuador never became a member of the UPEB.

[4] The UPEB set up an intergovernmental banana marketing company as a joint marketing venture, COMUNABNA, in 1997, which sold to Yugoslavia and shipped bananas from the Dominican Republic to the US, but it folded in 1983.

[5] Prior to 1974, the MNCs had had long contracts extending from 59 to 99 years. In Honduras, the United Fruit Company had an indefinite concession previous to 1974. These contracts included agreements on export taxes, which were set at US$0.80 t^{-1} of boxed bananas for many decades (FAO, 1986).

represent an important part of the agricultural output. Changes in the amount of cultivated land, yields and production are key endogenous factors influencing the policies and positions of Latin American governments and civil society in the 'banana wars' of the last decade.

Over the period 1996–1999, cultivated lands increased in Ecuador, Costa Rica and Guatemala, and decreased in Colombia, Honduras, Panama and Brazil. Between 1996 and 1999, Guatemala and Ecuador experienced a strong expansion of banana plantations, with yearly growth rates of about 4.46 and 4.22%. The rest of the producing countries maintained or decreased their cultivated areas. Colombia, Brazil and Costa Rica experienced a significant decrease in the amount of cultivated land between 1998 and 1999, at rates of 10, 5.68 and 1.08%, respectively. Countries with increasing amounts of land devoted to banana production were interested in larger markets, while the preferences of countries with decreasing amounts of land devoted to banana production tended towards securing higher prices.

Over the same period, banana yields increased in Ecuador and Panama, decreased in Colombia and Costa Rica, and remained the same in Guatemala, Honduras and Brazil. Costa Rica and Honduras showed the highest yields, with 42 and 39 t ha^{-1}, whereas Panama and Brazil show the lowest levels of productivity, with 26 and 11 t ha^{-1}, respectively. Countries with higher yields have shown a strong interest in ensuring sufficient markets in which they can sell their bananas.

Except for Ecuador (which experienced a 6% production increase between 1998 and 1999), production volumes have decreased in the remaining countries. Most countries have witnessed a sharp production decrease in 1998/99. The largest decreases occurred in Guatemala and Honduras, with 36 and 45%, respectively. Decreasing production volumes have created an incentive for countries to ensure current price levels or even to attempt to secure price increases.

The 1998 decline in production volume in most Latin American countries was the result of atmospheric conditions and natural disasters that hit the region.[6] These phenomena led to a slight decrease (3%) in the volume of worldwide banana exports in 1998. The only country to experience a significant increase in banana exports was Costa Rica, which took advantage of markets that could not be served by exporting countries negatively affected by natural disasters, and also sold to some Latin American countries. By 1999, however, the recovery of banana production in Latin American countries and market demand expectations were widely perceived in the world market, leading to a significant fall in international banana prices (FAO, 1999).

---

[6] El Niño in Ecuador; Hurricane Mitch in Honduras, Nicaragua and Guatemala.

Table 6.1. Latin American (LA) banana exports by country (1000 t). Source: FAO (1999).

Country	1994	1995	1996	1997	1998	1999
Brazil	51.8	12.5	30.0	40.1	68.6	61.4
Colombia	**1,572.0**	**1,335.6**	**1,406.5**	**1,509.3**	**1,435.8**	**821.8**
Costa Rica	**1,874.6**	**2,033.3**	**1,933.3**	**1,835.3**	**2,101.1**	**2,049.8**
Dominican Republic	95.0	94.2	80.2	63.9	65.1	58.5
Ecuador	**3,307.6**	**3,736.5**	**3,840.2**	**4,456.3**	**3,860.3**	**3,872.2**
Guatemala	**587.9**	**635.5**	**611.2**	**658.8**	**632.2**	**n.a.**
Honduras	**493.7**	**521.6**	**637.1**	**557.2**	**433.1**	**n.a.**
Mexico	52.3	110.1	162.9	240.2	280.3	n.a.
Nicaragua	27.1	54.3	78.2	69.8	102.5	n.a.
Panama	**756.6**	**692.9**	**634.0**	**601.7**	**463.4**	**460.8**
Venezuela	47.7	32.4	40.4	68.3	72.1	46.2
Total LA exports	8,866.3	9,258.9	9,454.0	10,100.9	9,514.5	n.a.
Total of world	10,844.7	11,374.5	11,701.8	12,145.0	11,387.8	n.a.
% of world exports	82	81	81	83	84	–

n.a., not available. Bold type indicates 'Major World Exporters'.

The main Latin American exporters of bananas are located in Central America and the Andean Pact Region (see Table 6.1). In order of importance, the six major exporting countries are Ecuador, Costa Rica, Colombia, Panama, Guatemala and Honduras. These countries account for 95% of total Latin American exports. Three Latin American banana-exporting countries, Ecuador, Colombia and Costa Rica, are key players in the international banana trade disputes.

The other three main producers of bananas in Latin America, Brazil, Venezuela and Mexico, devote over 90% of their output to domestic consumption.

Ecuador, the regional leader and chief exporter in Latin America and the world, and Colombia are two major banana exporters, located in the Andean Pact region. Colombia is the second largest regional exporter, with a 30% share of the market. Colombia's share of exports was 17% in 1994, 14% in 1995 and 15% for the following years. This country was also a beneficiary of the export quotas imposed by the EU.

Figure 6.1 shows the trend for an 18-year period of banana exports in millions of (18.14 kg) boxes in several of the countries in the region. Ecuador and Costa Rica are the countries with the highest rates of average yearly growth (5.9 and 4.6%, respectively) in exports.

In order of importance, historical export markets have included Europe, with a 61% share (of this, the EU accounts for 52%), the USA (28%) and Japan (11%). The historical and more recent differences in relative shares, in particular in the European and US markets are central in defining the different interests behind the positions taken by

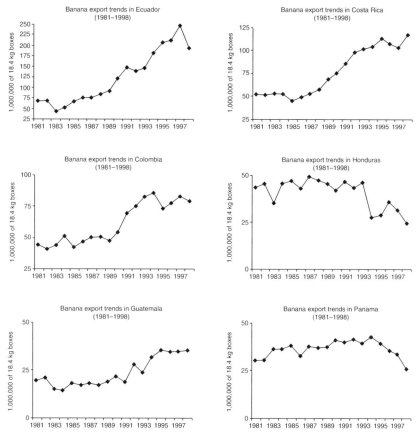

Fig. 6.1. Trend of banana exports in key Latin American exporting countries, 1981–1998 (million 18.4 kg boxes). Source: UPEB (1992) and FAO (1998).

Latin American exporters in the 'banana wars'. Environmental issues and multinational corporations exacerbate these differences.

Policies and Politics in Selected Latin American Countries

The recent reshuffling of interests, alliances and positions during the course of the 'banana wars' have put a spotlight on the differences, transitions and influences on trade policy in Latin American countries. The historical influences of colonial structures and multinational corporations have become intermingled with influences from trends in world consumption and production as well as domestic interests and actors and national policies.

The following sections attempt to identify characteristics, actors, interests and agendas that have been key in determining the policies and positions of Latin American banana-exporting countries in the recent 'banana wars'. The three cases described here are Ecuador, Costa Rica and Colombia, as these three countries are the major players in the recent WTO disputes. A summary of the major interests for each of these countries is presented in Table 6.2.

Table 6.2. Overview of major interests in three Latin American banana-exporting countries.

Country	Domestic interests	MNCs	Export destination/ % of exports[a]
Ecuador WTO 1996	Noboa Reybanpac Palmar	Chiquita Dole	US 34.8% Main EU destinations 29.6%, of which: Italy 14.6% Germany 7.9% Belgium-Lux. 7.1% Other 35.6%
Costa Rica UPEB 1974 GATT 1990	CORBANA (Corporación Bananera Nacional) CARIBANA (exporter, 12% market share) Comercial Bananera de Costa Rica (exporter, 4% market share) Chiriquí Land Co. (exporter, 1% market share)	Dole (exporter, 29% market share) Chiquita (exporter, 29% market share) Del Monte (exporter, 18% market share)	US 49.7% Main EU destinations 38.2%, of which: Belgium-Lux. 14.1% Germany 8.6% Italy 6.6% Sweden 6.5% UK 2.4% Other 12.1%
Colombia UPEB 1974	Independent Farmers (60% of producers) AUGURA – Banana Growers Association Uniban (Colombian owned exporter) Banacol (Colombian owned exporter) Sunisa (Colombian owned exporter) Bagatela (Colombian owned exporter) Banadex (exporter, owned by Chiquita) Conserba (exporter, owned by Dole) Proban (exporter, owned by Dole) Singrainagro (Labour Union)	Dole and Del Monte (40% of production) Chiquita (exporter) Del Monte (exporter) Dole (exporter)	US 28.7% Main EU destinations 49.7%, of which: Belgium-Lux. 40.7% Italy 8.8% Germany 0.2% Other 21.6%

[a]FAO Intergovernmental Group (1999). 1997 data are used for Guatemala and Honduras. 1998 data are used for the other countries.

Ecuador

Bananas became Ecuador's main agricultural export in 1947. Ecuador became the world's leading banana exporter in 1953.[7] The period from 1970 to 1984 was a period of substantial improvement in the quality of bananas produced in Ecuador. This increased quality was a key factor in the increase in Ecuador's share of the US market (FAO, 1986). Ecuadorian bananas also fared well in the more competitive atmosphere of the period due to the devaluation[8] of its currency between 1982 and 1985.[9] Ecuador never became a member of the UPEB formed by the other Latin American exporters in 1974. Ecuador became a member of the WTO in 1996.

Bananas became the leading Ecuadorian export product in 1997. In that same year, national banana legislation was passed,[10] which strengthened the role of government intervention in banana production and marketing.[11] This legislation forbade the establishment of new banana holdings and included specific price-setting elements. It established the right of the government to review and set minimum producer prices, and reference FOB prices for exporters. It also established sanctions for non-compliance with the minimum support price. In the following year, new producer prices and FOB reference prices were set by an interministerial agreement.[12]

Ecuador's cultivated area comprises nearly 160,000 ha, chiefly located in three provinces: El Oro (32%), Guayas (31%) and Los Ríos (29%). Plantations also exist in the spurs of the Los Andes mountain range in the provinces of Azuay, Bolivar, Cañar, Cotopaxi, Pichincha and, to a lesser degree, in Manabí and Esmeraldas (CORBANA, 2000).

---

[7] Ecuador is also a major producer of organic bananas (*Inside US Trade*, 2001).

[8] Some of the advantage resulting from devaluation is thought to have been offset by increased transportation costs (FAO, 1986).

[9] This is true in spite of the fact that Ecuador's share of total Latin American exports dropped 11.8% from 1973 to 1983. This decrease in shares possibly can be attributed to Colombia's 14.5% increase in shares of total Latin American exports.

[10] The legislation was passed in July 1997 and went into effect in August of the same year.

[11] Specifically, the Executive Branch through the Ministry of Foreign Trade and the Ministry of Agriculture.

[12] The producer prices of US$4.25 and US$3.35 were set for a 19.52 kg box for the high season and the low season, respectively. The FOB reference prices of US$5.95 (high season) and US$5.05 (low season) were also set in January 1998. Data and information on the 1997 and 1998 Ecuadorian banana price legislation are based on the FAO Intergovernmental Report (1999).

Ecuador's production structure may be characterized as follows:

- 40% of banana production is managed by small- and micro-producers, with land tracts not larger than 30 ha, although the mode is approximately 5 ha. These farms characteristically are artisanal, with cultivation as a family activity and not managed as a business. For this reason, family members only engage in banana production when prices are high. Thus, artisanal producers easily engage in production or leave it, depending on price.
- 35% of the production area is in the hands of middle-sized producers, with farms between 30 ha and less than 100 ha. Most of these producers lack adequate infrastructure and basic equipment, they are not integrated and they forward bananas to artisanal packers.
- 25% of the production area is owned by large producers with technical infrastructure[13] and adequate equipment, vertically integrated with carton manufacturing, fertilizer companies, shipping firms, fumigation fleets and packing plants, among other facilities.

Ecuador's share in Latin American banana exports increased from 37% in 1994 to 44% in 1997, but fell again to 40% in 1998. This reduction resulted from the application of the quota system by the EU to Ecuador and other Latin American countries, and the effect of climatic phenomena hitting Ecuadorian production. Like other producers, Ecuador exports bananas chiefly to Europe and the USA. In addition, it is the Latin American leader in terms of banana exports to Asia and Oceania. From 1996, Ecuadorian exports began entering the former USSR as well as China.[14]

Both multinationals and Ecuadorian companies carry out trade in bananas. Major companies are usually integrated from production to transportation to sales in the various markets. In order of importance, these include: Exportadora Bananera Noboa (with a 32% share, exporting mainly to the USA and Belgium); Reybanpac (16%, exporting to the USA and Russia); Ubesa (Standard Fruit Co. – Dole, 14%; exports chiefly to the USA and Italy); Brundicorpi (United Fruit Co. – Chiquita); Agro Comercio Palmar; Bandecua (Del Monte); Cimexesa; Costatrading; Exportadora Quirola; Comerban; and 99 other trading firms (see Fig. 6.2).

Exportadora Bananera Noboa,[15] the leading Ecuadorian banana-exporting company, was established about 50 years ago and is roughly

---

[13] Technical infrastructure means sprinkling irrigation, cable cars, central packing facilities, drainage and so on.

[14] Ecuadorian exports by destination are follows: the EU, 45%; NAFTA, 26%; Asia-Pacific Region, 24%; MERCOSUR, 6%; and Central American Common Market, 0.4%.

[15] Exportadora Bananera Noboa is the banana division of Grupo (*continued*)

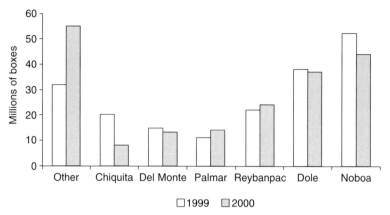

Fig. 6.2. Ecuadorian banana exports by trading company, 1999/2000. Source: CORBANA (2000).

estimated to have a trade volume of around 10–13% of the world market. It is the fourth biggest banana export company and controls over one-third of Ecuador's exports. It is one of the largest exporters to the European market, and has grown in importance since 1993. Noboa owns the biggest shipping operation in the banana industry and is the most diversified exporter of all the big companies. In addition to the US and the EU, Noboa exports to Japan, New Zealand, South-east Asia, Eastern Europe, the Middle East and the 'Southern Cone' of South America. The agricultural division of Exportadora Bananera Noboa owns over 7000 ha in banana production, with some of the highest productivity in the industry (averaging 2800 boxes per hectare per year). Noboa also buys from some 600 'Associated Producers' covering 36,600 ha.

In Ecuador, multinational corporations do not own a significant share of the 25% of farms with technical infrastructure that are integrated throughout the entire production chain. Dole owns 25,000 ha but Chiquita and Del Monte do not own banana farms. In 2001, Indrizo S.A., one of Grupo Noboa's eight subsidiaries, further reduced the role of MNCs in Ecuador as a result of the January 2001 acquisition of 7.58% of Chiquita shares.

The 1999 per-box cost for bananas in Ecuador approached US$5.16 in the case of large farms with technical infrastructure. Contrary to what happens in the rest of Latin America, Ecuadorian producers are fully integrated from banana production to trade, thus reaching significant economies of scale. On the other hand, given the characteristics and the production structure of the banana sector, per-box costs

---

[15] (*continued*) Noboa S.A. The Noboa group does not make accounts or other detailed information available to the public.

in small and middle-sized farms (which account for a significant percentage of total production) are, on average, much lower than those mentioned above.

The Ecuadorian market is a spot market selling to the highest bidder, with a large number of buyers and sellers competing with each other. Banana prices are not contingent upon technical or political decisions, but rather are influenced by production and trading structures that simultaneously have a substantial impact on the world price of bananas. On the other hand, small operators lacking adequate information regarding price and volumes carry out 40% of banana trade. They frequently make purchasing decisions in spot markets, such as that of Ecuador, under circumstances that do not favour the stability of world market prices and volumes. In addition, for the last few years the supply of merchant fleets has increased faster than demand. Ecuadorian merchants have skilfully taken advantage of this fact to overcome the main previous entry barrier to banana trade, the control of transport facilities.

While Ecuadorian farms with technical infrastructure and equipment experience production costs similar to those of all other producers in the region, a significant portion of Ecuadorian production takes place in small and medium-sized farms with production practices and structural and cultural features favouring costs per box much lower than the regional average. All of the above has contributed to very 'competitive' average purchase prices for Ecuadorian bananas, as compared to the rest of the regional countries.

Costa Rica

Bananas were first exported commercially from Costa Rica in 1879. In 1899, United Fruit was formed through the merger of the Boston Fruit Co. and the Tropical Trading & Transport Co. In the 1930s and 1940s, banana production was relocated from the Atlantic to the Pacific coast. In 1956, Standard Fruit began production in Costa Rica. The Corporación Bananera Nacional (CORBANA) was established in 1971 under the name Asociación de Bananeros (ASBANA), as a government-sponsored private association.

In Costa Rica, banana production was consolidated on the Atlantic coast between 1971 and 1984. Average yields declined during this period and a banana tax was introduced in 1974. These two events were primarily responsible for the 3.9% decrease in the Costa Rican share of total Latin American exports between 1973 and 1983. However, the effect of these two events was mitigated by the devaluation of the national currency, beginning in 1981. Costa Rica is a member of the UPEB and has higher export prices than Ecuador, in part due to export taxes that have their origins in the period after the formation of the UPEB.

Independent producers, on 50% of the cultivated lands, character-ize Costa Rica's production structure; the remaining 50% is in the hands of multinational corporations, chiefly Dole, Chiquita and Del Monte. Companies engaged in banana trading include Standard Fruit Co. (Dole, 29%); Compañía Bananera del Atlántico (Chiquita, 29%); Banana Development Co. (Del Monte, 18%); CARIBANA (12%); Comercial Bananera de Costa Rica (4%); others (3%); and Chiriquí Land Co. (1%).

Costa Rican exports go mainly to Europe and the USA; 58% of exports for 2000 went to the USA; 41% to Europe (including the Mediterranean region), and just 1% went to Asia. Between 90% and 95% of trading takes places through major multinational corporations. In 1999, 90% of exports were made through these companies, with a decrease to 87% in 2000 (see Fig. 6.3).

Costa Rica was one of the main beneficiaries of the export quotas imposed by the EU. Banana trade in Costa Rica accounts for 9.5% of total exports and 4.2% of the country's GDP.[16] In addition, the govern-ment receives a significant tax income from this sector.[17]

Colombia

United Fruit began banana production in Colombia in the 19th century in the Magdalena region. This region remained the main Colombian banana-producing region until the second half of the 20th century,

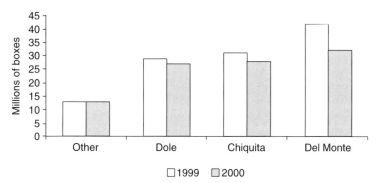

Fig. 6.3. Costa Rican banana exports by trading company, 1999/2000. Source: CORBANA (2000).

---

[16] Source: Costa Rica Central Bank.
[17] Costa Rica is the only country taxing banana production and trading.

when production declined and banana production moved to the Urabá region. Banana production began in the Urabá region of Colombia in 1909 under the German company Albingia Consortium.[18] United Fruit, together with its subsidiary Frutera de Sevilla, began production in 1916. The Urabá banana export market was consolidated in 1963. In Colombia, rapidly increasing yields in the Urabá region resulted in substantial growth in the Colombian banana export sector. From 1970 to 1984, exports increased from 296.3 million to 920.9 million boxes (FAO, 1986).

Colombia is a member of the UPEB. However, Colombia's policy of non-imposition of export taxes, in contrast to the export taxes imposed in Central American countries during the same period, also helped to spur the rise in exports. Colombia's share of total Latin American exports increased from 4.8% in 1973 to 19.3% in 1983. Urabá is also the home of the Banana Growers Association of Urabá (AUGURA), which was founded in 1963. Government incentives, such as soft loans and tax credits, were key elements in the establishment and consolidation of national export companies (FAO, 1986).[19]

In 1997, Colombia set an export subsidy (CERT) of 3% of FOB value for all banana exports. This subsidy is to be phased out completely by 2003. A new organization is planned to replace the subsidy and to facilitate increased productivity and export competitiveness as of 2003 (FAO Intergovernmental Group, 1999).

Under the Banana Framework Agreement, Colombia charged a 70% export certificate fee for Category A and C licences. This programme was expected to generate approximately US$31 million in 1998 alone (FAO Intergovernmental Group, 1999). The revenues were used to redistribute economic rents resulting from the EU banana regime to all growers through a system of direct payments based on individual export volumes without differentiation based on the destination of the exports. This certification programme was declared to be discrimina-tory by the European Court of Justice in 1998 and the programme was dissolved.

Independent farmers provide about 60% of Colombian production and the remaining 40% is under MNC control (chiefly Dole and Del Monte) (see Fig. 6.4). Many producers are vertically integrated with transportation and packaging. Banana trade takes place chiefly through the traditional MNCs.

---

[18] Albingia received the banana concession as a trade-off for the construction of a railroad track, but it later failed as a result of World War I (AUGURA, 2001).

[19] The soft loans were distributed by PROEXPO, the Export Promotion Fund, and were available to pre-finance banana exports and for on-farm investments. The tax credit was an export subsidy amounting to 10% of the export value (FAO, 1986).

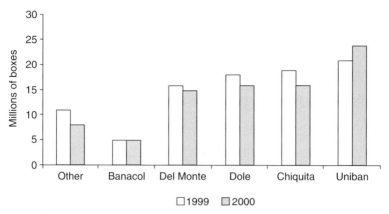

Fig. 6.4. Colombian banana exports by trading company, 1999/2000. Source: CORBANA (2000).

Four of the Colombian banana-exporting companies are owned by Colombian stockholders: Uniban, Banacol, Sunisa and Bagatela. The other two are owned by MNCs. Chiquita owns Banadex, and Dole owns 60% of Conserba de Del Monte and Proban. As shown in Fig. 6.4, 59% of exports in 1999, took place through multinational trading companies such as Chiquita, Dole and Del Monte, while 41% was carried out by national firms, with Uniban holding a 23% share of banana exports in Colombia. By 2000, the multinational share of trade decreased to 56%, while Uniban's share grew to 29% (CORBANA, 2000).

Colombia exports mainly to Europe and the USA. In 2000, export shares by destination were as follows: Europe, 40%; the USA, 39%; the Mediterranean, 16%; China, 4%; Russia, 1%; and the Baltic Region, 1%. Eighty-three per cent of exports were marketed through major MNCs. Banana exports account for 32% of Colombia's agricultural exports.

Urabá, located in what is known as the banana corridor, has remained the main banana-growing region in Colombia. Urabá is comprised of 11 municipalities, all of whose economies are dependent on agriculture. Ninety per cent of the Urabá economy is dependent on the banana industry (AUGURA, 2001). Urabá has its own port, which serves approximately 350 ships transporting bananas annually (AUGURA, 2001).

Banana policy in Colombia is influenced strongly by AUGURA, the Banana Growers Association of Urabá (FAO, 1986). AUGURA represents 83% of the total banana exporters. Five of the seven Colombian national exporting companies are associated with AUGURA: Uniban, Banacol, Bagatela, Banadex and Proban. AUGURA also manages the Colombian Social and Environmental Programme, BANATURA, which planned to start operations in 2001. Four of the banana-exporting companies have established social foundations: Banacol (CORBANACOL), Banadex (FUNDABANADEX), Probán (FUNDAPROBÁN) and Uniban (FUNDAUNIBÁN).

Environmental Issues in Banana Production

Banana production is associated with several environmental issues: use of pesticides, deforestation, soil depletion, flooding, waste disposal and water pollution. The loss of soil fertility after 3 or 4 years of banana cultivation without rotation has led to the continuous expansion of banana plantations, resulting in the related problems of deforestation and flooding. The issue of the disposal of the large amounts of waste created during banana production has not yet been resolved in an economically and environmentally efficient way. In addition, the extensive use of pesticides has led to soil and water pollution. Currently, very intensive methods of production, using large volumes of chemicals (second only to the cotton industry), are used in order to produce bananas for export. Environmental issues in Latin America affect production costs and are beginning to play a greater role as MNCs begin to participate in environmental certification programmes.

The costs involved with reducing the negative environmental impact of banana production strongly influence the decisions of MNCs in the highly competitive international banana export market. This is particularly true in the context of the 'banana wars', as many companies see an opportunity to secure increased market shares. While environmental issues have been raised in all of the three main Latin American exporting countries, Costa Rica is currently the main actor in this area.

Costa Rica is the Latin American leader in environmental development. Although other countries are also taking similar measures, they lag behind Costa Rica by at least 5 years. In Costa Rica, 100% of banana farms appropriately dispose of organic waste, 97% recycle plastics, 95% recycle plastic cord, 91% have buffer areas, 95% reforest riverbanks, 60% of production area is under certification, and it is the only country to levy an environmental tax. Investment in environmental programmes for banana cultivation and trade amounts to €353 million.

Costa Rica is the only country that actively considers ecological and human development in banana production.[20] For this reason, production costs are high compared with those of competitors. On average, banana farms are estimated to devote 26% of total investment to social

---

[20] This is true of all banana farms, both independent and MNC-owned, regardless of size. The value of this as a marketing advantage, however, has not been recognized in the market due to excess world supply of bananas.

investment, including housing, schools, drinking water, electricity, phones, roads, community centres, dining rooms, sport facilities and health-care centres. Likewise, social benefits are paid regularly by all banana farms, which increase salary costs by at least an additional 51%. Finally, 10% of per-box costs are accounted for by additional benefits to workers, including service subsidies, scholarships, school supplies, libraries and sick leave.

Only two firms are eco-certificated in Ecuador, under Eco-etiquetado Eco-Ok (Rey Banano del Pacífico) and ISO-14000 (UBESA). Colombia has a Social and Environmental Management Programme for the banana sector applied through BANATURA, a teaching tool to support and encourage management and operation teams of banana farms to develop and implement a sustainable development process.

Recently Chiquita decided to participate in an environmental certification programme in Colombia, Costa Rica, Guatemala, Honduras and Panama. In addition, 30% of Chiquita's independent suppliers are participating.

Labour Issues in Banana Production

From the beginning, labour issues have been a key factor of Latin American banana trade. The 'black legend', the exploitation of workers by United Fruit, has overshadowed the banana trade since the days of 'banana republics' and later the first 'banana wars'. Labour disputes also played a key role in the relations with United Fruit, which left Costa Rica in the wake of the 1984 strike.

The Ecuadorian banana industry provides direct and indirect employment to nearly 14% of the country's population, 28% of the population in the coastal area and 56.4% of the population of the three main banana-producing provinces (CORBANA, 2000). The country also has a wage rate significantly lower than that of other Latin American countries.

Banana production and trade in Costa Rica employs 2.5% of the labour force – 11%, if indirect employment is taken into account. Costa Rica, second to Ecuador in global exports, is particularly troubled as its higher wages and tighter labour regulations mean that it cannot compete on cost. Average salaries in the Costa Rican banana sector are much higher than those paid by the major competitors. For some tasks, the difference can amount to ten times as high. Wages[21] for agricultural workers have increased in Costa Rica from 37,470 (current) colones in 1994 to 62,843 (current) colones in 1998. Agricultural workers are the

---

[21] Wage data for Costa Rica is taken from the 1999 IMF Statistical Annex for Costa Rica.

lowest paid by sector of all Costa Rican workers. The next lowest paid by sector, construction workers, received 15% more money (73,909 current colones) than agricultural workers in 1998. The highest paid sector, public utility workers, received 61% higher wages (160,549 current colones) in 1998. Agriculture is responsible for 20% of the workforce, i.e. 261,600 total jobs. This represents a 1.4% decrease in percentage of total employment from 1994 to 1998.

The banana industry in the Urabá region of Colombia was disrupted by violence in 1992 and 1997, resulting in the destruction of banana production and shipping infrastructure and causing growers to leave their farms. This led to declining productivity (by up to 50%), unemployment and economic recession, and increased drug trafficking[22] in the area (AUGURA, 2001).

In 2000, the banana industry in Urabá[23] provided 16,500 (of the total 22,000) jobs directly in the banana industry and 52,500 (of the total 65,000) jobs associated with the banana industry in Colombia. The local labour union, Sintrainagro, has a membership of approximately 14,000. The National Agricultural Workers Union, SINTRAINAGRO, was established in 1975. SINTRAINAGRO currently has a membership of approximately 16,000, 78% of whom live in Urabá (AUGURA, 2001).

Worldwide oversupply of bananas is expected to continue. Prices are expected to be lower and to stabilize in the short and medium term, which would put strong pressure on MNCs production or purchases from independent producers with high production costs. Production costs in countries with labour and environmental guarantees are, by far, much higher than those in countries without minimum labour and environmental policies. As a result, the lower prices directly promote purchasing bananas from countries with a less-than-desirable labour and environmental situation.

International Trade Issues and Latin American Bananas

One of the major export markets for the banana output of continental Latin America is the EU. Consequently, the actions taken by the EU in changing its import regime have led to much instability. Latin American governments recognized that the EU trade policy focused on three key objectives: integrating the European market in order to increase its bargaining power; ensuring the banana supply from former

---

[22] According to AUGURA, 'around 40% of drug trafficking was done through Urabá and Panama'.

[23] Bananas are also produced in Santa Marta, the largest area of banana production in Colombia. However, this production is scattered and is not comparable with Urabá in terms of political and economic influence.

colonies in Africa, the Caribbean and the Pacific (ACP); and consolidating supplies through EU trading companies. Thus, expansion into this market was going to be difficult.

Another factor with a negative influence on the market for Latin American bananas was the high expectations related to the fall of the Iron Curtain, as a significant consumption increase was envisioned for transition economies and substantial improvement was anticipated for the Asian markets. Both expectations, however, proved overly optimistic. These optimistic demand estimates led to increased cultivation areas and improved productivity, which resulted in larger banana output. When the anticipated demand did not materialize, international banana prices fell, worsening the crisis of the banana industry in Latin America.

Due to the importance of the European market and the uncertainty it has created since 1994, describing the main changes and events in international banana trade as seen from Latin America is of paramount importance. Four stages can be identified in this 8-year period, each reflecting a different approach to banana trade in the EU. These are as follows: (i) the period before 1994; (ii) the Banana Framework Agreement; (iii) the changes resulting from the WTO ruling; and (iv) the recent US–EU Agreement.[24]

Latin American bananas in the EU before 1994

Prior to 1994, the EU had several distinct banana markets. Import controls existed for countries with former colonies producing bananas, namely, France, Spain, Portugal and the UK. As a result of the Lomé Convention, these countries purchased bananas exclusively from their former colonies.[25] On the other hand, while Italy maintained a quota system for the Latin American countries, Germany was Europe's chief buyer and dealer, also supplying the northern European countries. The system existing prior to 1994 was challenged in the GATT by Costa Rica, Colombia and Guatemala on 12 December 1992. The GATT panel ruled for the claimants on 19 March 1993. However, as a new trade system (Regulation #404–93) was to become effective beginning 1994, the judgement *per se* had no further relevance (see Chapter 8).

On 1 January 1994, the EU passed Regulation 404/93, allowing for the issuance of export licences with different tariff preferences for banana firms and a 2.2 million t quota. These licences were issued in line with the 1989–1991 banana trade volumes. As a result of having a

---

[24] Details of these regimes are found in Chapters 3 and 4 of this book.
[25] The UK had a small import quota for these same countries.

significant share of banana exports to the EU for that period, Dole benefited considerably from these quotas. However, Costa Rica and Colombia challenged Regulation 404/93, as they foresaw restrictions to their EU market share resulting from this new trade policy (CORBANA, 2000).

The Banana Framework Agreement

On 18 April 1993, Costa Rica, Colombia and Guatemala requested a panel under the GATT to examine the new EU policy. The panel subsequently ruled for the claimants on 14 January 1994, when Regulation 404–93 had been in effect for only 14 days. As a result of this ruling, the EU agreed to set a quota system assigning each country a given export share under a fixed tariff, plus a higher tariff rate for the surplus. This was chiefly favourable to Colombia and Costa Rica, which in the final ruling were granted 21 and 23.4% quotas, respectively. This, however, left out both Ecuador and Panama. Other less significant countries in terms of banana exports, e.g. Venezuela and Nicaragua, were also assigned quotas with percentages similar to their export levels.

This arrangement, known as the 'Banana Framework Agreement' was reached on 28 March 1994, and became effective as of 1 January 1995.[26] As a result, banana-exporting countries issued export certificates, forcing European operators owning import licences to purchase these certificates, or at least to match them with licences enabling them to trade bananas. Each country issued its certificates on a different basis; in some cases a small group of producers was favoured (as in the case of Colombia), in others, certificates were assigned based on each producer's historical share of exports (as in the case of Costa Rica). The effectiveness of the quotas resulted in a market for import licences and export certificates that artificially increased the price of bananas. This situation led major North American banana operators to engage in a fierce competition and, as a result, to purchase European companies that owned licences. Companies lacking enough import licences lost market share. That was, for instance, the case for Chiquita.

The WTO ruling and Latin American suppliers

Since the new regime excluded Ecuador from the quota system and, in addition, had a negative impact on Chiquita, both Ecuador and the USA

[26] Details of the Agreement are given in Chapter 7.

requested a panel under the WTO stating their disagreement with the quota system.[27] A judgement for the claimants was pronounced in 1997. As a result, the WTO proposed three alternatives: to assign country quotas to all major suppliers, including Ecuador; return to the trade system in place before 1994; or to implement a first-come, first-served system. No agreement was reached in relation to quota assignment on a per-country basis, given Ecuador's opposition to negotiating quotas with former BFA beneficiary countries. MNCs, on the other hand, had not reached an agreement regarding their individual shares of import licences, as the result favoured some of them more than others, depending on the assignment period chosen.

This lack of definition led to the suggestion of a first-come, first-served system in late 2000. All parties objected, as none felt it favourable. The system was complex both in terms of management and in terms of application, and would have led to inefficiencies in the production and logistics systems, as it set a reduction rate that negatively affected the product on its way to the EU (CORBANA, 2000). According to the system, a portion of this product in transit should be diverted to other markets if and when EU quotas were met.

Some people, however, thought this system could favour Ecuador for several reasons. In view of Ecuador's low prices, many traders would be willing to take the risk of shipping the product to the EU, even when aware of the fact that a portion could be diverted to other lower-price markets. In the long run, this would ensure a much higher average price than could be obtained if 100% of the product were shipped to the secondary market, as occurs today. This would give Ecuador a larger share of the EU market than it currently has. In addition, Ecuador is knowledgeable about the secondary market and feels confident in it, as at present it plays a significant role in the trading of Ecuadorian banana production.

US–EU Agreement and Latin American views

The first-come, first-served system that was to have been implemented by the EU, beginning on 1 July 2001, would have created disadvantages to almost all of the parties involved. The USA filed an appeal against it in Geneva and was authorized to apply a number of penalties on European products. The Latin American countries that were favoured by the quota system also challenged the new procedure.

---

[27] At the same time, a German trading firm filed a claim in 1996 with the European Court of Justice in Luxembourg, contending the application of a discriminatory system, as a result of restrictions on its banana import and distribution opportunities in northern Europe (see Chapter 4).

The US–EU conflict also revived talks on strengthening the Union of Banana Exporting Countries (UPEB). The members of UPEB hope that the organization will help in the process of modernization and diversification of the banana industry as well as ensuring them a greater share of the profits from banana exports (CAA, 2000). The UPEB was instrumental in increasing the influence of Central American governments in the banana sector and breaking the power of the banana multinationals in the 1970s. Perhaps the members hope that it will be similarly instrumental in increasing the negotiating power and bargaining positions of Central American governments in the current banana market.

After negotiating for several months, a temporary agreement was reached between the USA and the EU to be effective between July 2001 and 2006.[28] This agreement assigns licences on the basis of historical preferences.[29] As a result of this modification, there is be an A–B quota of 2.65 million t paying a €75 t^{-1} tariff, and a C quota of 750,000 t where ACP countries will not pay tariffs. The quota for Latin America will be managed through the licence programme. It consists of assigning these licences to primary importers or companies growing and buying bananas in Latin America to sell in Europe, according to historical per-country exports between 1994 and 1996.

Several different parties opposed the agreement. Dole said this was not the best way to free banana trade. Its opposition, however, is seen as linked to the fact that its major competitor, Chiquita, will be favoured by the new system, given the reference period used. Ecuador has opposed the licence system and, as a consequence, lobbied hard for an agreement on the application of the new system allowing it to receive significant compensation from the EU. Ecuador was fully aware that the new agreement would require its support with the WTO and so it enjoyed some bargaining power.

Although the system resulting from negotiations between the USA and the EU is not the most 'desirable' to exporting countries with quotas (Costa Rica and Colombia), it is seen in the region as less prejudicial than the first-come, first-served one. The licence system favours MNCs that, in the final analysis, will be the ones to define the market share for each of these countries, depending on convenience of purchase, number of plantations in each country, most convenient and

---

[28] Import quotas will disappear by 2006. Co-existence of quotas and tariffs until that time was approved by the WTO.

[29] The new system will continue to benefit the African, Caribbean and Pacific countries (ACP). In accordance with the agreement linking them to the EU, these countries will not pay tariffs but will witness a small reduction in their quotas, as these have often been under filled (see Chapter 5).

inexpensive transportation logistics, and the average cost of production and purchase. In addition, this system is considered to somehow benefit independent producers too, as typically multinational operations face higher production costs than independent producers. Thus, mixing products could ensure MNCs lower average costs, which would encourage them to continue buying from independent producers. Finally, countries where MNCs have other types of production activities are thought to have a chance to benefit from the impact of lower logistics costs shared by different products. The bargaining power, however, continues to be in the hands of multinational companies, so that in the short or medium term no improvement in banana prices is expected.

Conclusion

Latin America continues to play a key political and economic role in the global banana trade. Although the most recent 'banana wars' have been resolved, the market for Latin American bananas continues to be characterized by a level of uncertainty. Uncertainties in the Latin American world banana market result from a wide range of endogenous and exogenous political and economic factors. Some of them are common to many agricultural products, including changes in the world supply of bananas as a result of production conditions. Other, less obvious, factors include competition between countries with very different production structures resulting from differences in labour and environmental policies.

Latin American banana trade continues to be influenced strongly by external policies and prices. Multinational corporations remain a factor in trade in Latin American bananas through their indirect influence on international trade policy. Changes in EU trade policies and artificial price increases in the European market create inefficiencies, negatively impact developing economies in Latin America and lead to further distortions in the international market.

As the evolution of the banana dispute illustrated, even within the Latin American banana industry there are significant differences that affect the desirability of various trade policies. This is especially critical, since it can be argued that much of the profit in banana trade is associated with rents accruing to EU policies. While many participants have called for free or perhaps *fair* trade, it is not clear that this is really the case. Perhaps the Ecuadorian industry is most interested in truly free trade. Because of the limited presence of US multinationals, low wage rates, thus low costs, and acumen with spot markets, Ecuadorian producers would be formidable competitors in international markets. However, as their presence in international markets expanded, so too would the desire of US multinationals to acquire an expanded presence in Ecuador.

The US multinationals and, by corollary, industries in countries such as Costa Rica and Honduras, are less interested in free trade than fair trade. Of course, fair trade in this context is implicitly defined as some form of managed trade that favours the strategic position of the multinationals. Even in this case, as was seen in the banana dispute, the trade policies can favour the strategic position of one multinational over another. The incentives to pursue managed trade are strengthened by the competitive disadvantages (*vis-à-vis* Ecuador) the US multinationals face because of investments in environmentally friendly production technologies and high wages, as well as socioeconomic infrastructure.

The future of Latin American bananas in the global market is also dependent on the ability of Latin American countries to develop policies with appropriate mechanisms to deal with market uncertainties and external vulnerability. Exporting countries in Latin America will have to carry out at least two tasks in order to increase their bargaining power once the US–EU Agreement expires in 2006. First, they must achieve 'country of origin' recognition. This differentiation can be achieved through consistent high-quality standards and through emphasizing quality attributes such as labour and environment to final consumers. Second, Latin American countries must develop policies that will reduce their external vulnerability. This includes reducing their dependence on multinational companies so that independent producers can sell directly to European importers. These two strategies are not mutually exclusive and, implemented in conjunction, they provide a vital cornerstone of Latin American repositioning in a freer banana market.

References

AUGURA (2001) Asociación de Bananeros de Colombia, Urabá, Colombia.
CAA (2000) The economy: banana exports. *Colombian Newsletter* No. 5, May. Colombian American Association, Inc.
CORBANA (2000) Corporación Bananera Nacional, San José, Costa Rica.
FAO (1986) *The World Banana Economy 1970–1984: Structure, Performance and Prospects*. FAO Economic and Social Development Paper No. 57. Food and Agriculture Organization of the United Nations – FAO Commodities Division.
FAO (1999) *Banana: Informative Note*. Food and Agriculture Organization of the United Nations, Rome, December.
FAO Intergovernmental Group (1999) *Review of Policy Developments Affecting Banana Trade*. Intergovernmental Group on Bananas and on Tropical

Fruits: Committee on Commodity Fruits, First Session, Gold Coast, Australia. CCP: BA/TF 99/8. May.

Inside US Trade (2001) Commission approves banana regs after settling with Ecuador. *Inside US Trade* 4 May. Inside Washington Publishers, Washington, DC.

SICA/MAG (2000) *Balance of the Banana Sector in Ecuador.* SICA/BIRF/MAG Project, Ecuador.

Stanley, D.K. (1994) *For the Record: the United Fruit Company's Sixty-Six Years in Guatemala.* Centro Impresor Piedra Santa, Guatemala.

UPEB (1992) *Annual Statistics of Bananas.* Panama, 1991–1992, 1980–1990.

The Caribbean and the Banana Trade

7

Rachel Anderson, Tim Taylor and Tim Josling

Introduction

Bananas have played a significant role, second only to sugar among the export crops, in the economic history of the Caribbean. Indeed, the growth of exports of bananas is in many ways tied to the demise of the sugar sector. First in Jamaica and then in the Windward Islands, bananas were introduced as a replacement crop when profits from sugar exports decreased. Jamaica was among the first of the islands of the West Indies to establish a banana export industry, using sailing craft to supply the eastern seaboard of the US with fresh fruit. It is likely that the traditional banana of the 19th-century trade, the Gros Michel, was itself developed on the island. For many decades, Jamaica was the primary supplier of Caribbean bananas to the UK market, in competition with fruit from the Canary Islands.

The Windward Islands emerged in the post-war period as an alternative source of bananas to those from Jamaica, spurred on by the desire of the British authorities to counter the dominance of American multinationals in the marketing of Jamaican bananas. The recent story of the Caribbean banana trade, as impacted by the WTO conflict and the issue of preferential access for the region to the EU market, has been of particular importance to the Windward Islands, though Jamaica is also affected by the changes in market regulations.[1]

---

[1] Belize and Suriname are also significant suppliers of bananas to the EU. Belize, though having access to the EU market as a former British colony, (*continued*)

©CAB *International* 2003. *Banana Wars: the Anatomy of a Trade Dispute* (eds T.E. Josling and T.G. Taylor)

The focus of this chapter is on the economic and social impacts of bananas on the economies of the Windward Islands. The four countries that have been associated historically with the export of bananas to the United Kingdom are St Lucia, St Vincent and the Grenadines, Dominica and Grenada.[2] These countries share a strong concern for the future of the banana trade, based on a high level of economic dependence on exports of the fruit coupled with the deep social and political significance of the sector.

This chapter first overviews the history of the banana trade in the Windward Islands and the place of those exports in the economy of the islands. The structure of the banana sector is then described in order to highlight the range of issues that have been brought to a head by the banana dispute. The main implications of the WTO banana dispute for the Windward Islands are discussed in so far as they pinpoint the causes of current concerns. Some indication as to the possible future of the sector is attempted in a concluding section.

Evolution of the Windward Islands Banana Industry

The evolution of the banana industry in the Windward Islands stands in sharp contrast to that of Jamaica and Latin America. The American banana multinationals played a minor part in the development of the Windward Islands' export trade in bananas. While the dollar-zone banana industry evolved largely according to the dictates of market forces and the competitive dynamics of two dominant multinational companies, the banana industry in the Windward Islands developed with the help of considerable government intervention and under a variety of protective regimes. Despite these differences, marketing problems in both the Caribbean and Latin America have been similar, with the relationships between the growers and the shippers being a

---

[1] (*continued*) has a plantation and marketing system more like those of its neighbours in Central America. Suriname, until recently a Dutch colony, also has a more extensive banana system, but at a less advanced level of development. Bananas from Suriname have access to the EU market as members of the ACP.

[2] These countries comprise the southern end of the chain of small islands known as the Lesser Antilles (in contrast to the Greater Antilles, which comprise Cuba, Jamaica, Puerto Rico and the island which is shared by Haiti and the Dominican Republic). The more northerly part of the Lesser Antilles chain includes Anguilla, Antigua and Barbuda, Montserrat, St Kitts and Nevis, as well as the French Overseas Department (DOM) of Guadeloupe. In addition to the four independent countries discussed here, the French DOM of Martinique is also geographically in the Windward Islands group, though it has a different political and commercial status that will not be discussed here.

source of tension, and the tendency of the crop to be destroyed by disease or hurricane.

The origins of the banana industry in the Windward Islands date to the mid-1800s. Sugar production, which had been a staple agricultural activity in the Windward Islands for almost a century, was in serious decline. With the abolition of the slave trade and the rescinding of the preferences by the Sugar Equalization Act of 1845, sugar production became unprofitable.[3] By the end of the 19th century, sugar production in Grenada, Dominica and St Vincent was virtually non-existent, and in St Lucia was in serious decline (Nurse and Sandiford, 1995). As sugar exports declined in importance, the search for alternative crops began. This was perhaps the first attempt at agricultural diversification in the Windward Islands. Among the crops considered were bananas. Bananas had been grown in the islands for domestic consumption for some time.[4] However, bananas were considered to have ideal prospects as an export crop, as the climatic conditions were well-suited for production on a year-round basis. Transportation of tropical fruit by sea was becoming cheaper and quicker, opening up possibilities that had been impracticable before (Davies, 1990).

The first attempt at banana export production in the Windward Islands occurred in 1923, when the Swift Banana Company, a subsidiary of the United Fruit Company (UFCO), established production operations in St Lucia and began exporting bananas in 1925. An outbreak of Panama disease resulted in the effort failing 2 years later. In response to damage to its lime crops during the late 1920s (Wiley, 1998), banana production was also encouraged in Dominica.[5] In 1931, the Leyland Line began exporting Dominican bananas to the UK, and in 1933 the Canada Banana Company (also a UFCO subsidiary) began exporting bananas to North America under an agreement between Canada and the West Indies.

The move into banana production in the Windward Islands was encouraged by British policy, though the motives were a mixture of foreign and domestic concerns. The *Report on Marketing and Preparing for the Market of Foodstuffs Produced in the Overseas Territory*, issued by the Imperial Economic Committee in 1925, encouraged banana production in the Windward Islands as a means of breaking the UFCO monopoly in the UK banana market. The 1938/39 Moyne Commission

---

[3] A new source of sugar, the sugar beet, was being developed in Europe at this time and later became a heavily subsidized competitor for tropical sugar exports.

[4] As early as 1890, suggestions were made that bananas could be cultivated in Dominica (Clegg, 2000).

[5] During the 1930s, Dominica became the world's leading exporter of limes (Wiley, 1998).

encouraged banana production as a means of addressing socioeconomic concerns, the most important of which was employment (West
India Royal Commission, 1945). But the Canada Banana Company that
signed a 5-year contract to export bananas to Montreal was owned by
UFCO, raising issues about both dominance in trade and the activities
of this company in the Jamaican trade since the turn of the century
(Clegg, 2000). One significant development by the Canadian Banana
Company was the establishment of the banana-grower associations,
which acted as intermediaries in dealings with the marketing
companies (Davies, 1990).

Banana exports from the Windward Islands ended in 1942, due to
the loss of the use of shipping vessels during the second world war.
Banana exports did not resume until the late 1940s. In 1948, Paddy
Foley and Geoffrey Bland acquired land in Dominica to produce
bananas for export and established a British-registered firm, Antilles
Products Limited (APL), to market both their own and other farmers'
bananas. They signed a 15-year exclusive marketing contract with the
Banana Grower Associations (BGA) of all four Windward Islands to buy
and ship all export-quality bananas. They also hastened the introduction of the Lacatan (Puerto Rique) variety, to replace the traditional
but disease-prone Gros Michel. The Lacatan (a Cavendish banana) was,
however, more delicate and required careful handling.

Exports to the UK were not possible immediately, and the first
bananas were sold in Dublin and Antwerp. APL had no contract with
the Ministry of Food, which controlled both marketing and consumer
purchases. APL also lacked shipping facilities, and failed to get
adequate support either from the Crown Agents Shipping Department
in London (a British parastatal that favoured citrus production over
banana cultivation) or the (rival) producer groups in Jamaica (Clegg,
2000). By 1952, the company experienced severe financial difficulties
and was acquired by Geest Limited, a company that had been started by
John and Leonard Geest when they arrived in England in 1930 from
Holland to promote the family market-garden exports (Davies, 1990).[6]

As Geest controlled a large network for the distribution of fresh
fruit, the addition of banana imports fitted the company well.[7] In
addition, Geest represented a viable and credible competitor to UFCO
in the marketing of bananas from the West Indies. With its acquisition

---

[6] Apparently, the Foley family approached Elders & Fyffes (part of UFCO) to ask
whether they would be interested in the company. Fyffes reportedly declined on
the grounds that there was no long-term future in banana production in the
Windward Islands (Clegg, 2000).

[7] Geest acquired Dan Wuille and Company, Limited, of Covent Garden in 1954.
This company had considerable experience as banana ripeners and salesmen
(Davies, 1990).

of Antilles Products, Geest became the sole marketer of Windward Island bananas and made use of its monopsony status. The size of the Windward Islands industry in relation to Geest's shipping assets gave the company almost complete control over Windward Island banana exports. This enabled Geest considerable clout in negotiations over risk sharing and in determining its pricing arrangements with the BGAs (Grossman, 1998). It signed 10-year contracts with the BGAs, agreeing to purchase all export-quality bananas. From 1952 until the mid-1960s, banana exports from the Windward Islands increased their share in the UK market and successfully broke UFCO's (Elders & Fyffes) monopoly. The Windward Islands possessed some competitive advantages over their main competing region, Jamaica, in that the shipping time to the UK was shorter than from Jamaica and Geest enforced strict quality standards. However, the industry was also the beneficiary of Jamaica's inability to supply the UK due to the slow pace of its industry's post-war recovery.

When supplies from Jamaica eventually rebounded, a period of excess supply and falling prices created intense competition and tension between both the companies (Geest and Elders & Fyffes), and the governments of Jamaica and the Windward Islands.[8] The 'conflict' was eventually resolved with the 'WINBAN Agreement' in 1966. This agreement in effect guaranteed a protected market for bananas produced in Jamaica. Fyffes was allotted 52% of the UK market for Jamaican fruit exports, and the Windward Islands received the remaining 48% of the market. The agreement prohibited both companies from obtaining bananas from other sources except in times of supply shortfall. This market share agreement effectively removed the competitive element in the UK market for a generation.

During the 1970s, banana exports to the UK from the Caribbean declined due to the impact of a succession of droughts and hurricanes. The switch to field boxing of bananas, made necessary by the adoption of the Cavendish varieties, also forced the industry to make costly adjustments. The supply shortfalls from the Caribbean resulted in the introduction of dollar-zone bananas (dollar bananas) to the UK market. Dollar bananas were subject to a 20% tariff and were limited to the difference between domestic demand and total supply from all preferential suppliers.[9] A Banana Trade Advisory Committee (BTAC) was created in 1973 to monitor dollar banana imports. The BTAC was composed of representatives of the Ministry of Agriculture, Fisheries and Food, trade organizations from Jamaica (JAMCO) and the Windward Islands (WINBAN), and representatives from Geest and Fyffes. Import

---

[8] This period is known as the 'banana war'.

[9] Other suppliers to the UK market in the post-war period included the Canary Islands and other ACP countries such as Cameroon, Belize and Suriname.

restrictions on dollar bananas were controlled through licences administered by the BTAC.

   In 1973, the UK entered into the European Community and its preferential duty was replaced by the Common External Tariff.[10] A point of
contention at the time of entry was the status of trade from the Commonwealth countries. The incorporation of historical trade arrangements within those that the EC had set up for the former colonies of
France and other members was achieved in the Lomé Convention in
1975. The agreement guaranteed free access for most products from the
former colonies, though sensitive agricultural products were subject to
quota limits. Sugar from the Caribbean and beef from southern Africa
competed with domestic production of these products. Bananas did not
pose a direct threat to domestic producers, at least not in the UK, but
quantities were controlled as a way of keeping up the profitability of
the UK market for the marketing firms and their suppliers.

   As seen in Fig. 7.1, during the 1980s banana exports from the
Windward Islands increased significantly and the industry enjoyed
relatively good economic health. However, the monopsony power of
Geest in its dealings with WINBAN continued to place Windward
Island producers at a disadvantage, especially in terms of the sharing of
market risk. In the early 1990s, Geest began encountering financial
difficulties (Roche, 1998) and in 1996 was acquired by a joint venture
by Fyffes and the Windward Islands Banana Development and

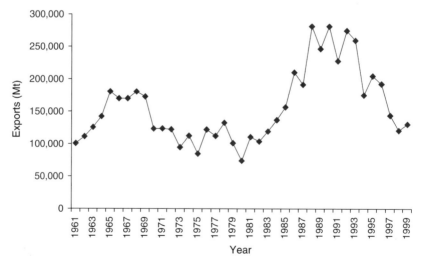

Fig. 7.1.   Windward Island banana exports, 1961–1999 (Mt). Source: FAOSTAT
(2000).

---

[10] A complete discussion of the evolution of EU policy towards bananas may be
found in Chapters 3 and 4 by Tangermann in this volume.

Exporting Company (WIBDECO).[11] Each partner acquired a 50% stake in the joint venture. The joint venture was organized into two companies: Windward Isles Banana Co. (UK) and Windward Isles Banana Co. (Jersey). Assets acquired included: all of Geest's UK green and yellow banana business, which ripens and distributes 8 million cartons of ACP fruit; nine ripening centres; a European dollar banana business of 11 million cartons sourced from Costa Rica, Colombia and Ecuador; 3500 ha of land in Costa Rica, with a production capacity of 6.6 million cartons; two island-class ships; and the Geest backhaul business, which transport 85% of non-banana cargo from the UK.

The past few years have been rife with uncertainty for the Windward Islands banana industry. In 1996, a rebel farmers' union in St Lucia went on strike over its desire to sell bananas to Chiquita Brands International.[12]

The strike was eventually settled; however, concerns remain. WIBDECO's contract with the St Lucia Banana Corporation (SLBC)[13] expired in the first quarter of 2000. It has been reported that the SBLC will begin shipping with the Maersk Lines of Denmark (EIU, 1998). Such a move would have severe impacts on WIBDECO.

The Place of Bananas in the Windward Islands Economies

The impact of changes in market access and the degree of competition on the Windward Islands depends on the role that bananas play in the economies of those countries. This section gives an overview of the economic structure of the Windward Islands banana industry.

Share in exports and GDP

As evidenced in Fig. 7.1, the level of exports has been decreasing steadily over the last decade. Overall, the four Windward Island exporters experienced a 57% reduction in the value of bananas exported between 1990 and 1999, from a total of US$153 million to only US$65 million (see Fig. 7.2). The largest Windward banana exporter, St Lucia, has seen a 56% reduction in the value of banana exports since 1990 from US$73.9 million to US$32.2 million in 1999. The two

[11] WIBDECO is itself a joint venture between the BGAs and Governments of the Windward Islands (see below).

[12] Banana producers in the Windward Islands are currently contractually bound to sell their bananas to WIBDECO (see below).

[13] Formerly St Lucia Banana Growers Association (SLBGA) until October 1998.

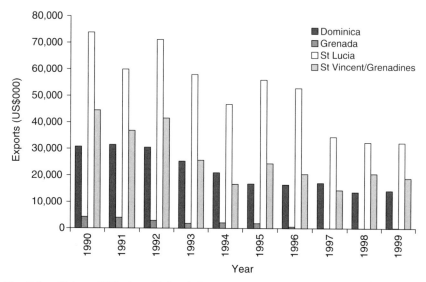

Fig. 7.2.   Value of Windward Islands banana exports, 1990–1999 (US$'000).

mid-sized banana exporters, St Vincent/Grenadines and Dominica have experienced reductions of 42 and 46%, respectively. The most extreme (97%) decrease in value of banana exports can be found in Grenada, which experienced a drastic drop from US$4.3 million to US$123,000 between 1990 and 1999.

Small economies are open economies and often have a relatively narrow commodity base, and export relatively few crops (Josling, 1998). This commodity concentration shows up dramatically in Fig. 7.3. The viability of St Lucia's banana industry has been undermined by the decline of production and exports.

Figure 7.4 illustrates the share of banana exports in both total exports and agricultural export earnings. The export dependency is greatest for St Lucia, where banana exports in 1999 accounted for about 55% of total export earnings and over 80% of agricultural export sales. In Dominica, export bananas accounted for almost 70% of agricultural exports in 1999, but accounted for only 26% of total exports. At the other end of the spectrum, banana exports account for only 0.6% of agricultural exports in Grenada.

The production and export of bananas also represent a significant share of Gross Domestic Product in the Windward Islands. This share, for the four islands, rose from around 10% in 1980 to almost 15% by 1987, falling steadily to less than 8% by 1998 (Sandiford, 2000). St Lucia is the major banana exporter in the Windward Islands, but the crop is also important in St Vincent and in Dominica. Grenada, by contrast, earns relatively little from banana exports at present. The role of bananas in GDP is the lowest in Grenada, where the value of banana

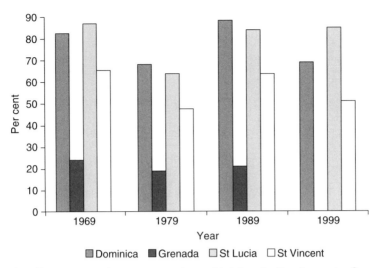

Fig. 7.3. Banana exports as a percentage of total agricultural exports. Source: FAOSTAT (2000).

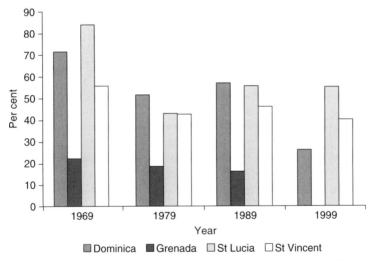

Fig. 7.4. Banana exports as a percentage of total exports. Source: FAOSTAT (2000).

exports has become insignificant in recent years, though there have been attempts to revive the industry.

Agriculture is one of the main economic sectors in St Lucia. Bananas comprise the largest part of agricultural exports, with a share of consistently over 80% in the 1990s. The contribution of bananas to GDP peaked in the mid-1980s at 34%, but has declined steadily since (FAO Intergovernmental Group, 1999). Banana exports as a percentage of GDP were at 10% in 1993 and reached a low of 5% in 1998. St Lucia has a major banana sector that represents about 5% of GDP although it is down from 10% in 1993. However, banana production contracted by one-third between 1993 and 1997, to less than 60% of the 1992 historical peak (IMF, 1999).

The viability of St Lucia's banana industry has been undermined by the decline of production and exports. The decrease in export levels results in a widening marketing margin between growers and importers to cover transportation and handling costs, which are inversely related to the shipment size. The decrease in export volumes from 1995 to 1997 caused a decrease in the prices paid to growers[14] from EC$ (East Caribbean dollars) 0.16 to EC$0.10. In a continuing spiral, the decrease in grower prices causes export levels to decline even further. The addition of higher quality requirements to declining prices and export levels has led to a drastic fall in the number of active growers from 7049 to 5698 to 5270 in 1933, 1996 and 1997, respectively (FAO Intergovernmental Group, 1999).

Banana exports are still important for the economies of St Vincent and Dominica, though this importance has been declining over time. The share of bananas in GDP in Dominica fell from 30% in 1980 to just below 5% in 1998. St Vincent has seen the importance of the banana sector decline from 11% of GDP in 1990 to slightly less than 3% in 1998 (Sandiford, 2000).

The steady decline in the share of the banana sector in GDP is not only due to stagnation in the banana market. Each of the four islands has been steadily diversifying its economy, based on a continual influx of foreign investment and increased exports of both tourism services and other export items. FDI in Grenada and Dominica has remained between 5 and 10% of GDP (except for a brief spurt in Grenada in 1995), but tourist spending has risen from 6% to nearly 20% of GDP in Dominica and has consistently been above 20% in Grenada since the late 1980s (Sandiford, 2000).

Figure 7.5 clearly indicates an inverse relationship between the banana industry and the tourist industry in terms of shares of GDP. The left side of the graph shows the steady decline of per cent of GDP contributed by bananas as opposed to the steadily increasing share of tourism. The graph on the right highlights the complementarity between the two sectors in recent years. From 1993 to 1994, while the banana shares of GDP dropped by 2.4%, the tourism shares of GDP rose by 3.9%. The change from 1994 to 1995 revealed the opposite effect: as banana shares of GDP increased by 0.4%, shares of tourism GDP decreased by 0.9%.

---

[14] Grower prices are based on the value of the bananas in the import market. In the case of Windward bananas, this is mainly the UK.

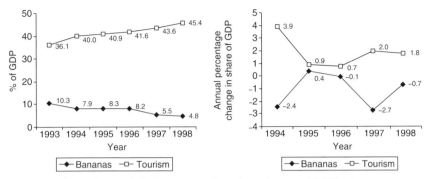

Fig. 7.5.   St Lucia trends in banana and tourism shares of GDP.

Tourist spending makes up over 40% of GDP in St Lucia,[15] and has risen to over 70% of GDP in St Vincent. The number of active banana farmers has fallen in St Lucia by more than 50% from 1993 to 1997, while employment in the tourist industry increased by 27% (IMF, 1999).

The largest increases in tourism expenditure occurred in St Lucia, where it rose 36% from 1993 to 1998. In St Vincent, tourism expenditure rose by 26% between 1996 and 2000. Increases in expenditure were more modest in Dominica and Grenada at 6.5% (1996–2000) and 13.5% (1995–1999), respectively (Fig. 7.6). In Dominica, however, the tourist industry has shown low growth in the past few years.[16] This has helped to spur efforts to achieve improvements in the banana industry, such as the Banana Recovery Plan.

The BRP is representative of more recent efforts to secure niche markets, such as those for organic[17] and 'fair trade' bananas (see below).

Employment in banana production and marketing

Bananas remain a major source of income and employment in the Windward Islands. The banana sector is by far the largest agricultural activity in three of the Windward Islands. Employment in the Grenada banana industry is now small relative to nutmeg and other more recent farm-based exports. Direct employment in the sector, however,

---

[15] Annual tourism earnings rose by 9.5% from 1993 to 1997. Tourism is the most important sector in St Lucia in terms of contribution to the economy (FAO Intergovernmental Group, 1999).

[16] The contribution of tourism to GDP has remained virtually the same over this period.

[17] Currently, the main suppliers for the organic market are the Dominican Republic, Mexico, Colombia, Honduras, Costa Rica and the Philippines.

underplays the impact that a drastic reduction in the banana sector would have on jobs. However, exact estimations of employment and wages are complicated by the use of family labour by some farmers.[18] For example, in Dominica unpaid household members are estimated to make up over 40% of the agricultural work force (FAO, 1995).

Table 7.1 provides estimates of the number of people employed in the banana industry in St Lucia, St Vincent, Dominica and Grenada.

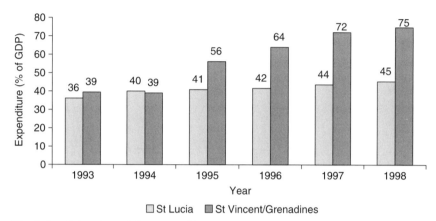

Fig. 7.6. St Lucia and St Vincent/Grenadines: tourism expenditure in per cent of GDP, 1993–1998. Source: IMF (1999b).

Table 7.1. Windward Islands population, labour force and banana industry employment. Source: Sandiford (2000).

	St Lucia	St Vincent	Dominica	Grenada	Total
Labour force	73,660	43,000	34,000	42,250	192,910
No. employed	57,307	34,400	26,112	35,076	152,895
No. unemployed	16,353	8,600	7,888	7,174	40,015
Unemployment rate (%)	22.2	20	23.2	16.98	20.74
Dependent population	92,314	76,824	49,415	64,424	282,977
Rural labour force	46,406	22,360	10,540	27,040	106,346
Urban labour force	27,254	20,640	23,460	15,210	86,564
Rural unemployment	10,302	4,472	2,445	4,591	21,811
Urban unemployment	6,050	4,128	5,443	2,583	18,204
Banana employment	13,836	12,704	9,040	216	35,796
Banana employment as % of population	9.25	11.42	12	0.22	8.21
Banana employment as % of labour force	18.78	29.54	26.59	0.51	18.56
Rural banana employment as % of rural labour force	23.85	45.45	68.15	0.64	20.2

---

[18] Most family labour is without wage.

Twenty-three per cent of all workers are involved in the banana industry. Banana employment as a percentage of the population is highest in Dominica, at 12%. It is also high in St Vincent (11.4%) and St Lucia (9.3%). Employment in the banana industry is particularly important in rural areas, where it comprises 23.9, 45.5 and 68.2% in St Lucia, St Vincent and Dominica, respectively. The provision of employment is one of the major impacts of the banana industry in St Lucia.

The importance of employment in the banana industry and ancillary activities has been emphasized by an International Labour Office (ILO, 1999) report on *Restructuring and the Loss of Preference*, which points out that many other people are temporarily involved in the transportation, harvesting and packing of fruit for export. An Oxfam report estimates that the 'livelihoods of over 60,000 people (one third of the population) depend on the banana industry in St Lucia. In St Vincent, the proportion is almost 70 percent' (Godfrey, 1998). Traditional agriculture is the main sector for employment and export earnings in Grenada. It employs almost one-third of the working population and ensures 60% of export earnings (CBEA, 1997). During 1988–1992, the banana industry in Dominica employed 60% of agricultural workers (CBEA, 1997).

The daily agricultural wage in St Lucia is between EC$25 and EC$40. Aggregate annual agricultural wages amount to approximately EC$53 million (US$19.63 million).[19] In St Vincent and the Grenadines, the wage rate for agriculture is about EC$20 per day (10% higher than the minimum[20] wage). However, the minimum wage paid to banana workers is approximately three times higher than the wage paid to banana workers in Latin America (IMF, 2000).

The reduction of the number of farms growing bananas has been noticeable in recent years (see Table 7.2). Between 1992 and 1998, the number of active growers drastically decreased (32%) in the Windward Islands. The largest drop of 80% was in Grenada, with the number of active growers falling from 600 to 118 in only 6 years. Although less dramatic, the reductions in the numbers of growers in Dominica and

---

[19] Using a daily wage of EC$35, a 4-day working week, 5300 full-time banana workers and 50 working weeks annually plus 3975 harvest workers (part-time) earning EC$40 per day (FAO Intergovernmental Group, 1999). This figure assumes that own and family labour are paid the same as hired labour and does not include the wages paid by the BGAs or other associations to their employees.

[20] The Wages Regulation Orders set the minimum wage for agricultural workers in St Vincent and the Grenadines in 1989. The minimum wage has not been changed since 1989. The number of workers receiving the minimum wage (10–13% of workers in agriculture, industry and shops) is gradually decreasing (IMF, 2000).

St Lucia are very substantial, 46 and 36%, respectively, and indicate a crisis in the Windward banana industry. The least affected by this trend was St Vincent, which none the less saw a reduction of 12% in the number of active growers (Liddell, 2000).

The Structure of the Banana Sector

As shown in Table 7.3, the banana industry in the Windward Islands is based firmly on smallholder operations. St Lucia's banana farms tend to be small and thus prevent the attainment of economies of scale. The industry is characterized by a large number of small producers with smallholdings in hilly areas. As a result, the average yield is less than half of that in Latin America and production costs are almost twice as high (IMF, 1999). In both Dominica and Grenada, most holdings with land are held by individuals or households, with 99 and 97%, respectively. Fewer than 1% of holdings are held by corporations in either country. Cooperatives, governments and others also have a negligible

Table 7.2. Reduction of the number of active growers. Source: Liddell (2000).

	Year	Dominica	St Lucia	St Vincent	Grenada	Total
Number	1992	6,555	9,500	8,000	600	24,555
of active	1998	3,533	6,061	7,048	118	16,760
growers	% change	−46%	−36%	−12%	−80%	−32%

Table 7.3. Holdings by size, number and area in St Lucia, Dominica and Grenada. Source: FAO (1995).

	St Lucia		Dominica		Grenada	
Holding size classes	Number of holdings	Area (ha)	Number of holdings	Area (ha)	Number of holdings	Area (ha)
Total	13,368	20,772	9,026	21,146	18,277	14,164
Holdings without land	1,628	–	592	–	5,829	–
Under 0.4 ha	–	–	1,635	263	6,828	971
0.4 and under 2.0 ha	9,172	5,476	4,495	4,716	4,249	3,562
2.0 and under 4.0 ha	1,711	4,409	1,412	3,679	849	2,266
4.0 and under 10.1 ha	700	3,794	689	3,923	374	2,145
10.1 and under 20.2 ha	92	1,243	86	1,156	73	971
20.2 and under 40.5 ha	27	658	54	1,486	43	1,133
40.5 ha and over	15	840	36	1,888	32	3,116
80.9 and under 202.3 ha	16	2,125	22	2,764	–	–
202.3 and over	7	2,227	5	1,271	–	–

number of holdings. In Grenada, St Lucia and Dominica, the majority of holdings are owned or are in owner-like possession, with 87, 82 and 76%, respectively. In St Vincent and the Grenadines, farms are generally small (< 2 ha) (FAO Intergovernmental Group, 1999).

Contractual relationships

The export of Windward bananas is regulated by contractual relationships. The Canadian Banana Company established the tradition of contractual relationships between the shippers and the banana growers' associations rather than between shippers and individual growers in the 1930s. The basis for the contemporary structure of the Windward banana industry has its roots in the signing of 10-year contracts[21] between the banana growers association on each of the Windward Islands and Geest in 1954. These contracts guaranteed both prices and a market for Windward bananas and are the basis for the UK as the historical destination of Windward bananas[22] (Grossman, 1998).

A banana growers association (BGA) that has exclusive export rights regulates the banana industry on each island. In 1958, the BGAs were unified under a regional alliance called Windward Islands Banana Growers' Association (WINBAN). WINBAN functioned as the intermediary between the growers and the shippers.[23] This structure has been taken over by the WIBDECO[24] (WINBAN's successor), which has contracts with the BGAs that entitle it to exclusive export rights.

The BGAs own 50% (5 million) of the capital shares of WIBDECO, the national exporting company for the Windward Islands. The BGA's individual shares of the capital stock was the ratio of their respective export volumes over the 3 years preceding the agreement. The resulting allocation of shares[25] was as follows: St Lucia Banana Corporation (SLBC), 24%; St Vincent Banana Growers' Association (SVBGA), 13.5%; Dominica Banana Marketing Corporation (DBMC), 11.5%; and Grenada Banana Cooperative Society (GBCS), 1%.

---

[21] 'Contracts were changed to fixed-price agreements in 1966–67 and in 1972–73 at the request of WINBAN, but they subsequently reverted back to their original formats' (Grossman, 1998).

[22] These guarantees stimulated rapid growth over the following 5 years and formed the basis for the term 'green gold' (Grossman, 1998).

[23] The existence of an intermediary resulted in fewer adversarial relationships between the Windward growers and Geest than were common among growers and shippers in other regions.

[24] WIBDECO has been the owner of the Geest banana business since 1995.

[25] The governments have waived their right to profit to optimize returns to growers.

Before the establishment of WIBDECO, production, packaging, assembly, transport and distribution were carried out by WINBAN in cooperation with Geest. The pricing schemes for farmers were regulated in the contracts between WINBAN and Geest. Until 1983, prices were set according to the 'Green Market Price' (GMP).[26] After 1983, the pricing system was reformed and a new pricing scheme was established based on the Green Wholesale Price (GWP).[27] Theoretically, the price scheme based on the GMP was supposed to offer lucrative benefits for both Geest and the Windward growers.[28] In practice, the GMP favoured Geest and, according to WINBAN, allowed Geest to consistently recover all costs, regardless of market trends or prices. The changes implemented in the price scheme and following contractual revisions based on the Green Wholesale Price (GWP) shifted a portion of the risks to Geest and helped to increase growers' profits. However, the disparity between the distribution of risks and profits remained and was not changed fundamentally until the 1994 agreement.

The 1994 agreement, and the resulting contractual changes, were achieved on the basis of the increased bargaining power of the Windward Islands as a result of the EU Single Market licensing schemes.[29] The new agreement transferred the responsibility for loading bananas in the Caribbean and unloading in the UK to WIBDECO. It also made provisions for WIBDECO to gain access to dollar licences in 1997, which provided substantial financial benefits. As a result, Geest's role became more like that of a link in the chain rather than the main actor and beneficiary. This transformation in the role and influence of WIBDECO, both political and financial, has fundamentally changed the position of the Windward Islands in the banana wars.

Place of the banana associations

The BGAs function as intermediaries between the growers and the shippers, in this case Geest. A unique characteristic of this arrangement

---

[26] The Green Market Price was the price at which Geest sold green Windward bananas to importers and ripeners (also known as 'green' handlers). Geest's costs were deducted from this price before the growers were paid.

[27] The Green Wholesale Price was a weighted average based on the sale price of ripe fruit by Geest in addition to the Green Market Price.

[28] Windward growers were supposed to receive a share of profits from Geest's UK ripening operations. According to Geest, the level of profits remained below that at which the Windward producers received a share (Grossman, 1998).

[29] The new banana regime under the EU Single Market resulted in the dependency of Geest on the importation of Windward bananas to gain access to dollar banana licences.

is that there is no formal written contract between the growers and the purchaser. The BGAs have been plagued by enormous debts, unfocused management, lack of direction, excessive costs, inefficient and expensive boxing depots, and high-cost overhead structures. Each of the four Windward Island countries has its own banana growers' association.

The St Lucia Banana Growers' Association was privatized in 1998 and renamed the St Lucia Banana Corporation. The privatization included the transfer of full management and ownership of the company from the government to the growers. Geest Bananas Limited also provided financial backing and technical assistance for the privatization of St Lucia's BGA.

The St Vincent Banana Growers' Association was founded in 1953 as a public company.[30] Unlike the structures common in most contract farming systems, there are no formal, written contracts with each farmer. Instead this is regulated by the SVBGA charter that requires it to purchase all bananas of exportable quality. It also provides a wide variety of other services as a buyer/coordinator.

In Dominica, the Dominica Banana Marketing Corporation (DBMC) is the government-owned banana export company (IMF). The Dominica Banana Association was established in 1934 to market, regulate and control banana exports, and it promptly signed a contract with the Canadian Banana Company. In 1959, the name was changed to the Dominica Banana Growers' Association. The DBMC is the sole purchaser of bananas produced in Dominica for export outside of the Caribbean.

The role of BGAs in marketing is quite limited, if not non-existent, as this task falls under the responsibilities of WIBDECO (see below). The BGAs also monitor and coordinate the production of the numerous individual holders on the islands. Services provided by the BGAs include the import and sale of agrochemicals, transportation for shipping of harvested, boxed bananas from rural areas to inspection stations. In addition, the BGAs also have an influential role in the determination of fruit quality and the setting of corresponding pricing schemes. Although independent in a day-to-day context, the BGAs remain subject to government influence.

The BGAs in Jamaica and the Windward Islands, the traditional suppliers to the UK market, were united through the formation of the Commonwealth Banana Exporters' Association in 1972. The name was changed to the Caribbean Banana Exporters' Association (CBEA) in 1975 after the Lomé Convention Agreement. Belize and Suriname also later became members. In 1988, the CBEA set up a London lobby office

---

[30] The Banana Growers' Association Ordinance transformed it into a statutory corporation in 1954.

that is financed 'by means of a levy paid equally by growers and by companies on the volume of bananas imported from each CBEA origin' (CBEA, 1997). Lobbying is carried out in cooperation with Fyffes, Geest and Jamaica Producers, and CBEA's marketing companies (CBEA, 1997). This coalition of governments, companies and growers may be unique in the history of lobbying in the EU. The cooperation between the governments and private bodies in lobbying the EU has blurred the lines between insiders and outsiders in the policy-making process.

The Windward Islands' Farmers Association (WINFA) is a sub-regional umbrella organization grouping of national small farmers' organizations in the Eastern Caribbean that was formalized in 1987.[31] Its members include: the National Farmers' Union (NFU) in St Vincent; the National Farmers' Association (NFA) in St Lucia; the Grenada Cane Farmers' Association (GCFA); the Dominica Farmers' Union (DFU); and the Patriotic Organization of Martiniquan Farmers (OPAM) in Martinique. WINFA has begun to take a more active role in advocacy with the establishment of the Banana Desk in 1997 and the Fair Trade Desk in 1999. WINFA works in cooperation with other organizations such as the German BanaFair.[32] This cooperation targets marketing in the German market in particular. WINFA is coordinating the Fair Trade initiative in the Windward Islands, together with WIBDECO and local associations.[33]

The Role of Trade Preferences

Preference into the UK market

Under successive Lomé Agreements and the successor Cotonou Agreement, the ACP countries have been granted duty-free access into the EU market. Of special significance to the Windward Islands industry is Protocol 5, which guarantees free access for bananas. In addition, the Treaty states that 'all advantages of preferential access and of price which ACP bananas enjoyed prior to the Lomé arrangements would be maintained over time' (Nurse and Sandiford, 1995).

---

[31] Loose grouping in 1982; founded in 1984.

[32] They have been working together since 1998.

[33] The EU 'newcomer' licensing practices under the banana import regime require the importers of 'fair trade' bananas to compete for the 8% of licences available for all newcomers. This fierce competition is an acute barrier to 'fair trade' bananas. This competition also forces 'fair trade' importers to purchase licences from other licence holders, pushing the prices down further to a level comparable to those in Switzerland, which does not require licences to import bananas (FAO Intergovernmental Group, 1999).

Until the introduction of the Single Market,[34] the Windward Islands were the main suppliers of bananas to the UK. As a result of the contractual relationship with Geest (and between the UK and Geest), the UK market was a guaranteed outlet for Windward bananas. The Single Market called these guarantees into question and caused changes in supply patterns. UK imports of Windward bananas dropped approximately 30% from 1992 to 1998. At the same time, UK imports of dollar bananas from Latin America increased.[35] Suppliers of bananas from other countries now claim to supply over 70% of the UK market: Fyffes, 33%; Chiquita, 13%; Del Monte, 12%; Dole, 16% (Liddell, 2000). While competing suppliers are entering into the UK market, which was traditionally supplied by the Windward Islands, the same cannot be said for the entrance of Windward bananas into other markets. Table 7.4 gives an estimate of the impact of an immediate and total liberalization of the European market for bananas.

Table 7.4. Impact of loss of preferences on the Windward Islands banana industry. Adapted from Sandiford (2000).

	St Lucia	St Vincent	Dominica	Grenada	Total
Banana employment before full liberalization	13,836	12,704	9,040	216	35,796
Banana employment after full liberalization	3,459	3,176	2,260	54	8,949
Banana unemployment after full liberalization	10,377	9,528	6,780	162	26,847
Unemployment before full liberalization	16,353	8,600	7,888	7,174	40,015
Unemployment after full liberalization	26,737	18,985	14,671	7,333	67,726
Dependent population before full liberalization	92,314	76,824	49,415	64,424	282,977
Dependent population after full liberalization	102,691	86,352	56,195	64,586	309,824
Rural banana employment before full liberalization	11,069	10,163	7,232	173	28,637
Rural banana employment after full liberalization	2,767	2,541	1,808	43	7,159
Loss of rural banana employment after full liberalization	8,302	7,622	5,424	130	21,478

[34] See Chapter 4 for details on the licensing scheme.
[35] This applies to both direct imports and imports that enter the UK by way of other EU member states.

The other large import markets, the US and the rest of the EU, are almost completely under the control of the big three multinationals, Chiquita, Dole and Del Monte, and the Ecuadorian Noboa. Thus, ensuring continued access to the key UK market is a policy central to the survival of the Windward banana industry.

Plans for restructuring

There have been several serious attempts to restructure the banana industry of the Windward Islands. Of these, the Kairi/Agrocon Action Programme[36] (1992/93) and the Cargill Technical Services Plan[37] (1994/95) are of particular importance in the context of the new EU banana regime. The underlying goal of both of these plans is the commercialization of the Windward banana industry.

The 1993 Kairi/Agrocon Action Programme focused on two key aspects: quality improvement and institutional strengthening. These measures targeted the economic viability and the international competitiveness of the Windward banana industry to ensure its survival in the face of the new banana regime in the EU. Quality improvement was to be achieved by a programme to establish targets, standards and incentives to be coordinated by WIBDECO. A Productivity Improvement Programme was suggested to increase yields (approx. $1.2–2$ t ha^{-1}) and reduce the unit cost of production through the use of technology to reduce the cost of labour (estimated to constitute 50–60% of production costs). In addition, the programme called for improved infrastructure (better roads) and marketing as well as the addressing of environmental issues (soil erosion and irrigation). Support was also given for increased R&D to improve quality and increase productivity.[38]

The most significant suggestions came in the area of institutional strengthening. This was to be achieved by: (i) the formation of WIBDECO as the regional mechanism for the development and management of the production and export of bananas; (ii) the establishment of an interim planning committee and a Restructuring Support Unit (RSU) to

---

[36] The full title is 'A Time-phased Action Programme to Improve the International Competitiveness of the Banana Industry of the Windward Isles'. The Kairi/Agrocon Action Programme was commissioned by the Caribbean Development Bank (CDB). The report was submitted 3 months before the implementation of the new European banana regime (Sandiford, 2000)

[37] The full title is 'Action Plan for the Restructuring of the Windward Islands Banana Industry'.

[38] The contribution of tertiary level research towards improving the Windward banana industry has been minimal. Stronger links could be forged between research and production and distribution in the context of trade liberalization. The Asian Tigers could serve as a model in this respect (Sandiford, 2000).

implement the Action Plan; (iii) the transformation of the BGAs into equity-based entities with farmers as the major shareholders in the long-term; and (iv) the improvement of marketing arrangements through negotiations with Geest, the implementation of tender procedures, joint ventures and the establishment of WIBDECO in Europe.[39]

The creation of WIBDECO was perhaps the highlight of the Kairi/Agrocon Action Programme's otherwise limited success. The large expenditures required by the programme proved to be an insurmountable hindrance.[40] In the hopes of obtaining sufficient funding, an appeal was made to the EU. However, EU assistance was contingent on a review of the industry. The Cargill Technical Services Plan[41] is the result of this review. The Cargill report focused on similar issues to the Kairi/Agrocon Action Programme, but placed a greater emphasis on addressing financial issues resulting from policies on price subsidies to farmers, as well as bad management of inputs. This included eliminating financial deficiencies and debt; eliminating the BGAs' working capital deficit to allow them to function with adequate liquidity; and ensuring that WIBDECO and BGAs function as cost rather than profit or investment centres. In addition, the report suggested the establishment of a new pricing structure of bonuses and penalties, the adoption of a debt reduction programme to solve the cash flow problem, and the retention of strong budgeting and cost controls while developing the financial database of the industry (Cargill Technical Services, 1998).

The emergence of WIBDECO

The Banana Growers and the Governments of Dominica, Grenada, St Lucia and St Vincent and the Grenadines jointly own the Windward Islands Banana Development and Exporting Company (WIBDECO). WIBDECO was registered in the four Windward Islands in 1994 and is a two-tier service company: the Windward Islands Banana Development and Exporting Company Limited in the Windward Islands (WIBDECO WI) and the wholly owned subsidiary, the Windward Islands Banana Development and Exporting Company (UK) Limited (WIBDECO UK). Box 7.1 gives an overview of WIBDECO's businesses.

---

[39] This proposal resulted in the establishment of WIBDECO UK.

[40] 'Neither the farmers, BGAs, WINBAN, nor the Governments of the Windward Islands were in a position, individually or collectively, to finance the Programme' (Sandiford, 2000).

[41] Contracted by the Overseas Development Administration (ODA), the plan was published just over 1 year after the new EU banana regime was implemented (Sandiford, 2000).

Box 7.1.   WIBDECO's businesses. Source: Sandiford (2000).

WIBDECO's businesses include:[a]

- The UK green and yellow banana business, which ripens and distributes eight million cartons of ACP fruit annually and includes the nine ripening centres in the UK along with the associated equipment.
- The European dollar banana business, which markets 11 million cartons of bananas sourced from Costa Rica for Colombia and Ecuador.
- The Costa Rican farm (3500 ha) producing 6.6 million cartons annually and employing 2200 people.
- Two island-class ships, the Geest St Lucia and the Geest Dominica representing 640,000 ft^3.
- The Geest backhaul shipping business, which in 1996 transported 85% of non-banana cargo from the UK and utilized four chartered ships making weekly stops in the Windward Islands.
- Geest Industries Limited, a private company limited by shares incorporated in England in 1932.
- Geest Industries (WI) Limited, a private company limited by shares incorporated in Dominica and St Lucia in 1949 and 1963, respectively.
- Geest de Costa Rica SA, a company incorporated in Costa Rica in 1991.
- Geest Limited, an international business company incorporated in Jersey in 1993.
- Geest Europe NV, a limited corporation incorporated in Belgium in 1992.
- IJ Co SRL, a company incorporated in Italy in 1991.

---

[a] Acquired during the purchase of Geest in December 1995.

The company's EC$10 million share capital, consisting of 1000 shares of EC$10,000 each, was allocated as follows: EC$5 million in equal amounts to the four WI Governments (12.5%) and EC$5 million to the BGAs as a ratio of their respective export volumes over the previous 3 years. The allocation of the shares to the BGAs is: SLBC, 24%; SVBGA, 13.5%; DBMC, 11.5%; and GBCS, 1%.

WIBDECO's main services are to (1) negotiate marketing and freight arrangements for Windward Islands fruit, (2) manage the industry's joint venture investments in WIBUK and WIBHJ, and (3) reinforce the Windward Islands' and Caribbean banana lobby in Europe. WIBDECO's secondary responsibilities are to (1) arrange payments from export sales and other trading activities to the BGAs, (2) manage receiving and loading operations in the four Windward Islands, (3) coordinate the Geest shipping agency and branch operations in these islands, and (4) provide technical services to the industry to enhance productivity and fruit quality.[42]

WIBDECO sells and markets Windward Island bananas in the UK. Geest Bananas (a joint-venture company equally owned by Fyffes and WIBDECO) is responsible for shipping and ripening of Windward bananas. WIBDECO also sells green bananas to Continental Europe under the 'Windward Islands' and 'Tropical Eden' brand names.

WIBDECO has taken steps to improve prospects for the sale of organic bananas in the UK through cooperation with the Sainsbury's[43] supermarket chain. Sainsbury's has offered WIBDECO a guaranteed market for organic fruit. It was expected that Windward organic bananas would begin to appear on Sainsbury's shelves from the middle of 2001. Geest estimates expect an initial volume of around 2500–3000 boxes per week in the short term and 30,000 in the long term.

The success of WIBDECO from 1994 to 2000 in fostering a more 'commercial' basis for banana operations and improved terms of market exchange appears limited. In June 2001, WIBDECO announced a new plan to restructure the banana industry.[44] The plan focuses on three key areas.

- A streamlined management and operational structure to reduce cost and improve efficiency, and respond in a timely manner to market demands.
- A streamlined, restructured and targeted grower base capable of producing to volume and quality specifications on the basis of commercial contracts.
- Significant investment in farm inputs, rehabilitation and replanting, and in off-farm and on-farm infrastructure.

The plan, which in essence calls for the elimination of the BGAs, will be funded by the EU (US$55.5 million). WIBDECO intends to purchase control of the reception, product management and certification currently in the hands of the BGAs and become the sole operator between the grower and the supermarket (RJR News, 2001). On 1 August 2001, WIBDECO announced that Geest Bananas, under the name Windward Islands, would, under a new arrangement, become a service provider rather than a marketer of Windward Islands bananas in the UK and Europe. WIBDECO UK will now be known as Windward Bananas (Seon, 2001).

---

[42] ILO (1999).

[43] Sainsbury's is the largest buyer of Windward Island bananas in the UK. It is also a leading player in the UK organic market.

[44] 'Wibdeco Unveils Strategy for Industry' in RJR News (www.radiojamaica.com/rjrnews/_rjrnews/000000c6.htm).

The Windward Islands and the WTO

Lomé and the WTO

The non-discrimination rule of the GATT, subsumed in the WTO, is somewhat of a paradox. Countries collectively agree that it is better to have a rule restricting discrimination for fear that the trade system would collapse in a series of favourable deals negotiated by powerful countries. But most countries in the world do have discriminatory policies, favouring some at the expense of others. The GATT had little success in defining the dividing line between the desirable rule and the almost universal practice. Two exceptions have emerged over the years: the formation of customs unions and free trade areas, and the help for developing countries through non-discriminatory preferences. Unfortunately, for the EC and the Caribbean, the Lomé Convention meets neither of these two accepted criteria. When the GATT was the arbiter of trade conduct, this discrepancy could be overlooked: the EC could have blocked acceptance of any panel report that threatened to undermine the trade arrangements with the ACP. The Uruguay Round changed the situation drastically. Panel reports could no longer be ignored. In its place, the EU had to apply for a waiver from the obligation under Article I to avoid discrimination.[45]

Windward Islands participation in panel hearings

Initially, the Caribbean countries were excluded from the panel hearings. It was deemed that these countries were not 'substantial suppliers' in the EU market. Eventually the importance of the case for the region was recognized, and representatives from the Windward Islands were allowed to take part.[46]

The reaction of the politicians in the Windward Islands to the threat to banana exports was unequivocal. Richard Bernal, at that time the Jamaican Ambassador in Washington, made the case on trade policy grounds. The issue

> has seriously strained U.S.–Caribbean relations . . . In every free market, governments make allowances for vulnerable producers such as small farmers and small businesses without violating the operation of free

---

[45] See Chapter 9 in this volume for a discussion of the WTO ruling on preferences, and Tangermann and Josling (2002) for a review of the place of preferences in the WTO system.

[46] This did not end the contention: the panel argued against the presence of hired lawyers from outside the region to attend the hearings, rather than the more usual representation by government employees.

markets. Given that the Caribbean accounts for 2 percent of the world market and about 8 percent of the European market it is possible to accommodate Caribbean exports without disrupting the free market in bananas.

(Bohning, 1999)

Dame Eugenia Charles, until 1995 Prime Minister of Dominica, raised the stakes well beyond the issue of trade rules. 'The Europeans face a choice. They either continue to buy our bananas or their children may well buy cocaine that comes through these islands' (Hansard – House of Commons Daily Debates, 27 February 1992). Her successor as Prime Minister of Dominica, Edison James, appealed to the world to recognize the banana issue as a matter of security.

> The Commonwealth of Dominica, my country, and other countries of the CARICOM (Caribbean Community and Common Market) group are threatened by the WTO's decision. Our main means of livelihood, bananas, has been placed on the shakiest of grounds by this decision. Such uncertainty brings about instability and can threaten peace.
> Clichés like 'desperate times call for desperate measures' and 'a hungry man is an angry man' may sound banal, but they cannot be ignored. Peace in our region and peace in the world depend much on the humanitarian dispensation of justice, and the action which has been taken against us in the WTO is not justice.

Other leaders tried a more direct approach, casting doubt on the commitment of the WTO to assist small countries. The Prime Minister of St Lucia suggested that:

> The WTO ruling is a capitulation to the machinations of those who are blinkered by free trade and sheer greed. We had looked to the WTO to respect the special social and economic circumstances of small, vulnerable economies and have been cruelly disappointed.

(CBEA, 1997)

The Foreign Minister of St Vincent stressed the same point.

> The recent WTO ruling has left us dazed and helpless. . . . Money and greed have been elevated to the status of a religion and care and concern are now regarded a vice. Our future is now on a life support system. However, I am confident that our resourcefulness and faith will see us through.

(CBEA, 1997)

In December 1999, the Caribbean and the US reached a framework proposal for resolving the dispute. The key features were:

- a two-tier tariff quota system;
- the first tier to be at a uniform tariff for imports from all sources;
- the second tier with duty-free entry for ACP bananas and a tariff of US$115 t^{-1} for Latin American bananas;

- the quotas would be allocated on the basis of historic reference periods; and
- eventual movement to a tariff-only regime with the Caribbean, suggesting a 10-year transition period.

The EU Commission has also made a number of proposals, the most recent on 5 July 2000. The most significant differences between these proposals and the Caribbean/US proposals are as follows.

- Licences should be allocated on a first-come, first-served, rather than a historic basis.
- Failure to reach agreement on such a tariff quota system would lead to the immediate movement to a flat-tariff system with no quotas.

Future Prospects for the Windward Islands Banana Trade

In the light of the WTO ruling and the US–EU agreement to settle the dispute, the Windward Islands banana industry finds itself in an all too familiar position. The industry evolved under preferential trade regimes and its survival appears to depend on their continued existence. Despite much of the rhetoric in the banana dispute, the debate is not so much about the legality of preferences as it is about the form of preferences. Though the future of trade preferences in general remains uncertain, there is little doubt that the Windward Islands banana industry will continue to receive some type of preferential access to EU markets for the next decade. The negotiations to determine the degree of preference and the nature of the competition for those preferred markets are in their early stages.

The longer-term outlook for the banana sector is clearly for more competition in the market for bananas. Thus the changes that can be made in the production and marketing of the crop from the Windward Islands are likely to be crucial. There continues to be talk of increasing the productivity of banana production in the Windward Islands through technological innovation and programmes to rationalize or privatize the sector, thereby improving competitiveness (Williams and Darius, 1999). While such initiatives may improve productivity and thus competitiveness, it is unlikely that the Windward Islands will ever be competitive with the dollar producers. The fact that the multinationals are developing production in ACP countries in Africa, as well as the competitive potential of banana production in Belize and Suriname, further complicate matters. ACP-wide policies may not provide adequate protection for the Windward Islands against other ACP producers.

References

Bohning, D. (1999) Caribbean nations accuse U.S. of breaking vow on banana sales. *Miami Herald*, 1 April.

Cargill Technical Services (1998) *Socio-Economic Impact of Banana Restructuring in St. Lucia.* Draft Report commissioned by the Government of St Lucia and the European Union, September.

CBEA (1997) *Windward Islands Prime Ministers Call for Continued EU Support.* CBEA Press Release, 24 October.

Clegg, P. (2000) The development of the Windward Islands banana export trade: commercial opportunity and colonial necessity. *The Society for Caribbean Studies Annual Conference Papers.*

Davies, P.N. (1990) *Fyffes and the Banana* Musa sapientum*: a Centenary History, 1888–1988.* Athlone Press, London.

EIU (1998) *Regional Developments: Disputes Plague the Banana Industry.* The Economist Intelligence Unit Country Report for the Windward and Leeward Islands. EIU, London.

FAO (1995) *Dominica Agricultural Census.* Food and Agriculture Organization of the United Nations, Rome.

FAO Intergovernmental Group on Bananas and on Tropical Fruits (1999) *First Session: the Impact of Banana Supply and Demand Changes on Income, Employment and Food Security.* Committee on Commodity Problems, Rome, May.

FAOSTAT (2000) FAO Agricultural Database. Available at: apps.fao.org/default.htm

Godfrey, C. (1998) *A Future for Caribbean Bananas – the Importance of Europe's Banana Market to the Caribbean.* Oxfam Policy Department, March.

Grossman, L.S. (1998) *The Political Ecology of Bananas: Contract Farming, Peasants, and Agrarian Change in the Eastern Caribbean.* The University of North Carolina Press, Chapel Hill, North Carolina.

ILO (1999) *Restructuring and the Loss of Preference: Labor Challenges for the Caribbean Banana Industry.* International Labour Organization (ILO) Caribbean Office and Multidisciplinary Advisory Team, Geneva.

IMF (1999a) *St. Lucia: Statistical Annex.* IMF Staff Country Report No. 98/33. International Monetary Fund, Washington, DC, May.

IMF (1999b) *St. Vincent and the Grenadines: Statistical Annex.* IMF Country Report 99/148. International Monetary Fund, Washington, DC, December.

IMF (2000) *St. Vincent and the Grenadines: Recent Economic Developments.* IMF Staff Country Report 00/163. International Monetary Fund, Washington, DC, December.

Josling, T.E. (1998) Trade policy in small island economies: agricultural trade dilemmas for the OECS. Paper prepared for the *IICA/NCFAP Workshop on Small Economies in the Global Economy*, Grenada, August.

Liddell, I. (2000) *Unpeeling the Banana Trade.* Fairtrade Foundation, UK, August.

Nurse, J. and Sandiford, K. (1995) *Windward Island Bananas: Challenges and Option under the Single European Market.* Friedrich Ebert Stiftung, Kingston, Jamaica.

RJR News (2001) *Wibdeco Unveils Strategy for Industry.* Radio Jamaica. Available at: www.radiojamaica.com

Roche, J. (1998) *The International Banana Trade.* Woodhead, Cambridge.

Sandiford, W. (2000) *On the Brink of Decline: Bananas in the Windward Islands.* Fedon Books, Grenada.

Seon, E. (2001) *WIBDECO to Take Over the Marketing of Bananas in Europe.* St Lucia One Stop News. Available at: www.sluonestop.com/news/feb02a%2001.html

Tangermann, S. and Josling, T. (2002) Trade preferences for developing countries: their nature and status in the WTO. *World Trade Review* (forthcoming).

West India Royal Commission (1945) *Report of West India Royal Commission.* Appointed 1938, HMSO, CMD 6607, 6608 (usually referred to as the Moyne Commission Report).

Wiley, J. (1998) Dominica's economic diversification: microstates in a neoliberal era? In: Klak, T. (ed.) *Globalization and Neoliberalism: the Caribbean Context.* Rowman & Littlefield, New York.

Williams, O. and Darius, R. (1999) *Bananas, the WTO and Adjustment Initiatives in the Eastern Caribbean Central Bank Area.* Inter-American Development Bank Working Paper, Washington, DC.

US Interests in the Banana Trade Controversy

8

John G. Stovall and Dale E. Hathaway

Introduction

Until 1994, the US government stayed on the sidelines as Europeans worked out trade arrangements and quelled disputes with banana suppliers. The reasoning was straightforward: the US is not a commercial banana producer or exporter, nor was it involved in any of the regional or international banana trade arrangements. As a major consumer of bananas and with no import restrictions, the US government seemed content to let the private sector compete for domestic markets with no government intervention. Quarrels about European banana trading arrangements were seen as someone else's fight – at least until 1994.

What brought about such an abrupt shift in the government's position and how did the US come to play such a central role in the international banana trade dispute? And why was the US willing to risk further souring of relations with a major trading partner and angering friends in the Caribbean (including their US political supporters) when the stakes for the US would seem to be so small? The answer to these questions involves a complex mix of politics, economic interests of US multinationals, frustration with the EU and the promise of the newly formed WTO dispute settlement system. This chapter examines these issues and attempts to explain why the US took the action it did and what some of the consequences may be.

In assessing these questions, the authors benefitted from, and were challenged by, the enormous number of written accounts of what transpired, and why. The benefit was that there was a wealth of source material. The challenge was that many of the accounts provided competing perspectives, if not conflicting stories. Our approach was to assess those accounts, supplement them through interviews with several of the key players who participated in the saga and then write our own version.[1]

Background

Historically, the US government has taken a *laissez faire* approach to the market for bananas and the firms that supply them to the US market. In the US, anyone can import bananas; there are no quotas and virtually no tariffs. Market forces operated free of government interventions. One notable exception occurred in the 1950s when anti-trust action was taken against the United Fruit Company, the dominant banana supply firm in the US (see Chapter 5). The main concern appears to have been a desire to maintain competition in the domestic banana market and therefore reasonable prices to consumers. Otherwise there has been no special interest by the US in the source of supply, or the economic performance of banana multinationals.

The US was an interested observer as the EU, when instituting a single market for trade in the early 1990s, was forced to develop a unified banana regime to replace the fragmented set of trade arrangements that existed in member states. The resulting complex regime (Regulation 404, adopted in July 1993) alarmed US-based banana multinationals, who saw their market share in the lucrative EU market threatened. Closely watched by staff at the US Trade Representative (USTR), this development was seen as a flagrant violation of GATT and one more grievance with their trading rival, the EU.

A short time before the EU enacted Regulation 404, five Latin American banana-producing countries filed a challenge against the banana regimes of several individual EU member states under the provisions of GATT. Although urged by US-based banana companies to take an active role, the US was not a party to that challenge, holding to the traditional policy of staying on the sidelines in what had been considered someone else's fight. Nor was the US a party to the second challenge, filed by the same five Latin American countries in

---

[1] Neither of the authors was involved in any of the deliberations or has any personal knowledge about them. We were interested observers, but were not privy to any inside information.

June 1993, before the first panel issued its ruling. In addition, it was said that the Latin American complainants had not wanted direct US involvement, fearing their interests would be lost in a US vs. EU battle.[2]

Meanwhile, US banana interests, led by Chiquita International, which had found the USTR reluctant to take action, opened another front in the war on the EU banana regime, lobbying the US Congress and Administration to take action on their behalf. No strangers to US politics, and with close ties to Democrat and Republican leaders, Chiquita CEO Carl Lindner stepped up political contributions and simultaneous pressure on the USTR to take action against the EU.

According to Common Cause, a Washington-based public interest organization, Lindner and his interests donated almost US$1 million to the two dominant political parties in 1993 and 1994, making him one of the largest contributors of soft money in the US during that election cycle (Larmer and Isikoff, 1997; Rosegrant, 1999). Although historically closer to Republicans, especially Senate Majority Leader and Presidential Candidate Bob Dole, Lindner reportedly was a frequent visitor at the Clinton White House and held meetings with White House officials, including Mickey Kantor, who served as the USTR during the first term of the administration (Council on Hemispheric Affairs, 1998).

In the summer of 1994, USTR Mickey Kantor held three meetings with Lindner, two of them hosted by Senator Bob Dole. An unnamed source in the Harvard Case Study (Rosegrant, 1999) quoted:

> the signals were becoming pretty clear that USTR was not going to pursue this, and I think it was probably about that time when Chiquita realized that raising the interest in this case politically would have an effect on the reaction of USTR as an executive branch agency.

The Republican-controlled Congress also got in to the act. In August 1994, a group of 12 Senators, including Bob Dole, wrote to Kantor urging a formal Section 301 investigation into the harm done to US-based banana companies by the EU banana regime. Fifty Representatives sent a similar letter which said in part:

> The express intent of the new export quota and licensing authority is to inflict additional revenue and market share loss on American companies . . . that have suffered a 50 percent decline in the EU market share . . .

---

[2] A former government official told the authors in an interview that Carla Hills, Mickey Kantor's predecessor at the USTR in the first Bush Administration, refused to get the US involved in the banana dispute despite urging by banana interests.

The Section 301 Case

The same day as the date on the Congressional letter (2 September 1994), Chiquita and the Hawaiian Banana Industry Association petitioned the Clinton administration to file a Section 301 case against the EU. According to sources, the USTR had already informally agreed to take the action, as is customary in Section 301 cases, and had, in fact, helped Chiquita prepare the petition (Rosegrant, 1999). Kantor announced in October 1994 that the US would initiate a Section 301 investigation against the EU that claimed, among other things, that Regulation 404 discriminated against Chiquita's ability to market and distribute Latin American bananas (Rosegrant, 1999).[3]

At first, according to one account, the USTR was not interested in accepting the 301 petition, following the traditional position of staying on the sidelines (Rosegrant, 1999). So acceptance of the complaint by Chiquita and the Hawaiian Banana Industry Association (a minor player in the drama presumably recruited to give the complaint domestic legitimacy) marked a turning point in US trade policy. Critics who attributed the policy change to political contributions pointed out that never before had the USTR taken a 301 action with so few US jobs at stake.

Interestingly Dole Foods,[4] the other major US-based banana company that had opposed Regulation 404 along with Chiquita, chose not to be a part of the 301 petition. Unlike Chiquita, Dole Foods had taken aggressive action to position itself to gain market share in the EU under the restrictive regime even before the new regime was officially unveiled. They invested in banana production in Africa and bought ripeners in Europe in order to qualify for import licences. An unnamed USTR official was quoted to have said, 'although Dole was extremely cooperative whenever USTR requested technical support . . . Dole had practical reasons for not taking part'. Thus, Dole apparently believed it was better to join and make the best of it than to fight and possibly lose even more. That strategy appeared to pay off in terms of market share for Dole in the EU (see Chapter 5 for more on Dole's strategy).

---

[3] Section 301 of the US Trade Act of 1974 provides a mechanism through which companies can ask the USTR to intervene if it can be shown that the company or companies have been harmed by discriminatory trade practices. A Section 301 investigation is triggered to determine if a country has imposed unfair trade measures and, if so, the amount of damage done. If the investigation finds damages from unfair trade practices, the USTR can withdraw trade concessions in an amount equivalent to the estimated damage.

[4] Dole Foods has no relation or connection with Robert Dole, former US Senator from Kansas.

In January 1995, USTR Kantor announced that a preliminary investigation showed that the EU regime was costing US companies 'hundreds of millions of dollars'. He wrote to the EU's Trade Commissioner, Sir Leon Britain, threatening retaliatory measures if the EU and US could not reach a compromise. As part of the 301 process, the US held consultations with the EU, but according to USTR staff who participated, the 'negotiations with the EU officials went nowhere . . . they were not interested in negotiations'. With the 1-year deadline for the Section 301 case coming up in October 1995 and no prospect for a negotiated settlement with the EU, the US would have to retaliate or drop the 301 case. No compromise was reached and no retaliatory action was taken. After nearly a year of fruitless wrangling, the Section 301 investigation lost impetus, having been overtaken by other events, most notably the formation of the WTO.

In January 1995, as the Banana Framework Agreement went into effect, the USTR brought a similar case against Colombia and Costa Rica, two of the countries that were a party to that agreement. (The US did not challenge Nicaragua or Venezuela, whose banana exports were apparently too small to affect Chiquita adversely.) This action alarmed the two countries, which feared that retaliation might jeopardize important preferential trading arrangements with the US. If they did not implement the Framework Agreement, the years of struggle to gain better access to the EU market would be lost. But if they did implement the agreement, the US might retaliate by withdrawing valuable trade concessions.

The WTO Challenge

According to the current and former USTR staff interviewed, the decision to drop the 301 case against the EU was based on their reasoning that the newly formed WTO, with its dispute settlement process, offered a better alternative for pursuing remedial measures. The choice, a WTO challenge, was a fairly easy call, even with pressure from Chiquita and congressional leaders still pushing for a Section 301 retaliation. The USTR believed that a WTO challenge was on strong legal and technical grounds. Two GATT panels had laid the groundwork for a favourable ruling and the new GATS offered another basis for challenge. In addition, to have gone the Section 301 route, the US would be open to criticism of ignoring the new international dispute mechanism that they had helped to create. A USTR official was quoted as saying:

> If we had gone with unilateral sanctions, all we would have done was raise the ire of all the other WTO members, including the member states in the EU who favoured our position. You can't have the Community and

the Commission united by antipathy to the US and their unilateral action. You always need some people on the inside helping bring about change.

If more reasons for going the WTO route were needed, unhappy Latin American countries that had not signed the Framework Agreement offered an opportunity to sign on as co-complainants. If other countries were a part of the complaint, maybe 'the EU would be shamed into complying with its international obligations', according to one USTR official.

Almost a year after beginning the Section 301 investigation, the US, along with Mexico, Honduras and Guatemala, initiated a WTO complaint against the EU banana regime in September 1995 (see Chapter 6). In announcing the action, Kantor said:

> We have repeatedly sought changes in the EU banana regime to address the discrimination against US companies, but unfortunately the EU has been inflexible. We think it is appropriate at this time to resort to WTO dispute settlement procedures and we are pleased that other countries in our region that are also adversely affected by the regime are joining us.
>
> (*Inside US Trade*, 1995)

A few months later, Ecuador, which had just been admitted to the WTO, joined the complaint. This strengthened the case because Ecuador, the world's largest banana exporter with a substantial EU market share, was severely disadvantaged by the Framework Agreement in which it had not participated.

Colombia and Costa Rica, countries that had signed the Banana Framework Agreement and facing US retaliation under the earlier Section 301 complaint, signed a Memorandum of Understanding (MOU) with the US in January 1996 to end the still active Section 301 case. The MOU committed the two countries to support an open EU market for bananas. An official of the Costa Rican Embassy in Washington was reported to say that both Costa Rica and Colombia were caught between the jockeying of the US and the EU with no leverage to influence events. 'The countries that suffered the most in the end were the small countries', the official said.

The briefs laying out the US challenge to the regime related to a number of claims,[5] covering both goods and services. Under goods, the US challenged not only the quotas but also the licensing system. The services claim focused on how the regime's licensing requirements had distorted the Latin American banana service market. There was more reason to feel confident on the goods side, given previous GATT rulings, but the services claim was more uncertain because the new

---

[5] A USTR source from the Harvard Case Study (Rosegrant, 1999) was quoted to say that they filed as many claims as possible in order to get maximum leverage against the EU.

agreement had never been tested. Latin American co-challengers, except for Ecuador, focused their claims on goods.

Why the US Challenge?

To understand why the US government became so involved in this international trade dispute over bananas, a commodity that by any measure was a minor factor in the US economy and even less in international trade, one must look at a number of political, economic and social forces at work and a confluence of events that gave rise to such counterintuitive actions. Our explanation is offered, not as definitive conclusions but as propositions that history may someday rewrite. But on one issue we are certain: no single explanation is sufficient – several factors were at play. Some of the key forces at work are discussed in the following sections.

Frustration with the EU

Trade disputes between the US and the EU go back several years. From the US perspective, the EU has a long history of using a variety of means to erect barriers to US exports. Over time, agricultural interests in the US have developed a deep-seated distrust of the EU based on a number of disputes that have festered for years. Many US trade-policy officials and staff have come to view the EU as their main adversary in the international trading arena. Under this unusual climate of distrust and with the new WTO in place, there was a strong desire among many US commercial interests to get tough with the Europeans. Frustrations with the EU created a favourable climate for the USTR to do battle with the EU over the banana regime, without which the strategy might have been more cautious.

The WTO credibility factor

Supporters had sold the WTO to reluctant congressmen, in part, with the argument that this new body would be able to make the EU and other trading rivals live up to their commitments. This argument resonated well with many in Congress who believed that US trading partners were using unfair measures to keep US products out of their markets. Under the GATT, any member could essentially veto a panel's recommendation, rendering enforcement measures weak at best. The WTO, it was argued, was a new body that would give the dispute settlement process more teeth. Thus, the credibility of the newly formed dispute settlement body was on the line and bananas (along with beef hormones) presented one of the first opportunities to put it to a test. To not challenge the EU banana regime would be seen as a lack of confidence in the mechanism the administration had lobbied hard to sell to the American people and the Congress.

Mixing bananas and beef

The banana issue came along at a convenient time to combine it with a particularly difficult trade dispute with the EU over hormones in beef. This dispute showed no promise of resolution and was a high priority and high profile issue for US farm groups. The reasoning was straight-forward. Wrap bananas and beef in the same package and hit the EU with the bigger more persuasive challenge. Farm interests, led by the Farm Bureau Federation (the largest farmer organization in the US), added to the pressure on the USTR to get tough with the EU on beef and bananas. In a January 1999 press release, Dean Kleckner, President of the Farm Bureau said:

> American farmers need trade disputes resolved in a timely manner. We expect the WTO to bring the banana dispute to an end and insist that the resolution of future disputes, like the EU beef case, not be delayed. This case and the WTO ruling on American beef exports are too important to let slide. The future of the American farm economy depends on the elimination of barriers to free and fair trade.
> (American Farm Bureau Federation, 1999)

It seems clear that Chiquita had found a convenient and powerful partner to help bring pressure on the congress and the USTR to take action against the EU.

Sympathy for Caribbean banana producers

A counter force to the momentum for aggressive action against the EU banana regime was an undercurrent of sympathy for the plight of ACP countries, especially for nearby Caribbean banana producers. Why should the US government undercut neighbouring smallholder produc-ers in Caribbean islands who are struggling to make a living, when no vital national interests were at stake, but rather only the economic interests of a large multinational corporation? This line of reasoning had a strong appeal in several segments of US society and to a number of political leaders.

Sympathy was strongest in Caribbean immigrant communities and among the 'Black Caucus', a politically potent coalition of nearly all the

African-American members of the US House of Representatives. Also sympathetic to this cause were many environmentalists, various groups opposed to multinational corporations and globalization, and those who identify with the plight of poor third-world countries.

A public relations campaign to get this message across to political leaders and their constituents was organized with support from the Caribbean Banana Export Association, the Washington-based Caribbean diplomatic community and other sympathetic groups. The 'Washington Establishment' was targeted for stories about Carl Lindner's large political donations, with the message that he was attempting to make up losses from bad corporate decisions by gaining political influence through political contributions. They also portrayed the poor Caribbean grower as the helpless victim of this transatlantic fight between economic giants.

The threat of increased drug traffic was also raised as a consequence of driving poor Caribbean farmers out of banana production. The small share of world banana production in the Caribbean and the minimal global consequences of the disputed trade preferences were emphasized. 'With the little bit we grow we couldn't put any other country out of jobs but it could make all the difference in the world to the Caribbean,' Dominica's former Prime Minister Eugenia Charles said in making the case for the Caribbean point of view. Other arguments were put forth in terms of equity, such as a statement by Jamaica's Ambassador in Washington: 'Every country, including the US, realizes that in a free market you make allowances for certain vulnerable participants. It doesn't affect the operation of the market if a small percentage of the participants are given some kind of specialized treatment.'

On Capitol Hill, the Black Caucus, mainly composed of democratic congressional members, spoke out against the USTR position and tried unsuccessfully to blunt legislative initiatives aimed at forcing the USTR to take firm action against the EU. But the Black Caucus had little impact on congressional leaders who were members of the opposing party. Neither were they successful in persuading a normally sympathetic administration to change policy direction. A Caribbean diplomat, commenting on the failure of their message to change the US government position, said 'we were never able to convince allies in the Clinton White House'.

The administration countered the Caribbean argument with analysis showing only a fraction of the benefits of the EU banana-trade preference actually going to Caribbean producers. The USTR frequently cited a study that found the EU regime returned only 7.5 cents to the ACP countries out of every dollar the programme cost the EU (Borrell, 1994, 1999). The administration argued that there were other more effective ways of assisting ACP banana producers. The State Department, which one might expect to side with Caribbean neighbours out of fear of the diplomatic consequences of alienating allies, apparently supported the USTR position. A State Department diplomat involved in the banana-trade dispute who discussed this issue with the authors indicated that the EU regime did more harm than good for the Caribbean islands.

Money and politics

Many observers assume that the US government position on the banana regime was a direct result of large political donations made by Carl Lindner and the political influence that those contributions bought. Caribbean participants in the dispute assert this direct connection emphatically. Yet, the case for this direct connection remains circumstantial.

There is little doubt, however, that political influence played a key role in forming the US position. Indeed, hardly anyone would argue that money and politics are not linked in the US system. So in this sense, Chiquita and Mr Lindner's influence on the US position is the 'American way' for participation in government policy. As a former senior USTR official who was directly involved in the banana dispute told the authors, 'Chiquita did what any good lobbyist does in this town to influence government policy. They made a strong technical and legal case for their position, they brought in data and analysis and mobilized congressional support for their position.' What was left unsaid was that political contributions were key in gaining this political support.

What can be concluded from this as to the role of money and politics? The mix of money and politics was probably a necessary, but not a sufficient condition for the favourable policy outcome on the part of Chiquita. There are numerous examples of strong political pressures for trade actions that were unsuccessful because the actions sought were inconsistent with US policy or because the technical and legal case was weak. On the other hand, it seems unlikely that the government would have pursued the EU banana case without high-level political support. Perhaps what was different in the banana case was the amount of political contributions and the unabashed lobbying effort on the part of those representing Chiquita's interests.

Legal and technical merits

Another factor that helps to explain why the US took the complaint to the WTO was that the USTR believed the case was sound and definitely winnable. Based on earlier rulings and the legal merits, USTR staff were confident that they would prevail. They were much more confident about claims filed under 'Trades in Goods' because of earlier GATT rulings. They were optimistic but more cautious about claims under the GATS, since these provisions were untested and had no legal precedents on which to rely. The GATS claims focused on how the regime's licensing requirements had reallocated, reconfigured and restricted the Latin American banana service market. Services traditionally had not been viewed as being involved in the transfer of goods, so it was not known how the WTO panel would interpret this concept. Despite these uncertainties, the USTR staff believed their case was strong and that the case was winnable.

After the WTO ruling

The WTO panel finding in May of 1997 in favour of US and Latin American complaining parties was viewed in Washington as a complete vindication of the hard line taken by the USTR. The dispute apparently had been settled in favour of the complainants; the EU had been unsuccessful in its appeal and an agreement was reached by the EU to honour its WTO obligations in October 1997.

However, when a new regime was unveiled in January 1998, while the Chiquita perspective was rather discriminating, optimism faded. Experienced negotiators and observers saw a long battle with the EU shaping up. The remainder of 1998 witnessed transatlantic protests, threats and counter claims. Before the year's end, the US Congress approved a resolution urging the administration to take strong action and threatened to pass legislation requiring the USTR to take retaliation against the EU if the dispute was not settled.

The administration responded with an ultimatum, promising to take retaliatory action if the EU did not comply by January 1999. Soon after the deadline, the US requested retaliation authority and the proposed amount was taken to arbitration. The arbitrated amount (US$191 million) was imposed on a selected list of imported goods, retroactive to March 1999. Before the year was over, the EU proposed another regime, which some of the complainants immediately called WTO-inconsistent.

The wrangling continued without resolution throughout the year 2000, despite the sanctions imposed on EU imports. It became more obvious that the EU faced an impossible task to come up with a transitional regime that would please all parties, including different interests of countries within the EU. The US continued to insist on outcomes favourable to Chiquita during the last year of the Clinton Administration's 8 years in power. And the US Congress, controlled by the opposition party, also pressured the administration to impose more painful sanctions on the EU.

The Carousel bill

Although the amount of the sanctions (US$194 million in tariffs) could not be increased, law makers reasoned that pressure against EU governments could be increased by rotating the product mix against which they were imposed, thereby increasing the number of important exporters who suffered. The stated intent of the so-called 'Carousel Sanctions' bill, enacted in May 2000, was to 'induce compliance with WTO dispute settlement proceedings' by requiring the administration to periodically rotate retaliatory tariffs among selected European products.[6] This legislation angered European exporters and officials and further escalated the transatlantic trade dispute. Although never implemented, the Carousel Sanctions bill was a constant threat throughout the remaining negotiation process.

The 'first-come, first-served' option

One of the options for distributing banana import licences that had been 'on the table' for some time for the EU was to distribute licences on a 'first-come, first-served' basis during the transition period, rather than on a historical base period. The base period, the previously favoured option, had been a source of considerable squabbling among interested parties as to which years to use for the allocation. In an effort to break the stalemate, the EU adopted the 'first-come, first-served' method in the summer of 2000. There were varying interpretations about just how the scheme would work but, in general, banana exporters would declare their intention to import a specified quantify when the vessel was loaded and on the water.

This scheme proved to be just as controversial as the base period option. Shippers from distant ports claimed that they would be disadvantaged. Those who saw this as an opportunity to gain a larger market share obviously favoured the option. The US was sceptical, Caribbean countries opposed it, fearing that they would lose out in the transatlantic race, while Ecuador viewed the plan favourably.

Chiquita and Dole go 'head to head'

The two big US multinationals were seriously split for the first time in the long running dispute. Until this time, both favoured the same policy position for the US government – vigorous opposition to the

---

[6] The formal name for the bill was the Trade and Development Act of 2000.

'illegal' EU regime, but using different tactics. Chiquita took the political route, while Dole worked behind the scenes to bring about essentially the same policy position. Now they were 'head to head' for the first time. Chiquita strongly opposed the 'first-come, first-served' plan, but Dole, better positioned to take advantage of the scheme, just as strongly favoured it. Financially stressed, Chiquita, facing default on debt payments, favoured a base period that would give the company a guaranteed share of the profitable EU market. Dole called the 'first-come, first-served' proposal a free and fair marketing system and accused Chiquita of favouring managed trade and wanting a 'guaranteed market share that is significantly greater than every other participant, including Dole'.[7]

During the waning months of the Clinton Administration, Chiquita and Dole pleaded their opposing cases with USTR, urging a position favourable to their respective interests. But Dole was no match for the politically savvy Chiquita operatives. The Clinton Administration opposed the 'first-come, first-served' scheme.[8] The USTR's special negotiator for agriculture, responding to the EU's proposed regime, said:

> We are disappointed that once again the EU is announcing that it is unable to comply with its WTO obligations on bananas by announcing yet again plans for more studies and more analysis. The Commission is further delaying any prospect for resolution of this long-standing dispute.

Other USTR spokespersons called the EU plan 'blatantly WTO inconsistent' (Yerkey, 2000). Some Washington observers speculated that the EU initiative was designed to bide time until after the US November elections.

Whether biding time was the driving motive or not, it had exactly that effect. No serious negotiations could take place following the bitterly contested November election until the new Bush Administration took office in January 2001. Washington trade observers anxiously awaited the Bush Administration approach to the long-running banana dispute that many believed needed to be cleared up quickly in order to get on with other trade issues. There was also speculation as to whether the Bush Administration would continue to support Chiquita's position as opposed to the Dole position.

---

[7] Statement by David Murdock, Chairman and CEO of Dole Food Company, Inc., News Release, 9 March 2001.

[8] An unnamed former senior USTR official who at the time was intimately involved in the banana dispute denied any White House or improper political pressure to favour Chiquita. Instead, this former official cited technical problems that USTR saw with respect to WTO compatibility.

Answers to these questions were not long in coming. Soon after his appointment, USTR Robert Zoellick began discussions with EU Trade Commissioner Pascal Lamy on how to resolve the banana conflict. The announcement on 11 April 2001 that an agreement had been worked out in which the EU agreed to drop the 'first-come, first-served' method of allocation caught many by surprise.

According to the *Wall Street Journal* (13 April 2001), Dole officials were among the most surprised – and bitterly disappointed. A Dole spokesman said the company 'got sold up the river'. The spokesman also had bitter words for the USTR, saying that for that office, 'the real issue was simply to get a system that would take care of Chiquita'. A former US trade negotiator in four previous administrations, Christopher Parlin, was quoted as saying: 'This is the classic example of "money talks" in trade and politics'. The *Wall Street Journal* article went on to note that in the last political campaign cycle, Chiquita's top executive, Carl Lindner, and his financial interests had contributed US$1.03 million to Republicans and US$677,000 to Democrats. Dole by contrast gave US$134,000 to Republicans and US$25,000 thousand to Democrats.

Dole Chairman and CEO, David Murdock, accused the USTR of blocking the EU from making real reform in a prepared statement: 'It [the agreement] gives one company, Chiquita Brands International, Inc., a dominant, fixed market share of the EU's closed, quota market and continues to allocate licences to protectionist EU traders'.

Chiquita, clearly the winner in the settlement, said little but reiterated their claim that the EU banana-import policies had cost the company US$1.5 billion since 1993. 'We had the largest market share in Europe and we had the largest expropriation. No matter what, in any legitimate resolution of this fight, we stood to gain the most,' according to Chiquita's president and CEO, Steve Warshaw (Cooper, 2001).

The long banana war was finally over, but the aftermath will continue and there are still scores yet to settle, including Dole's suit filed in the EU court. The extent of gains for the winners and losses to the losers will not be known until the 'tariff only' system is implemented in 2006.

Impact of US Action on World Trade Policy

Virtually every trade dispute filed with the WTO has an impact on the trade policy of the complaining country, the defending country and, in many cases, on the entire trade system because of the precedent established by the panel decision. The banana dispute, however, clearly had a greater impact than most on the concerned parties and on the system.

One impact of the case was on the domestic public, which is important because the entire WTO and the world trading system is under attack by many forces in the US. Unfortunately, the banana dispute has heightened the suspicion of some groups that the WTO is the handmaiden of special corporate interests. Unlike many trade disputes, this one did not involve US jobs or US products, which caused many to question the basic economic interests of the US in pushing the complaint. This impression was heightened by the publicity that pointed out that the losers in the complaint were small farmers in tiny Caribbean islands, who were being hurt to benefit the bottom line of a giant multinational. This led the Congressional Black Caucus to condemn the complaint and the US government persistence in pursuing the case.

Trade policy specialists recognized that the EU banana regime was inconsistent with WTO rules and that, despite losing earlier complaints under GATT, the EU had refused to alter its system and generally agreed that testing the new dispute settlement system was desirable. However, even this group questioned the wisdom of using the banana case because of the overt political influence used to push it into the forefront.

On the other hand, key members of both houses of congress responded strongly to the political influence of the Chiquita corporation. They continued to put pressure on the White House and the USTR to pursue the complaint and refuse the EU proposals for settlement, and to determine how the US retaliates for the damages found to be suffered. The case brought an unprecedented attempt at direct congressional intervention when legislation requiring that the Senate Majority Leader agree to any proposed settlement was attached to a major spending bill.

Trade relations with banana-producing countries

The countries that are the likely beneficiaries of revisions in the EU banana regime are of course pleased with the US intervention in a battle they had waged since the EU system was put into place. On the other hand, the CARICOM countries that are likely to be the major losers under a revised EU banana regime are furious over several aspects of the US action. First, they assert that they were misled by statements from the highest levels of the US government that no action would be taken without consultation and due regard for their interests. That did not occur and it left a long-lasting impression that the US promises on international trade issues cannot be believed.

Second, the ACP producers are convinced that the US action was motivated solely by political contributions from the Chiquita interests and that the claims of establishing WTO principles are a flimsy excuse to cover an overt political pay-off. They argue that the willingness of the US to sacrifice its interests in the political stability and the economic development of the small island banana-producing countries constitutes a serious disregard for international interests.

Finally, the ACP countries were upset greatly when the WTO dispute settlement rules prevented them from participating in the dispute settlement process. They argue that a dispute settlement process that does not allow the parties most affected by the outcome to participate is inherently unfair.

The impact on US–EU relations

From the outset of the US intervention in the banana dispute, the dispute has affected US–EU relations adversely. At the beginning, the EU was incredulous that the US was entering the dispute directly, and they claimed initially that the US had no standing in the dispute because the US does not produce or export bananas. EU displeasure increased when, after winning the dispute in the original panel and the appeal process, the US refused to accept the modest adjustments in the EU banana import regime. The EU proposed and insisted on an adjustment that the WTO panel found consistent, which restored significant market share to the countries that had been in the EU market prior to the establishment of the new regime.

The US insistence on retaliation and the request for substantial compensation further irritated EU officials. The banana dispute coming on top of the beef-hormone case, where the US also asked for and imposed sanctions, was a continuing irritant in US–EU trade relations. It presented the EU officials with two adverse dispute settlements in the new WTO dispute settlement process, and both cases involved almost insurmountable political difficulties within the EU to produce policy changes necessary to comply with the WTO panels and the US concerns.

It is unclear as to the extent that the ongoing disputes over beef and bananas contributed to the inability of the US and the EU to organize a common approach to the WTO ministerial in Seattle in December 1999. There is no doubt that these disputes were part of the reason that the US and the EU failed to agree on the scope of a new round of trade negotiations. There is no doubt that the distrusts among ACP countries over the banana dispute contributed to their unwillingness to agree to key elements of a new round desired by the US.

Informed observers are convinced that frustration with the US over the banana and beef disputes was the prime reason that the EU Commissioner for trade brought a formal WTO complaint against the US Foreign Sales Corporation (FSC), which was founded by a panel to constitute a form of illegal export subsidy. This dispute shocked the

US, which believed that there was an agreement that the FSC system was acceptable and would not be challenged. Now the EU is refusing to accept the proposed US measures to deal with the WTO violation and has threatened to retaliate with what would be the largest retaliation ever imposed in the GATT/WTO system. If that occurs, it is likely to spark a major trade war.

What has been learned?

A major reason given by the USTR staff for entering the banana dispute was to establish that the new WTO dispute settlement worked as a substitute for unilateral action of the type used frequently by the US in the past. The banana case has proven that the WTO system worked, but ironically it has also exposed the fallacy that retaliation or threat of retaliation will force powerful countries to change politically sensitive policies or to offend politically powerful economic interests. While the new WTO dispute settlement system may function much like a court, it lacks a crucial element of an effective court system – the ability to impose sanctions on an offending party sufficient to change behaviour or prevent further violations.

References

American Farm Bureau Federation (1999) Press release, January. Washington, DC.

Borrell, B. (1994) *EU Bananarama III*. Centre for International Economics, Canberra and Sydney.

Borrell, B. (1999) *Beyond EU Bananarama 1993: the Story Gets Worse*. Centre for International Economics, Canberra and Sydney.

Cooper, H. (2001) Dole fails to find much appeal in accord to end banana war. *Wall Street Journal*, 13 April.

Council on Hemispheric Affairs (1998) *The Spotlight Should Also be on Mickey Kantor. The Council of Hemispheric Affairs* [press release online]. Washington, DC. Available at: www.coha.org/Press_Releases/98–04.html

Inside US Trade (1995) US requests WTO consultations on EU banana import restrictions. *Inside US Trade*, 29 September.

Larmer, B. and Isikoff, M. (1997) Brawl over bananas. *Newsweek*, April.

Rosegrant, S. (1999) *Banana Wars: Challenges to the European Union's Banana Regime*. Kennedy School of Government Case Study, Harvard University, pp. 9–11.

Yerkey, G. (2000) U.S. turns down European offer to settle dispute over banana trade. *International Trade Reporter* 17(28), 1068.

Bananas and the WTO: Testing the New Dispute Settlement Process

Tim Josling

9

Introduction

Trade conflicts in bananas are nothing new. The European market for bananas has been a battleground for commercial and diplomatic confrontation for many decades. But the recent trade dispute elevated this conflict to new heights. In doing so, it challenged the structure of the trade system and its ability to solve disputes. How the WTO resolved this problem will have widespread implications for many other issues. Both as an indication of the ability of major countries to use the trade rules constructively and as a precedent in a broad range of practical trade conflicts, the banana case is of great significance.

The banana controversy in the GATT was stimulated initially by the changes in the European import rules implied in the EU's policy of 'Completing the Single Market', which were introduced at the start of 1993 (see Chapter 4). Moving from the varied import systems run by individual countries to an EU-wide policy that could be operated without internal trade barriers proved to be a challenge. 'Dollar' bananas appeared to lose some of their market access to those coming from the former colonies of France and the UK. Some countries in Latin America settled on a market-sharing deal with the EU, but others complained to no avail. The Uruguay Round, with its strengthening of the dispute settlement process, came along at an opportune time for the disaffected group. Two panel reports under the GATT, in 1993 and 1994, had failed to improve the market position for 'dollar' bananas.[1] The third panel, reporting on 22 May 1997, proved more effective. 'Bananas III', as the report became known, found the EU in multiple violation of trade rules. The various steps taken to resolve this conflict continue to this day. This chapter is an attempt to summarize and draw some lessons from this 7-year dispute that has raised fundamental issues regarding the trade system.

The main interest in the banana case stems from its wide-ranging implications for the trade system. There is little doubt that its interpretation of trade rules will be used as a precedent for other cases that go to dispute settlement panels. But, in addition, it addresses some fundamental issues of the type of trade system that has been created in the WTO. Its subject matter, preferential access for an export crop from former colonies, is clearly rooted in the older post-war problem of reconciling modulated decolonization with non-discriminatory multilateralism. But the case is also being interpreted as a test of the ability to manage the impacts of globalism. Are the rules agreed in the WTO to be interpreted as a legal system that has to be enforced, even if it can have unfortunate effects on certain countries or groups? Or are these rules political statements of intention that can be moderated by circumstance and from which the powerless states need occasional relief? And if the rules are treated as a legal obligation, how does this impinge on the ability of national governments to respond to constituency pressures?

There is little doubt that the banana panel elaborated the interpretation of the GATT/WTO in a useful way. Article I: 1, which outlaws discrimination among WTO members, is a fundamental right that countries have agreed to enforce with rigour. The exceptions to this rule, however, need also to be made clear.[2] The EU was granted a waiver from the constraints of Article I in order to continue with the policy of supporting former colonies (the ACP countries) through trade preferences attached to the Lomé Convention.[3] The panel did not call

---

[1] The panel reports had no impact. The EU effectively prevented their adoption by the General Council, following a long GATT tradition of blocking unfavourable reports. The Uruguay Round Dispute Settlement Understanding (DSU) removed the possibility of such blocking tactics. A panel report can be appealed, but the Council can only reject the appeal ruling by consensus.

[2] The other MFN exemption that has caused problems over the years is that for free-trade areas and customs unions, contained in Article XXIV. No panel has yet had the task of exploring the limits of this Article, and there is little of relevance in the banana case to its interpretation. But the two are linked in that the EU sees the long-run solution to the preference issue to be the establishment of Article XXIV free-trade areas.

[3] The Lomé Convention was the centrepiece of the EU's relationships with the 71 developing countries of the ACP (the African, Caribbean and Pacific countries which once had colonial links with Europe). It was premised on a 'preferential partnership', which includes both better access to the (*continued*)

into question the legitimacy of this waiver, but instead grappled with the question of the scope of such an exemption. Did it extend to the question of discrimination in favour of EU firms in the allocation of licences for banana imports? This would imply that the waiver removed the need for the EU to follow Article XIII on the allocation of licences that are needed to administer the quantitative restrictions. Did the waiver apply just to traditional trade flows or include new ACP suppliers who had entered the growing banana trade more recently? More fundamentally, how could one reconcile an agreement to guarantee ACP suppliers access equal to their 'best-ever' export levels and not have the effect of reducing the share for those that previously had been supplying the unrestricted parts of the EU market?

As a 'pure' market access case, the banana issue would have been interesting enough. But the case tackled much more than the conflicts between Articles I and XIII and the Lomé waiver. It was the first panel to consider an argument that a country had contravened the new GATS, the General Agreement on Trade in Services. By allocating import licences to domestic firms based on past shipments, the banana import regime gave valuable trading permits to the competitors of the US-based multinationals. The EU had agreed to end discrimination in 'wholesale trade services' in the Uruguay Round. This aspect of the case increased its importance and provided a potentially useful clarification of the relationship between rules for goods trade and those for trade in services.

Just as the banana report clarified goods and services rules, so the process from panel to appeal and arbitration tested the newly enhanced Dispute Settlement Understanding. The panel had to tackle some crucial questions of interest and representation before hearing the case. But much of the activity took place after the panel had reported. The steps for launching an appeal were straightforward, and the EU modified its policies in the light of the report as modified by the appeal. But the issue of how to tell whether changes introduced subsequently met the conditions laid down by the panel was new ground. And whether one country could go ahead with sanctions before that determination

---

[3] *(continued)* EU markets than other developing countries and special lines of development assistance. The Lomé Convention granted non-reciprocal free access to the EU market for all goods except those that might interfere with domestic policies such as the Common Agricultural Policy (CAP). For these products, access was limited by quantitative restrictions. Separate Protocols to the agreement covered access to the banana, sugar, rice and rum markets in the EU. The Fourth Lomé Convention (Lomé IV) was signed in 1990, reviewed at its midpoint in 1995 and expired at the end of February 2000. Negotiations on a successor Treaty were completed in the year 2000, and the new Treaty (the Cotonou Agreement) was signed in June 2000.

had been reached posed timing issues. In the event, the original panel was pressed back into duty as arbitrators of trade effects, evaluators of the new policy instruments and even proponents of measures that the EU could take to be in compliance. Besides accumulating mileage credits, the three panel members became involved in banana trade policy at a deeper level than perhaps was envisaged originally.

The complexity of the case may have helped to clarify some issues of trade rules. The political sensitivity of the case has ensured that it continued to demand the attention of politicians and diplomats as well as trade lawyers. The fact that the two main adversaries were the US and the EU, and that the conflict was over an agricultural product, guaranteed a level of rhetoric and defensiveness that was unlikely to be easily contained. But the thought of the US as the champion of a small number of multinational banana producers using trade rules to destroy the traditional exports of small island economies in the Caribbean raised the visibility of the case beyond even the normal transatlantic conflict. And the credibility of the WTO was likely to be called into question whatever the outcome. If the DSU did not work in this case, and firms could not rely on their governments pressing such cases to avoid loss of lucrative markets, the Uruguay Round achievements would be diminished. But if the interests of US firms were seen to win at the expense of the small island economies, then to these countries the WTO was indeed just another way of extending the hegemony of such firms over the powerless. Other interests, such as European multinationals, Central American producers and German consumers could watch the drama unfold without themselves being in the spotlight.

Chronology of the Banana Case

The banana case rambled on for 8 years. In addition to the three panel reports, there has been an appeal, three arbitration awards (two for damages suffered and the other for the time needed to bring policies in to conformity) and four recalls of the original panel to examine the EU's response. In the light of these multiple panel reports and the complex judicial procedures, it may be useful to lay out in brief the timeline of the banana case. This is attempted in Table 9.1.

Three different time periods can be distinguished. The first period is that leading up to the request for consultations in September 1995. During this stage, the dispute was essentially one of market access by Central American companies in the EU market as a result of the consolidation of import quotas when the Single Market regime was adopted. The process of accommodation of these bananas was not easy, but the Banana Framework Agreement (BFA) at least in part met these concerns. The second phase began when the impact of the BFA

Table 9.1. Chronology of the banana case.

Date	Report or event	Reference
3 June 1993	First Banana Panel (not adopted)	DS32/R
11 February 1994	Second Banana Panel (not adopted)	DS38/R
28 September 1995	Request for consultation by Guatemala, Honduras, Mexico and the US	WT/DS16
5 February 1996	Request for consultation joined by Ecuador	WT/DS27/1
11 April 1996	Request for panel	WT/DS27/6
8 May 1996	Panel established	WT/DS27/7
22 May 1997	Panel report issued	WT/DS27/R
9 September 1997	Appellate Body report issued	WT/DS27/AB/R
25 September 1997	DSB adopts panel and AB reports	WT/DS27
16 October 1997	EU agrees to conform, requests 'reasonable' time to comply	WT/DSB/M/38
17 November 1997	Request of Arbitration on 'reasonable' time	WT/DSB/13
1 December 1997	Arbitrator appointed	WT/DS27/14
23 December 1997	Arbitrator's Award on time period	WT/DS27/15
18 August 1998	Request for consultation on new EU regime	WT/DS27/18
13 November 1998	Request for further consultation by Ecuador	WT/DS27/30 and Add. 1
14 December 1998	EU requests panel under DSU (Art. 21.5)	WT/DS27/40
18 December 1998	Request for recall of original panel by Ecuador (Art. 21.5)	WT/DS27/41
12 January 1999	Panels established for Ecuador and EU	WT/DS27/45
14 January 1999	Request for retaliation by US	WT/DS27/43
20 January 1999	Complaint about new EU regime	WT/DS158/1
29 January 1999	Arbitration panel appointed to consider new regime	WT/DSB/M/54
9 April 1999	Arbitrator's report	WT/DS27/ARB
12 April 1999	Panel report (Ecuador)	WT/DS27/RW/ECU
12 April 1999	Panel report (EU)	WT/DS27/RW/EEC
8 November 1999	EU status report	WT/DS27/51 Add. 1
9 November 1999	Ecuador requests retaliation	WT/DS27/52
19 November 1999	EU requests arbitration	WT/DS27/53
24 March 2000	Arbitrator's report on Ecuador and EU requests	WT/DS27/ARB/ECU
8 May 2000	Ecuador announces retaliation list	WT/DS27/54
13 October 2000	EU outlines FCFS scheme	WT/DS27/51 Add. 12
11 April 2001	EU and US agree on new EU scheme	
20 April 2001	Ecuador requests consultation	WT/DS27/55
4 May 2001	EU details new banana import regime	WT/DS27/51/Add.18
2 July 2001	US announces suspension of retaliation	WT/DS27/59
14 November 2001	Waiver granted for transitional banana regime	G/C/W/269/Rev.1

became apparent and the firms that felt that they were losing market opportunities began to pressure their governments for action. This phase continued through the adoption of the panel report as amended by the appeal process and the EU's announcement that it would change its policies to comply. The third stage of the process started with the realization by the complaining parties that the change in regulations had not in fact solved the problem and that further action was needed. This stage continued for another year, and could only be resolved by a change in policy that was safe from WTO challenge. Such a change was finally agreed between the EU and the US on 11 April 2001, about 8 years after the deliberations of the first banana panel.

The Panels

Bananas I and II

The various import regulations governing the banana trade in Europe have been the subject of consultations, negotiations and disputes for many years. As late as June 1993, a GATT panel (Bananas I) issued a report on the individual national import regimes and their compatibility with the GATT, though the report was not adopted. The complaint had been brought by Colombia, Costa Rica, Guatemala, Nicaragua and Venezuela. The main complaints were about the regimes that were used to give preference for the former colonies of France and the UK into those markets. In question was the policy of the French government to control access through parastatal companies and the British through the allocation of licences. Moreover, the market for bananas in Spain was essentially closed to imports, and much of the Italian market was reserved for Somalian fruits. The consolation prize was the 'free' markets in Germany and in Belgium, Holland, Denmark and Ireland. A consolidated tariff of 20% *ad valorem*, which had been waived in the case of Germany, allowed these countries to enjoy access to cheaper bananas mainly from Latin America (see Chapter 3).

The introduction of the common market organization for bananas (CMOB) on 1 July 1993 brought the matter to a head. A formal complaint was lodged by Colombia, Costa Rica, Guatemala, Nicaragua and Venezuela in 1993. The panel (Bananas II) reported on 11 February 1994, but this report was not adopted either. But as the first panel to look at the CMOB, its findings and argumentation formed a basis for the later Bananas III panel. With respect to the allocation of quotas, the Bananas II panel found that the specific duties levied by the EU on imports of bananas were inconsistent with Article II (i.e. they were above the bound levels), and that the preferential tariff rates for banana imports from ACP countries were inconsistent with the requirements of Article I (i.e. they were discriminatory). The report of the Bananas II panel also examined in detail the allocation of import licences, which had been set up within the CMOB, and found the system to be inconsistent with Articles I (non-discrimination) and III (national treatment). In particular, the allocation of licences to firms that had purchased ACP bananas in the past was deemed to violate the principle of national treatment (WTO, 1997a).

Meanwhile, the EU negotiated the Banana Framework Agreement (BFA) with Colombia, Costa Rica, Nicaragua and Venezuela, which gave country-specific allocations to these countries in exchange for not pursuing the adoption of the Bananas II report. Guatemala did not sign the BFA, and reserved its rights under the GATT with respect to the EU banana market. It tried unsuccessfully to have the Bananas II report adopted. The BFA was incorporated into the EU's Uruguay Round Schedule in March 1994. It came into force on 1 January 1995, and was applicable until 31 December 2002.[4] The BFA plays a key role in the legal and diplomatic developments in the banana case. By attempting to satisfy some non-ACP suppliers the EU succeeded in alienating others. This division set up conflicts among the Latin American countries and between the firms that were active in the banana trade. On the other hand, by dealing the largest suppliers into the European market, the EU clearly hoped to defuse the issue. In the event, the BFA became the target for much of the complaint by the other Latin American suppliers and made a solution much more complex.

Bananas III

Though GATT and WTO complaints often cite more than one Article that the offending country is supposed to have violated, the banana case is unusual for the lengthy list of purported violations. To illustrate this, the list of legal bases for complaints in the banana case is given in Table 9.2. The essence of the case was the discriminatory allocation of quotas and the licence procedures used to effect the quotas. But non-discrimination as a principle recurs throughout the GATT and the GATS, and thus the same policy measures can be in multiple violation. The practical effect of this, besides making the documents in the case somewhat lengthy, is to make it much more difficult to 'get away with' a discriminatory policy. In this case, it also makes it more difficult to cover all the bases when granting a waiver from the principle of non-discrimination. The EU may have thought that the Lomé waiver was satisfactory cover, but this did not survive the scrutiny of the panel.

The failure of the BFA to satisfy the varied interests of the Latin American producers led directly to the request on 5 February 1996 by Ecuador, Guatemala, Honduras, Mexico and the USA for consultations

---

[4] WTO (1997a: 24).

Table 9.2.   Basis for complaints about the EU banana import regime.

GATT Article I: 1	Non-discrimination
Article II	Schedule of concessions
Article III	National treatment
Article X	Transparency
Article XI	Elimination of quantitative restrictions
Article XIII	Non-discriminatory administration of quantitative restrictions
Import Licensing Agreement Article 1	General provisions
Article 3	Non-automatic licences
Agricultural Agreement Article 4.2	No discretionary import licensing
GATS Article II	Most favoured nation treatment
Article XVI	Market access
Article XVII	National treatment
TRIMS Article 2	National treatment and quantitative restrictions

with the EU.[5] After the necessary consultations had reached no conclusion, the complainants requested the formation of a panel.[6] The panel was established by the Dispute Settlement Body (DSB) on 8 May 1996.

The complainants

The list of complainants is itself of interest. Colombia, Costa Rica, Nicaragua and Venezuela had been the 'beneficiaries' of the BFA, and apparently were not willing to risk the wrath of the EU by trying to better their access. But the EU had not managed to satisfy Guatemala, and that country joined with Honduras in an exactly parallel complaint. Ecuador had joined the WTO only on 26 January 1996, and so was anxious to test its newly acquired rights.[7] The US originally had

[5] Throughout the WTO documentation, the EU is referred to as the European Communities, or the EC. The more common post-Maastricht name of EU is used here, even though the WTO usage is technically correct. The EC still exists as the primary location of responsibility for trade: the EU includes the EC in a somewhat analogous way to the inclusion of the GATT in the WTO.

[6] The EU was to argue before the panel that this period of consultation had been inadequate: given the long gestation period of this conflict it seems unlikely that any further interchange of information or explanations would have improved the situation.

[7] The EU indicated in its submission to the panel that Ecuador had been persuaded with undue haste (only 2 weeks after its membership) to join the others as a co-complainant. But one imagines that the Ecuadorian government had anticipated such action before its membership was approved.

intended to stay on the sidelines: it would not have been consistent with the attempt to build up relations with the Caribbean to be seen to challenge the EU's preferences in that region. But 1996 was an election year. Having sold the WTO to the US Congress partly on the basis of the strengthened DSU, it was vulnerable to the argument that holding the EU to the trade rules was an important aspect of US trade policy. Direct pressure from the US-based multinational corporations, in particular the Chiquita corporation, swung the Clinton administration behind the complaint. At a stroke, this raised the stakes and turned a thorny issue of preference systems into a matter of high principle and policy.[8] Along with the beef-hormone dispute, the banana case focused attention on the willingness of the EU to subjugate its policy preferences to the judgement of a WTO panel. If it proved unwilling, this would not be lost on those whose support for the extension of multilateral trade rules was tenuous at best.

Preliminary issues

All panels grapple with some preliminary procedural issues to convince themselves and the parties to the dispute of the ground rules. In the case of the banana panel these procedural issues took on an even greater significance. The most significant question was that raised by the EU as to why the US had any 'interest' in the banana import regime.[9] It produced few bananas and exported none to the EU. The trading interest of US-based multinationals did not constitute an excuse for the US government to get involved. The GATT and WTO dealt with goods, not companies. The intention of the DSU was not to examine 'abstract legal questions', but to deal with actual trade impediments. The US claimed that if Chiquita and Dole suffered in the EU market, US interests were involved. And, moreover, that its producers in Hawaii and Puerto Rico (within the customs area of the US) were impacted indirectly by the effect on world banana markets. Mexico took an even more direct line: consistency of a provision with the WTO should be examined in legal terms regardless of the extent of the commercial interest involved. In the end, the panel had no difficulty in establishing that the sale of bananas to the EU was not the sole criterion for having an interest in the case. The US

---

[8] Mexico followed the lead of the US in part because of the Mexican ownership at that time of one of the firms (Del Monte) and in part as an expression of North American solidarity on a matter of WTO principle.

[9] Other procedural issues related to the extent of consultations and whether separate reports were needed if there were multiple complainants. Both these issues raised relevant questions for the DSU, but will not be discussed here.

and Mexico both had an interest that gave them status as complainants.[10]

Less easily solved was the question of third-country interests and the presence of lawyers for private firms. Some 20 countries asked for their views to be taken into account. They argued to be included at all stages of the process and to be heard on a range of topics. The panel decided that these countries should be allowed to be present and be heard through the second session of the panel, in the light of the obvious and vital interest that many of these countries had in the case. They would not, however, be asked to comment on the interim report. Private lawyers were, however, banned from the proceedings to preserve the intergovernmental nature of the dispute settlement process.

Substantive issues

The substantive issues covered by the GATT that were considered by the panel were of three types: (i) tariff questions; (ii) quota allocation questions; and (iii) the legality of the import licensing regime. Several of these issues had also to be considered in the light of agreements that came out of the Uruguay Round, including the Licensing Agreement as well as the Agreement on Agriculture and the Trade-related Investment Measures (TRIMS) Agreement. In addition, the panel considered the compatibility of the licensing regime with the EU's obligations under the GATS.

Tariffs

The tariff issue was perhaps the easiest of the three. The complainants charged that the differential tariff rates that applied between third-country bananas and non-traditional ACP imports was a violation of the most favoured nation (MFN) principle.[11] No objection was lodged against the duty-free imports from the ACP where these were necessary to conform to the requirements of the Lomé Convention. The WTO had granted the EU a waiver from its Article I obligations in December 1994 (extended in October 1996): the EU argued that this was adequate to cover the whole import regime, and not just the traditional ACP imports. The only tariff question of particular interest to the panel,

---

[10] The important point of principle established by the panel was that the DSU does not require actual trade interests to be involved before a member can request consultations.

[11] Guatemala and Honduras, in their joint complaint, added a further tariff issue: that the tariff on third-country bananas was above the bound rate of 20%. This was in violation of Article II, which refers to the schedules of bindings.

then, was whether this waiver covered non-traditional imports from ACP countries. They decided that as the waiver was not specifically limited to the traditional trade quantities, it must be assumed that 'the preferential tariff for the non-traditional ACP bananas is clearly a tariff preference of the sort that the Lomé waiver was designed to cover' (WTO, 1997a: 333). As a consequence, the EU 'won' the tariff argument and defined in part the relationship between the Lomé Convention and the WTO.

Quota allocation

The EU was less fortunate in the case of quota allocation. The argument over the allocation of quotas went to the heart of the complaints over the EU banana regime. At its simplest, the argument revolved around whether the quotas under which banana imports are allowed were allocated in a way consistent with Article XIII of the GATT, which stipulates that they should be allocated in a non-discriminatory way and in one that disturbs trade as little as possible. The chapeau of Article XIII: 2 states that:

> In applying import restrictions to any product, Members shall aim at a distribution of trade in such product approaching as closely as possible the shares which the various Members might be expected to obtain in the absence of such restrictions . . .
>
> (WTO, 1995)

The complaining parties charged that the EU had allocated the banana import quotas in a way that was inconsistent with this Article. Some countries (the ACP and those that had signed the BFA) had country-specific quotas, while other countries had no such quotas but had to compete for the 'other' category of imports. Moreover, they argued that the quotas given to those countries were too large and did not reflect market developments. The allocation method also gave the BFA countries exclusive right to fill any shortfall in supplies under the BFA quotas.

The EU argued that the WTO waiver covered any discrimination under Article XIII as well as Article I. It further argued that it was in effect running two import regimes in parallel, and thus any discrimination between countries covered by different quota schemes was not in violation of the GATT. The traditional ACP bananas were given preference, but this was undoubtedly covered by the waiver and thus could be put on one side: the rest of the banana imports were covered by a tariff quota as entered in the EU schedule, even though ACP countries received a (waiver consistent) preference on the tariff to be paid. The panel pointed out that this was the first time a whole quota regime had been called into question, as opposed to the operation of an isolated quota provision. It could also have been said that the spread of tariff quotas that emerged from the Agreement on Agriculture made this issue of much greater significance. The allocation of quotas (as well as the distribution of licences, as discussed below) is of increasing interest in agricultural trade policy.

The panel found that the EU only had one quota regime for the purposes of analysing its compatibility with Article XIII, regardless of how the EU has chosen to administer the different quotas (WTO, 1997a). The EU had reached an agreement with the BFA countries, allocated shares in respect of non-traditional ACP bananas and granted country-specific quotas to ACP countries. This was the regime as laid down in Regulation 404/93. Moreover, it discriminated against the countries outside the BFA and the ACP. Colombia and Costa Rica had a substantial interest in the EU market and thus could reasonably have been included in the BFA: Nicaragua and Venezuela did not have such a substantial interest and had less of a claim than some of the complaining countries (Guatemala, Honduras and Mexico).[12] The EU's quota allocation scheme thus violated Article XIII and would have to be modified. On the other hand, the panel found that the quota allocation for the ACP bananas, even if in violation of Article XIII, was covered by the WTO waiver for the Lomé Convention.[13]

Import licensing system

If the quota allocation system ran afoul of Article XIII, the licensing system that gave expression to the quotas came in for the most severe condemnation by the panel. This system was judged with respect to its transparency and its tendency to discriminate. The system was complex, which in itself made for a lack of transparency. But the complaining parties charged that the intention of the licence system was to favour firms that historically had imported bananas from the Windward Islands and French overseas territories. This discrimination was contrary to Articles I (non-discrimination) and III (national treatment) of the GATT. It was also claimed that the COMB violated Article X of the GATT, which requires that countries administer trade measures, including licences, 'in a uniform, impartial and reasonable manner'. Moreover, it was argued that the EU's licensing system contravened the Agreement on Import Licensing Procedures (Licensing Agreement) that had been incorporated into the basic rules of the WTO

---

[12] Ecuador and Panama were not GATT/WTO members at the time of the BFA. Ecuador was deemed by the panel to have the right to challenge the quota allocation of the BFA upon joining ('all Members have rights') though, as the EU pointed out, it might have been better to have dealt with this issue in the Protocol of Accession.

[13] The Appellate Body later reversed this finding (see below).

at the conclusion of the Uruguay Round.[14] In addition it was charged that the arrangement violated the TRIMS agreement, which contains a list of trade-related investment measures such as purchasing requirements that are deemed to be inconsistent with national treatment in the GATT. The requirement that firms have to purchase bananas from the ACP in order to apply for 'B' licences was therefore a violation of this provision.

Perhaps the most significant challenge to the import licensing regime was the suggestion that it was inconsistent with the General Agreement on Trade in Services (GATS). The GATS was one of the major innovations of the Uruguay Round, putting service trade on a similar footing to that of goods. Non-discrimination and national treatment are fundamental principles of the GATS, as they are in the GATT. But the GATS contains some restrictions on the applicability of these principles. The banana case was the first major test of the scope of these rules and their relation to those in goods trade.

The first task of the panel was to clarify the relationship between the GATT, with its emphasis on the conditions under which goods are traded, with the GATS, which deals with services. Clearly, the trading of goods requires a number of services. If goods markets are distorted by discriminatory trade policies, does it follow that the provision of services that accompany those goods and effectuate the trade is also distorted? Or would that constitute 'double jeopardy' for the country implementing such contested regulations? The EU argued before the panel that it should not be made to justify its policy under both the GATT and the GATS, as it was not imposing any measure that discriminated directly on the provision of services. The fact that the 'necessary' quota system impacted service providers was not enough to establish a violation of the GATS. The US argued that, to the contrary, the way the licence system worked was to make it much more difficult and expensive for the US corporations to compete with those based in Europe.[15] Thus the licensing system was indeed contrary to GATS.

---

[14] The Licensing Agreement provided more detail on the way in which licensing measures were to be administered, and is included as an Annex 1A agreement in the Marrakesh Agreement, which established the WTO.

[15] The US had a particular reason to push the GATS complaint, as it had championed the inclusion of services in the WTO. As with the DSU, the GATS was a major selling point within the US to convince sceptics that the WTO was worthwhile. To have at hand a convenient case to explore the implications of the GATS was fortunate. The EU, in general content to include services in the Uruguay Round, chose to nominate 'wholesale trade services' as one of the sectors in its liberalization offer. This meant that it was subject to the general 'national treatment' provision of the GATS, along with 'non-discrimination'.

The panel had little difficulty in deciding that the same measure can both violate GATT and the GATS. Indeed, the specificity with which the import regime for bananas distributed licences, by operator category and activity, made it difficult to argue that measures had no effect on the competitiveness of particular firms.[16] The panel found that the EU regime did indeed violate the non-discrimination and national treatment provisions of the GATS. The Lomé waiver was of no help here, of course, as it related to the obligations under the GATT, specifically Article I. Once again, though, the issue was not so much the import of traditional ACP bananas but the BFA quotas and the third-country quotas. The panel ruled that the EU be required to change its import regulations to avoid conflict with the GATS. Box 9.1 lists the major findings of the panel with respect to both GATT and GATS challenges.

The Appeals

To no one's surprise, the EU appealed the panel decision, both its findings and legal interpretation. The US and other 'complaining parties' joined the appeal, though they obviously had problems with different aspects of the report. An appeal is only possible on points of law. But the Appellate Body nevertheless found itself considering most of the panel findings in its effort to resolve legal issues. Subsequently, the panel report, as amended by the Appellate Body, was adopted and the EU indicated its intention to modify its import policy to comply. Controversy surrounded the time that was reasonable for the EU to bring its actions into compliance, and that formed the subject of an arbitration hearing. This section discusses these steps in the banana saga.

Appellate Body report

The Appellate Body was asked by the DSB to consider the legal issues raised by the EU and the complainants and issued its report on 9 September 1997.[17] Their report in effect gave the original panel a grade of 'B plus': most of the important points were correct, but a

---

[16] An important aspect of the GATS is that it takes the WTO a significant step towards considerations of the impact of policies on firms as opposed to goods. Thus the arguments that the panel had to consider dealt with the competitive position of companies and involved commercially sensitive information.

[17] WTO (1997e).

number of errors in detail were spotted.[18] Box 9.2 lists the major findings of the Appellate Body.

Arbitrator's award

The EU had little choice but to accept the panel report as modified by the Appellate Body. On 16 October 1997, the EU informed the DSB that

---

Box 9.1. Main findings of WTO banana panel.

- Allocation of national quotas to ACP required by Lomé is not inconsistent if limited to pre-1991 'best ever' import levels.
- Allocation of national quotas to ACP above pre-1991 'best ever' levels is not required by Lomé, and is not protected by Lomé waiver.
- Non-traditional preferences for ACP exports are protected by Lomé waiver.
- Allocation of national quotas under BFA (e.g. to Nicaragua and Venezuela) rather than to others (such as Guatemala) contrary to Article XIII: 1.
- Allocation of 30% of licences to category B operators is inconsistent with Article III: 4.
- Application of operator category rules for non-traditional ACP and third-country quotas but not for ACP inconsistent with Article I: 1, as well as Article X: 3(a).
- Application of activity function rules for non-traditional ACP and third-country quotas but not for ACP inconsistent with Article I: 1.
- Matching of import licences with export certificates inconsistent with Article I: 1.
- Limiting hurricane licences to ACP and EU operators is inconsistent with Article 1.3 of Licensing Agreement.
- The allocation of 30% of licences to category B creates less favourable conditions of competition for others and is inconsistent with Article XVII and Article II of GATS.
- The allocation of 28% of category A and B to ripeners creates less favourable conditions of competition for others and is inconsistent with Article XVII of GATS.
- The exemption of category B operators of EU origin from matching import licences and export certificates is inconsistent with Article II and Article XVII of GATS.
- The allocation of hurricane licences exclusively to EC producers is inconsistent with Article XVII of GATS.
- The allocation of hurricane licences exclusively to ACP producers is inconsistent with Article II of GATS.

---

[18] The Appellate Body, a standing group of justices empowered to consider WTO panel appeals, has shown no hesitation in criticizing the performance of panels. The beef-hormone panel, in particular, suffered the fate of having some major interpretations of the Sanitary and Phytosanitary Agreement overthrown.

Box 9.2.   Major findings of the Appellate Body in the banana case.

- Upholds the panel's conclusion that the US has standing in this case.
- Upholds the panel's conclusion that there is only one EU import regime for the purposes of Articles I and XIII.
- Reverses the panel's conclusion that certain GATS claims by Mexico, Guatemala and Honduras were to be excluded.
- Upholds the panel's conclusion that the Agreement on Agriculture does not allow countries to act inconsistently with GATT Article XIII.
- Upholds the panel's finding that the allocation of quota shares under the BFA to some but not all suppliers with substantial interest violated Article XIII.
- Strengthens the panel's finding that the reallocation of unused BFA quotas violates Article XIII (inconsistent with XIII: 2 as well as with XIII: 1).
- Confirms the panel's interpretation of what access is required under the Lomé Convention, to provide preferential treatment for non-traditional ACP bananas but not to provide access for ACP bananas above the 'best-ever' pre-1991 levels nor to maintain licensing procedures on third-country bananas.
- Reverses the panel's finding that the WTO waiver covers inconsistency with Article XIII, as well as Article I.
- Reverses the panel's findings that Article 1.3 of the Licensing Agreement and Article X: 3(a) of the GATT preclude different licensing systems for different supplying countries.
- Upholds the panel's finding that the EU's activity function rules and the BFA export certificate requirement violate Article I: 1 of the GATT.
- Upholds the panel's finding that the EU's import licensing procedures and hurricane licence measures violate Article III: 4 of the GATT.
- Upholds the panel's conclusion that the GATS applies to the EU's regime and that banana firms are providing 'wholesale trade services'.
- Upholds the panel's finding that the allocation of 30% of the licences on non-traditional ACP and third-country bananas to Category B operators violates Articles II and XVII of the GATS.
- Upholds the panel's finding that the allocation of some of the Category A and B licences to ripeners violates Article XVII of the GATS.
- Upholds the panel's finding that the practice with respect to hurricane licences is inconsistent with Articles II and XVII of the GATS.

---

it would fully respect its international obligations in this matter. But they indicated that, in view of the complexity of the changes required, they would need a 'reasonable period of time' in which to examine all the options and to make the necessary changes. Consultations as to what constituted a reasonable time period broke down and the matter was referred to binding arbitration, as allowed under Article 21.3 (c) of the DSU. The Director General of the WTO appointed an arbitrator (one of the justices who had heard the appeal).

The EU requested a period of 15 months and 1 week (i.e. until 1 January 1999) to make the changes in its import regime, arguing that it would take that long to consult member states and the ACP countries and to conclude the various legislative steps. They further indicated that time was needed for firms to plan changes in their own operations as the licensing system was modified. This did not impress the complaining parties, who suggested that the necessary changes in EU regulations did not require extensive consultations, but could be proposed by the Commission quite speedily. More fundamentally, the EU had never said explicitly that it would change the offending regulations (presumably for fear of upsetting domestic sensitivities) and therefore needed no grace period.

The Arbitrator apparently was impressed with the argument that the complexities of the EU decision process would require several months to yield a new regime. The guideline of Article 21:3 of the DSU, under which the arbitration had been initiated, suggested 15 months as a maximum for the 'reasonable period of time', except under particular circumstances (WTO, 1999a). The Arbitrator saw no reason to require a shorter period, as the complaining parties had requested, and gave the EU the full 15 months plus the extra week that they had suggested. At least the EU could not claim that they had insufficient time to implement a WTO-compatible regime for the importation of bananas.

The EU response

The EU did modify its policy in the light of the panel report. The new banana regime was incorporated in Regulations 1637/98 and 2362/98. Regulation 1637/98 continues the tariff quota of 2.2 million t bound in the EU's WTO schedule and an additional 'autonomous' tariff quota of 353,000 t.[19] The total MFN quota was thus 2.553 million t. This quota was unchanged from the previous regime. An Annex to Regulation 1637/98 specifies a quantity of 857,700 t as traditional imports from the ACP. However, there were no longer to be any country-specific quotas for the ACP countries. Attempts to negotiate country-specific quotas for the 2.553 million t quota were unsuccessful, and the EU allocated them to third-country suppliers. The share and volumes are shown in Table 9.3, below.

More significant were the changes in the licensing procedure. Gone were the operator categories, activity functions, export certificates and hurricane licences. In its place was a 'single pot' system, under which reference quantities claimed for the MFN quota are pooled with those

---

[19] An autonomous tariff quota is one that can be changed by the EU without recourse to the WTO.

Table 9.3.   EU tariff quota allocation for third-country and non-traditional ACP banana imports under new regime. Source: WTO (2000b).

Country	Share (%)	Volume (000 t)
Costa Rica	25.61	653.8
Colombia	23.03	588.0
Ecuador	26.17	668.1
Panama	15.76	402.4
Others	9.43	240.7
Total	100.00	2553.0

for the traditional ACP quota. Thus all importers may use reference quantities from past imports to bid for current quota allocations. Moreover, an expanded 'newcomers' licence allocation could allow new entrants into the market to compete with the established firms. On the face of it, the new licence system appeared to be crafted to meet the criticisms of Bananas III. The Council of Ministers passed Regulation 1637/98 on 20 July 1998 and the Commission followed with Regulation 2362/98 on 28 October 1998.

The Challenge Renewed

It soon became clear that the end of the dispute was not at hand. The changes introduced by the EU in its banana import regime did not meet with universal acclaim. The US was openly sceptical that the new regime was WTO compliant. The EU agreed to talks in August 1998, but only on those parts of the new policy that had been agreed. Barely 2 weeks passed before Ecuador requested, on 13 November 1998, further consultations with the EU. The talks again were inconclusive. Apart from Mexico, none of the other complainants took part. Instead, the talk was of sanctions and retaliation. The protagonists were gearing up for battle: the EU decided to take a proactive stance.

The EU panel under Article 21.5

On 14 December 1998, the EU raised the issue of whether a WTO member should be deemed to be in compliance with a ruling unless a panel found to the contrary. In their eyes, they had responded to the original panel by making changes in the import regime for bananas. To be sure, the US had declared that the changes were not enough, but that was a unilateral declaration with no WTO significance. In fact the US, by threatening to go ahead with sanctions, was misusing the system so carefully devised in the Uruguay Round. The EU therefore requested a panel, under Article 21.5 of the DSU, with the mandate to find that the new regime of the EU 'must be presumed to conform to WTO rules unless their conformity has been duly challenged under the appropriate DSU procedures' (WTO, 1999c).[20] The EU looked in vain for someone to join in this action: Ecuador had requested a panel on its own complaint (see below) and the other complainants declined to be drawn in. The US argued that the EU, as respondent in the banana case, could not bring an Article 21:5 complaint to establish conformity of its own policies with the WTO.

The panel (the same three members from Bananas III) argued that they had no way of compelling the US and other complainants to seek a panel to challenge the EU changes. They agreed with the EU that there was an assumption of consistency implied in the DSU as in the WTO more broadly. A trade measure was indeed deemed to be consistent with the WTO if not challenged. But that did not imply that the absence of a challenge at any particular time could be taken as an indication that all parties agreed to its consistency. The panel therefore declined to support the EU's contention that its new banana import regime must be ruled consistent with the WTO. In any case, as it pointed out in its report, when convened as a panel to consider Ecuador's complaint, it had reached the conclusion that the EU's changes did not bring it into conformity.

The second arbitration

Having declined to take part in an Article 21.5 challenge to the EU's new regime, the US announced, on 14 January 1999, its intention to 'suspend concessions' (i.e. to apply trade sanctions through higher tariffs on EU goods) to the extent of its lost banana trade. It requested of the DSB approval of suspension to the extent of US$520 million. The EU protested at the amount, not least because it argued that the US was not a banana exporter and therefore its rights were not 'nullified' or 'impaired'. Using the provisions of Article 22.6 of the DSU, the EU asked for arbitration on the matter by the original panel.

The panel from Bananas III duly reconvened to arbitrate on the issue of the value of concessions that the US could withdraw to offset the loss of trade.[21] But to do this they had to establish that the new

---

[20] Article 21.5 allows for a panel to be set up if there is disagreement on whether measures taken in response to a panel ruling are consistent with the WTO. One would expect a complainant rather than a respondent to initiate such a panel.

[21] It is interesting to note that the other complainants did not at this time request withdrawal of trade concessions (i.e. higher tariffs on EU goods).

regime was in fact still not WTO-compatible. For, if the regime had been changed in an adequate way, no retaliation would have been authorized. The EU clearly had an incentive to seek a ruling on this matter. At the worst, more changes might be needed. At best, they would be given a clean bill of health.

The arguments before the reconvened panel were not unfamiliar. The new formulation of the quotas in Regulation 1637/98 did not convince the US, who argued that the split in the tariff quota between the non-country-specific ACP quota and the allocated MFN quota still contravened Article XIII.[22] The new licence procedure also drew criticism. The reference quantities, imports in the 1994–1996 period, were established under the old, WTO-inconsistent regime. The new regime merely perpetuated the inequity, in spite of an apparent change in mechanism. The 'single pot' system did nothing to level the playing field: it was *de facto*, if not *de jure*, discriminatory. Even the expanded 'newcomer' licences seemed to go to EU-based firms under the rules for establishing competency. The EU argued that its ACP quota was required under the Lomé Convention, and is therefore outside the MFN quota and the reaches of Article XIII. The new licence system had been introduced to meet WTO criticism: the use of a newcomer reserve was not intended to be discriminatory. But the Arbitrators sided with the US in their judgement of the new EU regime. They held that there was still discrimination in the allocation of licences, in violation of Article XIII, and that there was still lack of national treatment in the licensing procedures that acted against the competitive position of the non-EU shippers and thus contravened the GATS.

When it came to arbitrating the value of nullification and impairment, the panel settled on a figure of US$191.4 million per year, somewhat below the US claim of US$520 million. In doing so, they emphasized that suspension of concessions is designed as a temporary measure designed to induce compliance. It should be appropriate and have regard to the 'equivalence' of the impairment suffered. To calculate this, the panel had to establish a 'WTO-consistent counterfactual' and compare actual trade with this hypothetical situation. After some interchange with the parties to the conflict, the panel finally chose as a counterfactual a situation where the EU established a global quota of 2.553 million t (subject to a €75 t^{-1} tariff) and unlimited access for the ACP at a zero tariff (with this ACP preference covered by the WTO waiver). A relatively simple calculation led to a value of US-based trade that would be US$191.4 million greater than at present. This level of suspension was therefore allowed to the US under the DSU rules.

---

[22] It is significant that the Appellate Body had ruled that the Lomé waiver did not cover Article XIII.

The arbitrated level of trade sanctions did not end this aspect of the controversy. The US imposed retaliatory 100% tariffs on a range of European goods worth US$520 million on 3 March 1999. This anticipated by some 7 weeks the Arbitrators report, which cut the estimated trade loss to US$191.4 million. The US scaled back its retaliation at that time, but argued that it did not have to make good any interim losses suffered by the EU as a result of temporary over-retaliation. A panel was asked to consider, at the request of the EU, whether the US interpretation of the DSU was appropriate. The panel found in favour of the EU in April 2000.

The Ecuador panel

While the EU was intent on showing that the US had overstated the value of trade displaced by the EU's regulations, and other complaining parties were maintaining that the EU regime changes did not correct the problem of discrimination, Ecuador was forging its own path. On 13 November 1998, Ecuador had requested reactivation of the consultations with the EU that had taken place in September. Receiving no satisfaction from these bilateral contacts, Ecuador requested that the original panel be convened yet again to examine whether the findings of the report had been implemented (WTO, 1999b).[23] An added task was given to the panel, to assist the DSB in recommendations that might resolve the issue once and for all.

The panel, meeting at the request of Ecuador, came up with a similar conclusion to that which they were developing in the EU Arbitration hearing. They found that the EU policy change still fell short of WTO rules, both with respect to the allocation of quotas under Article XIII and with regard to the national treatment clause of the GATS. The Lomé waiver covered Article I violations, as it always had, but the Lomé obligation did not extend to banana imports above the pre-1991 'best-ever' quantities. The 'newcomer' licences were still *de facto* discriminatory to Ecuadorian exports and the firms that handled them.

At Ecuador's request, the panel also tried its hand at policy recommendation, or at least engaged in some speculation as to what it might find WTO-compatible. Three such options were mentioned, though without much elaboration.

---

[23] The panel had already reconvened to consider the EU's complaint about the level of US retaliation, as discussed above. Ecuador had declined to join the EU in its Article 21.5 request, and the other complainants had refused to join Ecuador in its challenge.

- A tariffs-only system without a tariff quota. This could include a tariff preference (at zero or another rate) for ACP bananas. A waiver would thus be necessary, unless this were to be part of an Article XXIV free trade area (or customs union).
- A tariffs-only system with a tariff quota for ACP bananas. A waiver would be needed for that tariff quota.
- A tariff-quota system like the current one (as revised), but either without any country-specific quotas or with such quotas subject to agreement by all substantial suppliers. If ACP bananas still received duty-free status, then there would be an issue as to whether this was 'required' by the Lomé Convention and hence whether a waiver was needed.[24]

The options outlined by the Ecuador panel had a significant impact on the subsequent discussions about the resolution to the problem. They, at the least, gave a framework for the discussion that followed, even if such policy suggestions may have appeared to be beyond the normal remit of an adjudicatory body.

Emboldened by the favourable outcome of the panel, Ecuador continued to push a somewhat independent line. In November 1999, it requested agreement from the WTO to impose sanctions on the EU of up to US$450 million (WTO, 1999e). But as total imports of consumer goods from the EU were only US$17 million, retaliatory tariffs would have hardly been effective. The answer was to retaliate by 'withdrawing concessions' in the fields of services (as negotiated in the GATS schedules) and intellectual property (under the TRIPS Agreement).[25] The EU considered the amount excessive and the method of dubious legality, and the well-travelled panel reconvened to consider the arguments. In March 2000, the Arbitrators settled on a sum of US$201.6 million, but agreed that Ecuador could retaliate on trade other than goods (WTO, 2000b). Sensing that the issue could get further out of hand, the panel ended its report with another plea for a solution.

In the light of the Ecuador panel and the award, the EU announced its intention to modify its regime yet again to see whether it could come up with a system that would be acceptable to the WTO and to

---

[24] The panel pointed out that such a waiver would be similar to that accorded to the US for the Caribbean Basin Initiative and other such non-reciprocal schemes.

[25] Specific targets for such retaliation were specified as wholesale trade services (GATS) and protection of performers rights, recordings, geographical indications and industrial design (TRIPS). In effect, Ecuador could have become a centre for 'European' goods made without the licences and patent fees mandated under TRIPS. It is worth noting that goods from Holland and Denmark were not to be targeted, presumably in recognition of their votes against the revised banana regime in the Council of Ministers.

traditional banana suppliers. This proved as difficult as ever. The options were becoming clear, but that merely highlighted the dilemma. At one extreme, a 'clean' WTO-compatible regime would avoid tariff quotas altogether, and their associated licences, and merely allow the ACP countries to sell bananas at zero or preferential tariff rates. But a high tariff would be needed to make it profitable to ship high-cost bananas into the EU market, and this would create problems for third-country suppliers (and perhaps German consumers). At the other extreme, a system of tariff quotas regulating ACP and third-country bananas would have to be negotiated with those countries to avoid continued challenges. But without creating new demand there was not enough room in the EU market to give everyone the quota to which they thought they were entitled. In practice, the logical next step was a mixed system based on a move toward a 'tariffs-only' regime with temporary safeguards for vulnerable ACP countries. The EU Commission held numerous bilateral discussions with the parties concerned but was unable to reach agreement on a mutually acceptable solution (WTO, 2000d).

The Solution to the Banana Conflict

The conflict finally has been resolved (at least for the time being) by means of an interim regime leading, after 4 years, to an arrangement that is less likely to be challenged under the WTO. The Commission had been consistent for some months in proposing a 'tariffs-only' regime after a transition period. Though this was not universally popular, the logic was compelling. ACP countries could still have tariff-free entry, but no quotas or licences would be needed. But an abrupt switch to such a system seemed out of the question. Some transition period was necessary, both for the countries concerned and also for the companies. Tariff rate quotas would have to stay for a few years. Which meant that there had to be a licence allocation system to manage the quota. After floating a rather controversial 'first-come, first-served' proposal, which would have led to a 'boat race' across the Atlantic, the Commission finally agreed an allocation mechanism that relied on historical shares for a limited period of time, before introducing 'tariff-only' access by January 2006. After an initial challenge by Ecuador, who felt that the bilateral EU–US deal had been biased against their interests and requested consultations (WTO, 2001c), the compromise was accepted by all parties to the dispute.[26]

---

[26] The text of the agreement between the EU and the US was reported to the WTO on 2 July 2001 (WTO, 2001e), along with the suspension of the retaliatory tariffs conditional upon the EU keeping to the agreed timetable.

Conclusion

The banana case had rumbled on for 7 years. In the course of this dispute the countries concerned had explored every corner of the DSU and tried an impressive array of diplomatic manoeuvres. Sensitive issues of foreign policy had come into conflict with trade rules and there appeared no easy way to resolve the problem. But the credibility of the system was at stake. Transatlantic relations were suffering in a conflict that had marginal economic interest to the US. The case clearly became an albatross around the neck of the WTO and the parties to the dispute.

Listing the significant aspects of the banana case is not difficult. Any challenge under the non-discrimination clause (Article I) is likely to be important in defining the nature of the trade system. The granting of non-reciprocal preferences is clearly discriminatory, and thus generally requires a waiver from the WTO. But the members collectively have some discretion as to how strictly to interpret this exception, and in which direction to move the trade system. The trade policy of many countries is centred around such preferences, and the stability of the trade system for them is closely tied to the long-term acceptability of these arrangements. An argument can be made that the trade system should be limiting these exceptions, either by consolidating them in the other broad MFN exemption, free trade areas and customs unions that are compatible with Article XXIV, or by phasing them out altogether. But if so, then this needs to be pursued consistently and transparently. The banana case has had the effect of raising the concern among supplying countries about the stability of the system. Rather than being seen as a rule-based organization of particular value to small and vulnerable countries, the WTO now is widely portrayed as a playground for the large countries to pursue commercial and political rivalries with endless disputes. Perhaps there is no consensus on the future of preferences, but it is not clear that the banana dispute served the function of illuminating this debate.

The banana case clearly did illuminate some aspects of the GATT, in particular the interpretation of Article XIII. The administration of tariff quotas has always been contentious. But now a new set of tariff quotas has emerged from the Uruguay Round as a result of the Agreement on Agriculture. These quotas are administered in a wide variety of ways, and the licences are distributed largely at the whim of national authorities. The ruling that tariff quotas under the Agreement on Agriculture have to conform to Article XIII is potentially significant. If the intention of that article is followed with any consistency, quotas based on historical market shares that do not reflect underlying shifts in costs are vulnerable. Thus a country that reduces costs (or even one that corrects an exchange rate distortion) could make a case for improved access. Cosy deals with favoured suppliers may be challenged; and changes in technology that could dramatically shift production costs may add to the pressures on periodic reallocation of quota rights or an auction system that gives low-cost suppliers the ability to penetrate quota-controlled markets.

References

WTO (1995) *The Results of the Uruguay Round of Multilateral Trade Negotiations: the Legal Texts.* World Trade Organization, Geneva.

WTO (1997a) *European Communities – Regime for the Importation, Sale and Distribution of Bananas. Complaint by the United States. Report of the Panel.* WT/DS27/R/USA. World Trade Organization, Geneva, 22 May.

WTO (1997b) *European Communities – Regime for the Importation, Sale and Distribution of Bananas. Complaint by Ecuador. Report of the Panel.* WT/DS27/R/ECU. World Trade Organization, Geneva, 22 May.

WTO (1997c) *European Communities – Regime for the Importation, Sale and Distribution of Bananas. Complaint by Guatemala and Honduras. Report of the Panel.* WT/DS27/R/GTM. World Trade Organization, Geneva, 22 May.

WTO (1997d) *European Communities – Regime for the Importation, Sale and Distribution of Bananas. Complaint by Mexico. Report of the Panel.* WT/DS27/R/MEX. World Trade Organization, Geneva, 22 May.

WTO (1997e) *European Communities – Regime for the Importation, Sale and Distribution of Bananas. Report of the Appellate Body.* WT/DS27/AB/R. World Trade Organization, Geneva, 9 September.

WTO (1998) *European Communities – Regime for the Importation, Sale and Distribution of Bananas. Arbitration under Article 21.3 (c) of the Understanding on Rules and Procedures Governing the Settlement of Disputes.* WT/DS27/17. World Trade Organization, Geneva, 7 January.

WTO (1999a) *European Communities – Regime for the Importation, Sale and Distribution of Bananas. Recourse to Arbitration by the European Communities under Article 22.6 of the DSU. Decision by the Arbitrators.* WT/DS27/ARB. World Trade Organization, Geneva, 9 April.

WTO (1999b) *European Communities – Regime for the Importation, Sale and Distribution of Bananas. Recourse to Article 21.5 by Ecuador. Report of the Panel.* WT/DS27/RW/ECU. World Trade Organization, Geneva, 12 April.

WTO (1999c) *European Communities – Regime for the Importation, Sale and Distribution of Bananas. Recourse to Article 21.5 by the European Communities. Report of the Panel.* WT/DS27/RW/EEC. World Trade Organization, Geneva, 12 April.

WTO (1999d) *European Communities – Regime for the Importation, Sale and Distribution of Bananas. Status Report by the European Communities. Addendum.* WT/DS27/51/Add.1. World Trade Organization, Geneva, 8 September.

WTO (1999e) *European Communities – Regime for the Importation, Sale and Distribution of Bananas. Request by Ecuador for Authorization of*

Suspension of Concessions or Other Obligations Pursuant to Article 22.2. WT/DS27/52. World Trade Organization, Geneva, 9 November.

WTO (1999f) *European Communities – Regime for the Importation, Sale and Distribution of Bananas. Recourse to Arbitration by the European Communities under Article 22.6 of the DSU. Decision by the Arbitrators.* WT/DS27/53. World Trade Organization, Geneva, 19 November.

WTO (2000a) *European Communities – Regime for the Importation, Sale and Distribution of Bananas. Status Report by the European Communities. Addendum.* WT/DS27/51/Add.5. World Trade Organization, Geneva, 11 February.

WTO (2000b) *European Communities – Regime for the Importation, Sale and Distribution of Bananas. Recourse to Arbitration by the European Communities under Article 22.6 of the DSU. Decision by the Arbitrators.* WT/DS27/ARB/ECU. World Trade Organization, Geneva, 24 March.

WTO (2000c) *European Communities – Regime for the Importation, Sale and Distribution of Bananas. Recourse to Article 22.7 by Ecuador.* WT/DS27/54. World Trade Organization, Geneva, 8 May.

WTO (2000d) *European Communities – Regime for the Importation, Sale and Distribution of Bananas. Status Report by the European Communities. Addendum.* WT/DS27/51/Add.9. World Trade Organization, Geneva, 9 June.

WTO (2000e) *European Communities – Regime for the Importation, Sale and Distribution of Bananas. Status Report by the European Communities. Addendum.* WT/DS27/51/Add.12. World Trade Organization, Geneva, 13 October.

WTO (2001a) *European Communities – Regime for the Importation, Sale and Distribution of Bananas. Status Report by the European Communities. Addendum.* WT/DS27/51/Add.15. World Trade Organization, Geneva, 19 January.

WTO (2001b) *European Communities – Regime for the Importation, Sale and Distribution of Bananas. Status Report by the European Communities. Addendum.* WT/DS27/51/Add.17. World Trade Organization, Geneva, 26 March.

WTO (2001c) *European Communities – Regime for the Importation, Sale and Distribution of Bananas. Recourse to Article 22.7 by Ecuador.* WT/DS27/55. World Trade Organization, Geneva, 20 April.

WTO (2001d) *European Communities – Regime for the Importation, Sale and Distribution of Bananas. Status Report by the European Communities. Addendum.* WT/DS27/51/Add.18. World Trade Organization, Geneva, 4 May.

WTO (2001e) *European Communities – Regime for the Importation, Sale and Distribution of Bananas. Communication from the United States.* WT/DS27/59. World Trade Organization, Geneva, 2 July.

Conclusion

Tim Josling and Tim Taylor

10

What can the banana trade conflict tell us about commodity trade and trade policy conflicts in the year 2002 and beyond? Is it a unique case where increasing commercial pressures to sell bananas clashed by accident of fate with delicate diplomatic relations between countries, and therefore is of little relevance outside its own market environment? Or is it an example of an inevitable tension between public policy and private profit of a type that can easily arise in other areas? Is the banana market a relic of the colonial past, when primary product trade flows went from tropical producers to markets in the US or in Europe, caught in a time-warp as countries struggle to define a stable post-colonial trade regime? Or is it a reflection of the new global marketplace, where multinational firms look for reliable and low-cost supplies from whatever country is willing to make (or accept) the investment? Does the banana case demonstrate the weakness of a global trade system that can threaten the livelihood of small island economies in the name of efficiency? Or is it an example of necessary rules that transform the trade system from one of power relations and hierarchical access to one of equality for all countries and constraints on market exploitation? There are no simple answers to such questions, but the act of raising them is itself a useful exercise for the understanding of trade policy.

The fascination of the banana case is precisely that it cannot easily be classified as one or other type of trade dispute. The banana case blends together the issues of developing country preferences, quota allocation schemes, trade dispute rules, multilateral trading firms, competition for market shares, political sensitivities, small islands in a global market and small-farmer alternatives to traditional crops.[1]

This concluding chapter attempts to draw some lessons for trade policy from the banana case. If indeed the conflict illustrates so many facets of trade, there should be something to learn from the protracted negotiations and discussions that the conflict has generated. Five of these facets are discussed below.

1. The question of preferences and the integration of former colonial trade patterns into the multilateral system.
2. The issue of market structure and the dominant place that some firms have acquired in the marketing of agricultural products.
3. The dilemma of the multilateral trade system poised between a rule-based and a power-based structure.
4. The state of the transatlantic relationship and the bilateral hegemony developed over the post-war period.
5. The influences on the conduct of trade policy in the largest countries.

Preferences and the Global Trade System

The EU banana trade is largely a reflection of a post-colonial European trade policy designed to benefit former colonies as they leave the protection of the metropolitan power. Guaranteed access to markets at a preferential tariff rate (or more commonly tariff-free) was intended to maintain the flow of goods to the metropolitan market and preserve the value of prior investments. Once initiated, there is never a good time to relinquish such preferences. But over time the preferred trade flows become less interesting to the recipient, and there is the danger of falling behind those countries that do not enjoy such privileged access.

---

[1] The closest commodity to bananas in terms of the complexity of trade issues is sugar. As in the case of bananas, sugar is grown both within and outside Europe. Sugar is also covered by a Protocol to the Lomé Convention and is of great importance to several small island economies. Multinational firms are active in the market and buy much of the output from developing countries. Some of the quota allocation methods might also be criticized under the WTO rules if a country or trader thought that there was an inconsistency with Article XIII. But to date it has not been in the interest of either the EU or the US to stir the sugar marketing arrangements that they have with preferred suppliers, nor has it apparently been deemed beneficial for new suppliers such as Brazil or established exporters such as Australia to challenge the status quo. Two GATT cases in the early 1980s targeted the sugar export regime of the European Community (as it then was), but neither panel report was able to find the EC regime in conflict with GATT rules.

So, independently of the banana dispute, there has been an ongoing debate about the need to perpetuate post-colonial preference schemes and whether such schemes are still in the interests of the apparent beneficiary countries (Tangermann and Josling, 2002).

The US regime (and the German regime prior to the Common Banana Market) reflects the absence of such colonial obligations and the desire to serve the consumer with low-cost tropical fruit. But the American banana-trade regime, based on private companies that developed export sectors in Central and South America, though not overtly designed to spur development in the exporting countries, was in its own way a form of preferential trade system. It rested on a pattern of development that was based on opening up lands and building infrastructure to service export markets. But such development was aided by political elites in the producing country and the US, as well as by financial structures that would have otherwise not have been available to the countries of Latin America.

Perhaps the main difference between the systems was that US multinational companies could source bananas in other countries, such as Jamaica, whereas the Latin American countries had less opportunity to compete in the European market. In other words, the European colonial trade system relied on keeping non-colonial producers from having access to the consumer market, whereas the American system gave the benefits of market access to the firms and allowed them more freedom as to where to produce. The banana case finally brings to a head the simmering tensions between two systems of colonial development in the Americas, the one based on imperial preference and naval power and the other based on private enterprise and access to almost unlimited capital.

The WTO has been the unwitting stage for this clash of colonial systems. The European post-colonial system is under challenge in the WTO because it appears to favour one group of developing countries that happened to have historical ties with Europe. Preferences in favour of one group of developing countries are usually at the expense of other developing countries. Latin American countries, perhaps more than those in Asia, consider the European preference system embodied in the Lomé banana regime to be basically unfair. But such systems do not change quickly: the conflict is too deeply rooted in the past. EU policy is certainly heavily constrained by an obligation to the ACP countries. The 50-year-old question of what to do with colonial preferences in a multilateral, non-discriminatory trade system has never been far from the surface. But then that same history has seen a struggle by the Latin American producing countries to take charge of their own production and marketing facilities. Even if the Windward Islands were to decide to abandon the production of bananas, the tensions that are currently felt in Latin America would probably continue.

Does the banana case throw light on the question of how the WTO should deal with the future of preferences and the trade problems of those developing countries that benefit from them? The EU's Lomé Convention needed to be granted a waiver from the application of the 'non-discrimination' principle that is at the heart of the WTO. The banana case has helped to clarify the terms of the waiver, specifically whether it applied to the non-discriminatory allocation of quotas. The end of the dispute has seen the question of the renewal of the waiver again become contentious. The Doha Ministerial took up the issue of a continuation of the waiver for the Lome and its successor treaty. In the end, the Latin American banana-producing countries agreed to drop their objections to the Cotonou waiver and the ACP countries were able to shift their support to the start of a new round of trade negotiations.[2]

Bananas and Market Structure

A theme throughout the history of bananas in Latin America and the Caribbean has been the divergent paths that the two regions' banana industries have followed and the differences between the attendant market structures and competitive dynamics that have evolved. The US–EU banana dispute brought these two aspects of the banana industry into juxtaposition.

The Caribbean banana industry arose from England's colonial system and the desire to find a solution to the social turmoil arising from the decline of sugar. Indeed, it may be argued that bananas represent the first diversification crop introduced into the Windward Islands. Within this context, the industry evolved less in response to market signals than in response to continued EU policy initiatives designed to ensure the viability of the Windward Islands industry in the face of competition from Latin American producers. The most important of these policies have been the banana protocols contained

---

[2] As one might expect, the actual situation was more complex than suggested here. The Ministers in Doha had to consider two waivers. The first was to allow the new trade regime embodied in the Cotonou Agreement, which included the regime for bananas, to be sheltered from challenge. This has an additional provision that allows the Latin American banana exporters to request arbitration prior to future EC banana tariffs going into effect on January 2006 (ITCSD, 2001). In addition, there is a provision for the suspension of the waiver if the EU does not grant current access for Latin bananas. The second waiver relates to the compatibility of the interim arrangements, beginning in January 2002, and only extending until the end of 2005. These two waivers were enough to satisfy the Latin banana producers that the EU could not postpone the 'tariffs-only' regime, and also allow the ACP to withdraw their objection to a new round of negotiations.

in the Lomé Convention. Over the course of time, the industry has made many attempts at rationalization in order to improve competitiveness and reduce its dependence on preferences in the EU market. However, all of these attempts have met with limited success at best. By the admission of their leaders, it appears that the Windward Islands have little hope of ever becoming competitive with the Latin American countries because of their high cost of production.

Without a means for differentiating their product, it does not appear that the Windward Islands banana industry will survive if the EU market is liberalized in 2006, as currently planned. This suggests that the Windward Islands is likely to continue to pursue political remedies to ensure the continued existence of the industry. It should be noted that although the current policy scenario has the EU market being liberalized in 2006, the Everything But Arms (EBA) agreement contains a provision that may allow the Windward Islands to retain some type of preferences. Additionally, as part of the banana settlement, an agreement was made that EU requests for WTO waivers on preferences for ACP countries would not be contested by the US or Ecuador.

The Latin American industry grew primarily in response to market forces. As the industry evolved, technology, economies of scale and competition, both fair and at times less so, has led to the oligopolistic structure that characterizes the industry today. Though the industry evolved in a competitive environment, the corporate strategies of the major players, especially in response to EU trade policy have been remarkably diverse. Upon implementation of the NBR, Chiquita realized it had made a miscalculation on the nature of the Single Market banana regime and found itself financially unable to adjust to the NBR. The company eventually chose to pursue a solution to its corporate difficulties through the policy arena. The other major players, such as Dole and Fyffes, which had the requisite financial resources, responded to the implicit economic signals contained in the structure of the NBR by acquiring assets that provided access to the EU market. As a result, they were able to garner market share primarily at the expense of Chiquita. Del Monte, due to corporate management difficulties, generally did not respond to the NBR in any direct manner.

Though the evolution of the Latin American industry was largely market driven, it is important to remember that it did so within the context of the EU banana protocols. The significance of this can be found in the terms of the final resolution to the dispute that left some form of managed trade in place. Dole and Del Monte supported a first-come, first-served result that clearly would have favoured them over Chiquita. However, they supported the final agreement precisely because of the benefits that managed trade creates for the multinationals.

Few of the major banana markets are particularly profitable. Indeed, as noted by Lavery (2001), as a result of the banana protocol, the EU historically has been the most profitable market for the multinationals. This suggests that, from the perspective of the multinationals, the banana dispute was less about the issue of extending preferences to the Windward Islands producers than about how the rents accruing to the multinationals were to be allocated. It also suggests that the multinationals may have less interest in genuinely free trade in the EU banana market than might be assumed.

This conclusion is, perhaps, relevant beyond the banana industry. In many markets where preferences are granted on the basis of colonial relationships, there can be significant rents that accrue to other market participants, especially multinationals. Thus a trade policy shift toward more competitive markets can be impeded to the extent that multinationals attempt to capture the policy process in order to preserve the attendant rents they enjoy.

Bananas as a Challenge for the WTO

The banana issue may be a reflection of historical tensions, but the topic is also rather current, if not avant garde. The dispute was perched in the GATT machinery just waiting for the changes wrought by the Uruguay Round to take effect. The banana case was the first to test the services agreement, GATS. It touched on issues of trade and competition that have not yet been discussed fully, let alone put into WTO rules. So the outcome of the banana conflict may have helped to clarify a number of important issues in the relationship between companies at different levels of the production marketing chain.

The dispute settlement regime has been put to the test by both the banana and beef-hormone cases.[3] So far the system has survived. The strengthening of the rules in the Uruguay Round has made the procedures more important. The banana case explored many issues, ranging from the nature of consultations to the standing of countries and the presence of third parties to a dispute. The appeal and arbitration processes have been tried and the issues of timing and the calculation of the appropriate suspension of concessions have been explored. But, more substantially, the issue of credibility of the WTO as a forum for resolving trade disputes has been brought to the fore. Here the record is not so positive. The lengthy nature of the proceedings and the fact that no satisfactory conclusion has been reached has cast doubt in some circles on the effectiveness of the DSU. Did the EU make a

---

[3] The more recent panel ruling on the US use of Foreign Sales Corporations also has raised the political temperature and added to the pressures on the DSU.

serious attempt to correct the deficiencies of its banana import regime? Or did it engage in delaying tactics and legal manoeuvres to avoid giving non-EU firms their rightful market access? Did the US have a serious concern for the sanctity of the trade system when it joined a case for a tropical product? Or had it found a convenient way of satisfying domestic electoral politics, demonstrating the power of the new WTO and bashing the EU at the same time?

Did the WTO serve the small countries well in this case? The countries of the Windward Islands clearly have doubts about both the impartiality of the WTO process and its ability to help protect them from the dominant powers of the region. But on the other hand a trade system based on rules is designed precisely to help the small and weak against the large and strong. So what went wrong in this case? The small countries of the Caribbean basically made the decision that their own interests were in preserving a system that had buffeted them against competition from Latin America. To have done otherwise would have been difficult both in political and economic terms. But in doing so, they challenged the rule system that prevents them from being left outside when others form preferential trade clubs. No one can believe that the Caribbean alone will be allowed special treatment in the markets of the EU. Already preferences have been eroded through trade liberalization and the extension of benefits to all least developing countries via the EBA initiative.

A major reason given by the USTR staff for entering the banana dispute was to establish that the new WTO dispute settlement worked as a substitute for unilateral action of the type used frequently by the US in the past. The banana case has proven that the WTO system worked, but ironically it has also exposed the fallacy that retaliation or threat of retaliation will force powerful countries to change politically sensitive policies or to offend politically powerful economic interests. While the new WTO dispute settlement system may function much like a court, it lacks a crucial element of an effective court system – the willingness of those who are found in violation of agreed rules to change behaviour or prevent further violations.

Transatlantic Trade Relations and the Banana Dispute

From the outset of the US intervention in the banana dispute, the dispute has adversely affected US–EU relations. At the beginning, the EU was incredulous that the US was entering the dispute directly, and they claimed initially that the US had no standing in the dispute because the US does not produce or export bananas. The EU displeasure was increased when, after winning the dispute in the original panel and in the appeal process, the US refused to accept the modest adjustments in the EU banana-import regime that the EU proposed and insisted that only an adjustment that the WTO panel found consistent and which restored significant market share to the countries that had been in the EU market prior to the establishment of the new regime.

The US insistence on retaliation and the request for substantial compensation further irritated EU officials. The banana dispute coming on top of the beef-hormone case, where the US also asked for and imposed sanctions was a continuing irritant in US–EU trade relations. It presented the EU officials with two adverse dispute settlements in the new WTO dispute settlement process, and both cases involved almost insurmountable political difficulties within the EU to produce policy changes necessary to comply with the WTO panels and the US concerns.

It is unclear as to the extent that the ongoing disputes over beef and bananas contributed to the inability of the US and the EU to organize a common approach to the WTO ministerial in Seattle in December 1999. There is no doubt that these disputes were part of the reason that the US and EU failed to agree on the scope of a new round of trade negotiations, and there is no doubt that the distrust sown among ACP countries over the banana dispute contributed to their unwillingness to agree to key elements of a new round desired by the US.

Informed observers are convinced that frustration with the US over the banana and beef disputes was the prime reason that the former EU Commissioner for Trade brought a formal WTO complaint against the US Foreign Sales Corporation (FSC), which was found by a panel to constitute a form of illegal export subsidy. This dispute shocked the US, which believed that there was an agreement that the FSC system was acceptable and would not be challenged. Now the EU is refusing to accept the proposed US measures to deal with the WTO violation and has threatened to retaliate with what would be the largest retaliation ever imposed in the GATT/WTO system. If that occurs, it is likely to spark a major trade war that would make the banana dispute pale into insignificance.

Bananas and the Conduct of Trade Policy

The banana case also raises important issues for the internal conduct of trade policy. Did large companies, such as Chiquita, have too much influence on trade diplomacy in this case? Did the US allow domestic electoral politics to cloud the foreign policy issue? Are there private sector solutions to what appears to be a public policy problem?

More broadly, the banana case has implications for the politics of globalization. It was not on the agenda at Seattle, but to many both inside and outside the WTO Ministerial the banana issue represented a significant aspect of the WTO. In this sense, the case is not just one of tidying up some 1960s era trade policies, but one that relates to the type of global trade and economic system that countries wish to build for the 21st century. The fact that the players in the wider game include multinational corporations and small farmers adds to the interest in the case. Moreover, the fact that one aspect of the dispute involves environmental and labour conditions in the Caribbean and Central America gives it a further saliency in the debate about global economic policy, and many small countries in the Caribbean see the banana case as an indication of their lack of voice in the WTO. For all these reasons, the banana case has influenced opinions and events way beyond the sector itself. This suggests that the impact of this dispute will be felt for years to come.

References

ITCSD (2001) EC–ACP Cotonou waiver finally granted. *Bridges Weekly Trade News Digest* 5 (39). International Centre for Trade and Sustainable Development, 15 November.

Lavery, B. (2001) Trade feud on bananas not as clear as it looks. *New York Times*, 7 February.

Tangermann, S. and Josling, T. (2002) Trade preferences for developing countries: their nature and status in the WTO. *World Trade Review* (forthcoming).

Index

Browse Read and Buy

www.cabi.org/bookshop

ANIMAL & VETERINARY SCIENCES
BIODIVERSITY   CROP PROTECTION
HUMAN HEALTH   NATURAL RESOURCES
ENVIRONMENT   PLANT SCIENCES
SOCIAL SCIENCES

CABI *Publishing*
A division of CAB International

Online BOOK SHOP

Subjects

Search

Reading Room

Bargains

New Titles

Forthcoming

Order & Pay Online!

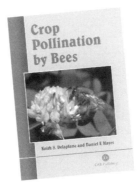

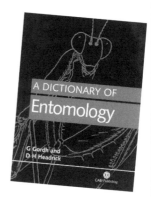

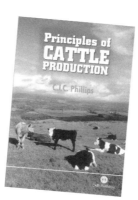

 FULL DESCRIPTION   BUY THIS BOOK   BOOK OF THE MONTH

Tel: +44 (0)1491 832111   Fax: +44 (0)1491 829292